S0-EXQ-385

SOCIAL STUDIES
IN SCHOOLS

SUNY SERIES, THEORY, RESEARCH, AND
PRACTICE IN SOCIAL EDUCATION
PETER H. MARTORELLA, EDITOR

SOCIAL STUDIES IN SCHOOLS

A History of The Early Years

DAVID WARREN SAXE

STATE UNIVERSITY OF NEW YORK PRESS

Published by
State University of New York Press, Albany

© 1991 State University of New York

All rights reserved

Printed in the United States of America

No part of this book may be used or reproduced
in any manner whatsoever without written permission
except in the case of brief quotations embodied in
critical articles and reviews.

For information, address State University of New York
Press, State University Plaza, Albany, N.Y., 12246

Production by E. Moore
Marketing by Theresa A. Swierzowski

Library of Congress Cataloging-in-Publication Data

Saxe, David Warren, 1953-
    Social studies in schools : a history of the early years / David
Warren Saxe.
        p.   cm.—(Suny series, theory, research, and practice in
social education)
    Includes bibliographical references and index.
    ISBN 0-7914-0775-6 (CH : acid-free).—ISBN 0-7914-0776-4 (PB :
acid free)
    1. Social sciences—Study and teaching (Secondary)—United States—
History. 2. Social sciences—Study and teaching (secondary)—
United States—History—Bibliography. 3. Civics—Study and
teaching (Secondary)—United States—History. I. Title.
II. Series.
H62.5.U5S29   1991
300'.71'273—dc20   90-48101
                                                            CIP

10 9 8 7 6 5 4 3 2 1

H
62.5
.U5
S29
1991

To Laura Ann, with love

34/3824

CONTENTS

FOREWORD

I was struck on my reading of Professor Saxe's manuscript with a set of appreciations. "How lucky," I thought, "to be invited to an association with a document that will be 'required reading' for decades." The "lucky" part is a personal indulgence; but the prediction that Professor Saxe's book will be "required reading" is an appreciation grounded in the author's finesse in choosing and grooming the topics and issues to characterize the nascence of the field of social studies. The more interesting of the two content designations used above is "issue" inasmuch as the intellectual and emotional vigor of a field of study is reflected in its issues. I will showcase a few of these issues in the paragraphs following.

In Professor Saxe's interpretation, the primal issue of the field of social studies was reflected in a conflict between the traditional historians and the insurgent social studies proponents over control of the social curriculum in schools. Though purportedly an intellectual issue involving the purpose of history in schools, its resolution by the 1916 committee on social studies had powerful social, political, and moral consequences in the education of citizens.

As Professor Saxe carefully unfolds this professional controversy, he stimulates our appreciation for the wisdom of the founders of the field. Although he encourages us to recognize a more generalized distribution of wisdom, Professor Saxe endorses for the field a distillation of social studies heroes. Some of these persons—John Dewey, for example—are well known. However, among the names of Kingsley, Dunn, Barnard, Robinson, and Jones, despite the key roles these persons played in defining social studies in 1916, none may generate an easily recognized image among social studies practitioners in 1990.

As Professor Saxe notes, some enterprising antiquarians among us have recently begun to disinter a few of the "Old Masters" who helped in a more recent past to shape the field of social studies and to settle or sharpen its issues. Thanks to these biographers and editors, an important group of latter-day saints is now properly canonized. Professor Saxe's contribution here, however, is to take one giant step backward to analyze and interpret the ideas and attitudes of an earlier group of persons who worked together to invent a field of educational interest. They, he insists, are the founders of social studies.

Indeed, Professor Saxe leads us to see social studies emerging at the turn of the century out of a network of professional collegiality. Kingsley, Barnard, Jones, Dunn, and Robinson were professional and philosophical colleagues who cooperatively forged an educational instrument (social studies) worthy of the challenges of an industrializing nation. Professor Saxe suggests, moreover, that the 1916 Report of the Social Studies Committee (sans Kingsley) "may have directly influenced the preparation of the . . . Seven Cardinal Principals," the centerpiece of the later report of Kingsley's mother-commission on school reorganization.

While Professor Saxe's interpretation celebrates the importance of "group work" in the invention of social studies, the evidence may not support the allegation that social studies emerged not from a "network of professional collegiality," but from a *web of professional intrigue.* That is, the evidence may not be *quite* strong enough to say that for the committee on social science, Kingsley handpicked a gang of like-minded cronies who had long since decided what was required for the exercise of citizenship and what sort of school work might put students in the frame of mind to act like citizens. The "intrigue hypothesis" would also assert that Kingsley knew that chairman Jones would change the committee's name to "social studies." There would also have been an understanding that Kingsley's men would persuade the committee to adopt what Professor Saxe calls the "social efficiency prototype" based largely on Jones's, Barnard's, and Dunn's civics courses, which had been developed previously at Hampton, Philadelphia, and Indianapolis. Moreover, Kingsley and his four horsemen of the apocalyptic social studies committee were in agreement that they stood in harm's way; the mischief of the traditional historians had to be stopped.

Fanciful interpretations aside, the issue of the disciplines, which, according to Professor Saxe, was joined initially in the 1916 committee by the production of the "social efficiency prototype," remains to be dealt with in 1990. This great curriculum compromise of 1916, featuring the famous problems of democracy course, the centerpiece of the social studies insurgency, in tandem with near traditional courses on U.S. and European history and whatever other social science courses that a school could afford, provided for no permanent solution. With that centerpiece long gone and its citizenship rationale in shreds, the battle of the disciplines continues today with even more complexity.

Nonetheless, the competition among disciplines for curriculum space in social studies does not come close to matching the dilemmas and uncertainties generated by the socialization issue in social education. Whether demonstrated in the cultural estrangement of school teachers from their college mentors or in the ambivalence of students between commitment to and criticism of their society and country, this issue, which appears to pit the person against the society, has always been a part of the social studies saga. Professor Saxe suggests, however, that that perspective may be much too narrow. The socialization issue in social studies education may simply be a reflection of the fundamental issue in American democracy.

Professor Saxe foreshadows this socialization issue when he indicates early in his narrative some major components of the disagreement between traditional history and social studies. Among these components were the very attractive claims that history provided for the intellectual development of the individual and that social studies aimed to enhance the social awareness of students. Later, when Professor Saxe pulls together the loose ends of the debates over social control, social service, civic responsibility, citizenship, and social efficiency, each and all contenders for the catbird seat in social studies and in public education, he shows us that the real issue all along in social education is a mirror image of what he calls the twin paradoxes of American democracy, freedom versus conformity and the individual versus society. That a curriculum area harboring these paradoxes has recurrent internecine conflicts should not come as a surprise to anyone.

Perhaps it is a consequence of its efforts to probe the full range of human experience as well as the whole of social events that social studies remains a conflicted field. The ills of humanity and the diseases of society become the aches of the discipline. If that truly is the case, who now will instruct us that it is the conflicts within ourselves that command the attention of social studies?

C. Benjamin Cox

PREFACE

History is a lifeline to the past; it bonds us with those who have come before us. Although it is imperfect, it can serve many purposes. This book attempts to serve one of those purposes. This is not a history of the turn of the century, nor is it a history of the major national committees related to the foundational and social studies. It is not a history of public schools, of muckrakers, of the progressive movement, or of Columbia University. It is not a history of immigrants, of urbanization, of industrialization, of John Dewey, or of any other issue. It is, however, a history of the beginning years of social studies in American public schools from the 1880s to the 1920s. Social studies often takes on different dimensions. For example, to some, social studies is the content, curriculum, or courses of study. To others, it is methods and theories of pedagogy. Or, more simply, social studies is what children are taught in school and nowhere else. All these dimensions of social studies, including the above elements, as well as a host of others come to bear on the evolution of the field, and where and when they play a part in the history they are represented.

From a historical perspective, it is often helpful to divide time into useful periods. In this effort, the examination of the history of social studies reveals peaks and valleys that suggest four temporal divisions. One division of the field would place the context, generation, and formulation of social studies in one period, the experimentation and implementation phase in the next, the maturation and emergence of social studies as a discrete field of school studies in the third, and finally the development of new paradigms and theses in the present day. Roughly speaking, this division corresponds to these overlapping time frames: 1880s to 1910s, 1910s to mid-1950s, mid-1950s to mid- or late 1970s, and the present era.

Without giving away too much of the story, the first period ended with the founding of the National Council for the Social Studies in 1921. The experimentation and implementation period began with the dissemination of the 1916 Committee on Social Studies report and gained momentum when the mainstream historians of the American Historical Association (AHA) joined the social studies education movement with the formation of the AHA Commission on Social Studies in January 1929. The second period spans the work of that commission as well as the Great Depression, World War II, and beginnings of the cold war. This period ended loosely with the publication of Maurice Hunt and Lawrence Metcalf's methods textbook that postulated social studies from a new dimension. Their text and its social and cultural context ushered in the new social studies movement.

After great efforts and many federal dollars, the new social studies era apparently died an unmourned death at some point in the 1970s. At that time social studies, together with history and geography, were about to be assigned to elective status. The *Nation at Risk* study of the early 1980s, however, changed all that. As the call went out for a "return" to a more foundational approach to social studies, the field entered into its present phase and a new leasehold within the school curriculum.

With regard to limitations there is another important issue to grapple with. The 1880s may be a reasonable place for beginning a history of social education, and, in particular, social studies. But why end this particular history with the late 1910s? Why not continue the history through the present or at least in to the new social studies era? Have not most of the history and contributions to the field occurred since 1921? Would not an approach centered on more contemporary issues and individuals be a more fitting context for a viable history of the field?

These are valid questions. But if we chose to simplify the early history of the field, to avoid placing it in its rich context, to diminish the accomplishments of those who laid the trail, to avoid discussing why social education was established, or, worse yet, to ignore the origins of the field altogether, we shall miss the point. One important purpose of this text is to avoid perpetuating the persistent ahistorical mythology of the field's origins, not to extend it. The study of the antecedent and prototype of the social studies is a necessary part of our professional educational heritage and it is justified on several counts. For example, collectively social studies teachers handle content that relates to historical matters and issues, but to teach history without an understanding of one's own curricular history is to present an ahistorical model. Practitioners also deal with curricular ideas, yet if they ignore the ideas and practices of our forerunners, then the wheel needs to be reinvented with each social studies teacher.

Finally, to continue without an understanding of the social, philosophical, and political underpinnings of the social studies movement is to wander hopelessly without a sense of connectedness, without knowing that social studies practitioners are related to the cause of furthering a democratic education. Additionally, an underlying assumption is embedded here for those being inducted into the practice of social studies education. One critical attribute of any profession is the study of the field's theory; the foundation of this theory should include some knowledge and understanding of the field's history.

The history of social studies is vital to our researchers and practitioners. For reasons often unexplained, social studies teachers know that social studies must have a history, but for the most part they are ignorant of whatever this history might entail. Despite the recent attention on the foundations of social studies, social studies teachers persist with an ahistorical comprehension of the field's beginnings. The treatments currently available, although certainly sympathetic to historical analysis, may have unintentionally added to the ahistorical phenomenon because they are largely centered on individuals, not contexts and issues (see chapter 6, note 99, for a list of publications). In contrast to this biography of individuals and their connections and accomplishments in social studies, perhaps practitioners and researchers alike would benefit from a historical interpretation of the contexts, issues, and individuals that this history of social studies endeavors to portray.

In this effort, by separating the inauguration of social studies from our more recent past, this history attempts to set off and highlight the context, issues, and individuals of the early years of the social education/studies movement. As more attention, focus, and reflection are centered on the origin and development of social studies, it is hoped that this special treatment of the field's nativity will contribute to the practitioner's professional understanding of the long and difficult struggle for social studies, then and now.

ACKNOWLEDGMENTS

The research and writing of this book involved the talents and efforts of many persons. For providing excellent service with their outstanding collections, I should like to single out the libraries at the University of Illinois at Champaign-Urbana, Teachers College-Columbia University, and the University of Chicago. For encouragement and council, I should like to recognize the efforts of Professors S. Samuel Shermis of Purdue University and C. Benjamin Cox of the University of Illinois at Champaign-Urbana, both of whom read the entire manuscript. For contributing a keen eye for detail, I truly appreciated the work of Theta Baughn and Nita Dotson of the University of Oklahoma. For their excellent comments and insight, I should like to thank the readers who offered their talent toward the publication of this book. In addition, for their understanding and patience, I should like to thank my sons Danny and Andy. The most credit, however, is due my wife Laura Ann, who, over the four years of this project, offered editorial assistance, expert guidance, and undying faith and love.

1. SOCIAL SCIENCE, SOCIAL EDUCATION, AND SOCIAL STUDIES: DESCRIPTIONS, DEFINITIONS, AND ORIGINS

THIS INTRODUCTION TO the history of social studies begins with an important task: to unravel the origins[1] of the central conceptualizations used to fashion the program of the seminal 1913–1916 Committee on Social Studies, produced under the auspices of the National Education Association.[2] Among many writers of social studies literature, it is popularly held that the field was an outgrowth of the traditional history curriculum[3]—that is, that the roots of social studies can be found with the examination of the development of history as a field of study in the nineteenth century and its extension into the twentieth century.[4] The search for the genesis of social studies, however, did not begin with nor extend from the development of the traditional history curriculum. Instead, the birth and growth of the social studies movement had its own set of unique beginnings.

Nonetheless, despite the separate origins of social studies conceptualizations, there are strong parallels between the growth and development of the traditional history curriculum and the social studies.[5] The prehistorical account of social studies ideas—that is, those that existed before the term was introduced by the 1913–1916 Social Studies Committee in 1913—can be divided into three branches. The first, like that of Thomas Jesse Jones's Hampton curriculum,[6] is linked directly to the creation of the program of the 1913–1916 committee. The second, as expressed in the 1892 Madison report of the Committee of Ten[7] and the 1898 report of the American Historical Association's Committee of Seven,[8] although related in part to the 1916 Committee's program, belong more in the longer tradition of foundational studies centered in the subjects of history and geography.[9] Finally, the third branch, as exemplified by individuals like Noah Webster, Emma Willard, and Peter Parley (Samuel G. Goodrich),[10] which, although related to both traditional history and social studies curricula in spirit and intent, can claim no direct lineage to the genesis or development of the 1913–1916 Social Studies.[11]

This chapter traces the beginnings of the social studies movement prior to 1913. Chapters 2 and 3 take up and include that portion of the emerging "traditional" history curriculum that later social studies insurgents annexed as part of the movement to place social studies into the public schools.

One particularly nagging problem that has plagued social studies research, one that Robert Barr, James Barth, and S. Samuel Shermis worked to clear up, is the problem of zeroing in on the varying definitions of social studies.[12] The concern over definitions, however, is more one that followed the introduction of social studies into the public schools after 1916 than it was for the 1913–1916 Social Studies developers. Still, although a definition of social studies was thought to be clearly stated by the 1913–1916 Social Studies conferees (see appendix p. 204), the term itself and its origins requires delineation and expression. Two other terms, *social science* and *social education*, often used as synonyms for social studies, also require definition and description. Each of these terms will be examined in the order of their appearance in educational and professional literature.

SOCIAL SCIENCE

Social science ideas, like social studies ideas, have a record antedating the beginnings of the discrete social sciences as found in the professional literature of the nineteenth century.[13] Given this heritage, it is helpful to expose those roots of the social sciences that are directly related to the notion of applying social science findings through formal education. The 1913–1916 Social Studies Committee concept of social science can best be characterized as the use of social science data to define the limits of freedom and support of the status quo, as well as the means to promote the social welfare of the masses. Formal education in this model utilized social control for social service.[14] The program was designed to encourage students to identify and analyze social problems, as well as to present solutions that not only contributed to the cause of sustaining individuals and groups from the ravages of urbanization and industrialization, but also led to beneficial social progress. In addition, with citizenship education as a major emphasis, students were to be socialized (learn the rules of society); acculturated (learn to adopt the culture of others); and enculturated (learn to be part of their own culture). Democratic principles were to be used as a guide for all learning within the social studies.

The foundation of social studies education stems from the attempt to utilize education for the promotion of social welfare. This concept had its beginnings in Great Britain after the 1820s and quickly spread to the United States.[15] Typically, social welfare leaders lobbied government and industry to protect women, children, families, and workers in general from the social, economic, and political exploitation commonly associated with a rapidly expanding urban and industrial environment. In this context social science provided reformers with a special purpose as watchdogs over human welfare.

An example of this function can be found in the creation of the National Association for the Promotion of Social Science that was formed in Great Britain in 1857 for the purpose outlined in its title. Its American counterpart, commonly known as the American Social Science Association (ASSA), was started in 1865 essentially for "treating wisely the great social problems of the day."[16] This new group of dedicated individuals, inspired by the work and mission of the British organization, recognized the importance of developing education as a vehicle of social progress and welfare. Here, through various social science subjects, ASSA thinkers proposed solutions to significant social problems of the day, such as crime, poverty, and social injustice.

The ASSA worked to efficiently disseminate its ideas through education and public debate. Although the primary function of the ASSA was to "accommodate social theory and social practice,"[17] an important consequence of its efforts forged a union between social science and educational reform. Indeed, in 1887, one of the earliest calls for social science in secondary schools was made by Carroll D. Wright, the first U.S. Commissioner of Labor. Wright argued that movement into the school curriculum would clearly further "broaden [the] public appeal" of the association.[18] Additionally, Wright's plea also emphasized the link between social science instruction and good citizenship.

Formal investigations in anthropology, political science, economics, sociology, social statistics, social psychology, and social geography comprised the bulk of the social science fields that materialized in the nineteenth century.[19] Social science, which first appeared as a self-contained field of study with a broad outlook, became the title of a group of discrete sciences in the 1880s, as researchers carved a niche in the emerging modern university for their particular specialty.[20] Largely because history and geography were more established during the nineteenth century, history, stemming from the tradition of the humanities, and physical geography (often labeled "pure geography") were largely excluded from social science characterizations, essentially standing apart and distinct from social science.[21]

Social Science and the Social Sciences

The beginnings of social science and the subsequent development of the individual social sciences can be attributed to the changing social, political, and economic elements of society in the Western nations. Historians of the social sciences tell that the social revolutions of the nineteenth century were directly related to changes in population, labor practices, technological advances, the factory system, urbanization, growth of political ideologies, and modern warfare.[22] Although many of these factors benefited Western societies, for social reformers there were clearly undesirable social consequences. The self-appointed task of these reformers was to seek solutions to societal problems as well as to expose what were perceived as evils that dissolved the fragile fabric of humanity.

As the conditions of life affected by these sweeping changes worsened, social reformers institutionalized compassion into the social notion of humanitarianism.[23] In general, this socially founded expression of thought and action sought to improve the human condition as found in slums and factories, and to provide relief for the poor, the insane, and the imprisoned. In addition, social reformers set out to abolish slavery, to spread literacy, and to extend suffrage. The social, political, and economic conditions of nineteenth-century America provided a ready intellectual and political climate for the secular extension of Enlightenment social theories, as well as those who wished to spread the religious version of the social gospel. Nonetheless, the "good society" was possible, social commentators explained; science taught us that humanity was not bound, that truth could set us free. As Edward Bellamy later predicted, the "golden age" was "before us and not behind us, and [was] not far away."[24] The power to reform society through its fundamental restructuring was within the grasp of citizens.

Given the extreme positivistic social utopias of Bellamy and Henry George,[25] among many others, two key points require explanation with social theory. What was the relationship of the individual to society? And what was the relationship of society to the individual? As the social sciences developed in the nineteenth century, the answers to these two questions came to define one's political, economic, and social orientation as well as one's philosophy of education. For the social reformers, the individual was responsible to join other individuals in a concerted effort toward social reform. For the Social Darwinists, the individual followed the relentless ebb and tide of social evolution. For the traditionalist Emersonians, the individual was supreme. Each of these perspectives can be found in the formation of the social studies program of 1913–1916. The social theories written during the nineteenth century are complex, and often appear contradictory to readers. Nevertheless, there were two strands of thought centered in social science that gave the 1913–1916 Social Studies its distinctive character. A third strand of thought (individual as supreme) is discussed in the following chapter.

The first strand of thought is found in the positivistic outlook of Auguste Comte. He proposed and defended a "science of society," wherein society was perceived to be on a steady progressive march. Comte's science of society—which he named sociology—sought a natural law to account for this progress. This view of social progress advanced that the investigations of social science provided the raw material from which new dynamic paradigms of society could be generated and applied. Education in this model was to be used not only as an "intellectual" force, "but also, and more emphatically, [as a] moral" force.[26] As a theoretical descendent of Comte, the early John Dewey[27] did much to further the use of social ethics and scientific method in education through his attention to identify and analyze social problems, as well as to examine the process of working out possible solutions or alternatives.[28]

Another strand of social thought developed in the nineteenth century by Herbert Spencer and continued by William Graham Sumner affected education. Departing from Comte's notion that there was a natural law of progression and could be manipulated for social purposes—that is, social progress—Spencer and Sumner pictured a rather pessimistic view of society and social change. Social reformers in the Lester Frank Ward tradition, which was derived from Comte, believed in an optimistic society in which institutions could be created, altered, or changed in response to societal change. The Spencerians, by contrast, held that society could not be guided or controlled through conscious human efforts. Moreover, for the Spencerians any interference or attempt at governing societal change could actually work against and retard the natural eventual evolution of society.

At best in the laissez-faire tradition of Spencer and Sumner, education could only insulate individuals from the ravages of civilization by explaining the natural order of things. As with societal change in the holistic sense, education would not mitigate the conditions of life. "Evil," Sumner wrote, "only alters its form."[29] To Social Darwinists like Sumner, men and women could exercise no meaningful effect upon the problems of society; they could only protect themselves against the inevitable.

Eventually these thoughts extended into pedagogic theory in which education was viewed as the best tool to instruct the mental development of the individual's "mind [as it] unfolds in a definite order fixed and controlled by some great natural law."[30] The relationship of the individual to society was defined by a "great natural law" that ultimately rendered the individual powerless. Social science for the Social Darwinists revealed and outlined the "great natural law." Education as defined by Spencer's disarming but central question, "What knowledge is of most worth?,"[31] was used to explain to individuals how the universe was organized and what place the individual held in this organization. Spencer wrote:

> It must not suffice simply to *think* that such or such information will be useful in after life, or that this kind of knowledge is of more practical value than that; but we must seek out some process of estimating their respective values, so far as possible we may positively *know* which are most deserving of attention.[32]

"In the order of their importance," Spencer classified the steps toward this knowledge as: (1) self-preservation (health); (2) economic security (vocational training); (3) child rearing and family responsibilities (preparation for parenthood); (4) civic-mindedness (citizenship training); and (5) leisure activities (preparation for the proper use of "free" time).[33] For example, to Spencer, educators were not to offer students half-baked notions of how to raise children. Rather, drawing from the social sciences, educators were to direct students to *the* way to raise children, *the* way to maintain a sense of social cohesiveness, *the* way to prepare for life. In the end, Spencer, as well as Sumner, had no interest in teaching students to turn the social, political, or economic tables to favor a harmonious society.

Some obvious problems with this line of thought were apparent, even for the Spencerians. What was *the* way? How do we recognize it when we find it? How was *the* way then taught to children? Despite these and related critical questions, Spencerian thought enjoyed great popularity in the later years of the nineteenth century.

Spencer's fourth step, however, was to become particularly instrumental in the development of the social studies. By the late 1890s Spencer's "civic-mindedness" was translated into a variety of conceptualizations that ranged from overt indoctrination to a reasoned decision-making model (as later found in the 1916 Committee suggestion of a course in Problems in American Democracy). In the context of an intensifying nationalism, by the 1890s citizenship education had become a dominant idea in American educational thought for both the traditional history advocates and the emerging social studies insurgents. The distinction between citizenship as the general purpose for schooling, and citizenship as a specialized school offering was formulated in these years. The social studies insurgents, however, centered their curriculum on citizenship, whereas traditional historians assigned citizenship education to a secondary role.

Spencer believed that citizenship training should be founded in a course he labeled "descriptive sociology." He noted that the content of such a course would be "drawn from the broad materials of history, economics, political science, sociology, psychology, and anthropology."[34] By adding geography and contemporary problems to this list, Spencer's subjects would essentially match the content of the 1916 social studies. Much later educational thinkers, such as David Snedden, were particularly influenced by Spencerian thinking toward citizenship education. Using Spencer as a base, Snedden sought to develop a curriculum from what thoughtful adults felt was needed for proper citizenship. In this view, the needs and interests of the child were not considered essential in curricular matters.

For social reformers like Lester Frank Ward, the Spencerian

search for the laws of social evolution proved too elusive. To Ward, Social Darwinists wrongly focused upon looking for and explaining a consistent law that could account for why the rich were rich and the poor were poor. Any educational application that stemmed from this theory would ultimately be flawed. "The object of education," for Ward, was "social improvement." Education was "really needed for the purpose of making better citizens."[35] The spirit of humanitarianism that flowered in the tradition of Ward eventually recognized the importance of education as a vehicle to attend to the needs of society.

The notion of humanitarianism, as it was voiced in Great Britain and the United States during the nineteenth century, laid the foundation for the development of an American educational system whereby the knowledge gained by social science investigations could be used to instruct and enlighten future generations in the necessities of attending to social welfare. Individuals had a duty to service society, to provide for the needs of the group over the interests of the individual, to guard against the exploitation of nonsocial individuals who sought to advance their personal agendas without regard to social consequences.

In sum, social science theory, as it emerged from the nineteenth century, posited two opposing views of change that were relevant to education. Both strands of thought acknowledged change as phenomenon. The amount and speed of social progress, however, divided social scientists. For the Spencerians, social progress was slow and steady, and could not be directed. For the followers of Ward, social progress could be bent and shaped. Without the human possibility of making any conscious effort to direct or channel change, the value of education for the Spencerians was at best a conserving agent to filter the harsh realities of change; it was not a core or central institution of society. In the Ward model, however, where meaningful involvement in change was possible, education played a vital role in society as a vehicle for guiding social progress.

In this latter view reconciliations were discussed to what may be called the related paradoxes of freedom versus conformity, and individual versus society. These paradoxes emerge simultaneously wherever individuals seek to maintain their freedom while society-authority imposes restrictions. As paradoxes, no permanent resolution is possible; they continue to persist regardless of any attention. In their application to education, these paradoxes could be described in the form of two sets of questions. First, How much freedom should be allowed in school curricula (and the class) that will not thwart the creative energies of students and teachers? How much conformity must be instilled through instruction to prevent chaos? And secondly, How do teachers foster and encourage the intellectual, physical, and psychological growth of the individual? How do teachers instil a sense of social responsibility that favors the welfare of the group over the individual? Ostensibly, to educators, the modern democraticlike school needed answers to all these questions to function, but At what point was the balance to be set? Notwithstanding other variations of these questions reflecting diverse educational interests, the paradoxes of freedom versus conformity and individual versus society were consistent themes in educational theory then, and, of course, persist today.

Social control efforts are a *natural* response to the freedom versus conformity and individual versus society paradoxes. In a general sense, social control efforts are means used by the status quo to move citizens on the freedom-conformity continuum. The question is whether or not a particular move in one direction is warranted; not that social control is an evil. Social control is not an evil in and of itself; it is merely a response to the paradoxes of social life. What is critical is *how, when, to whom,* and *for what purpose* the response is given. Society does not exist in a steady state; it is a dynamic entity. This nature requires repeated adjustment and readjustment to maintain any semblance of fragile order. Thus, social control is not only necessary, it is inevitable. The twin paradoxes help organize the context of social reform. In this context, then, formal education is inescapably an element of social control.

During the nineteenth century, in the complex arguments that developed from the effort to reconcile these paradoxes, the philosophical division between the nonsocial individual and the social individual unfolded and took significance. Education for the nonsocial individual was specialized and personal, resulting in the growth and maturation of individual characteristics. Education for the social individual, by contrast, led directly to the improvement of society and, by association, to the individual.

Self and Society

At this point it is important to clarify two issues. For the Spencerians directed social change was a nonissue; it led to no meaningful social progression. In this view, the paradox between self (individual) and society (social individual) had little significance. For the followers of Ward, though, the difference was sharp and distinct, and required progress toward reconciliation if society was to advance.

The program of the 1913–1916 Social Studies ultimately revealed its philosophical orientation through the attempt to argue both sides of the seemingly contradictory but necessary notion that education could be used as a tool for social control.[36] It fostered a benign conformity, as well as a system for social service that attended to the welfare of society and extended freedom.[37] Here social control and social service were vehicles used to attend to the twin paradoxes. Social control, first identified and discussed by Edward Ross,[38] may be placed on a continuum where, on the one hand, it could be identified as a direct, prescriptive, indoctrinative method of teaching the views of the political and economic status quo. Social control in this context essentially rendered the student passive. It was not compatible with social service that sought to extend freedom. On the other side of the scale, social control could be seen as an open-ended, guiding system of education that attempted to address inevitable social, political, and economic change through an enlightened method of experimentation and questioning. This view of social control enabled students to participate. It dovetailed nicely with the version of social service that extended freedom.

Through the mechanisms of this less overt social control and social service, the 1916 conferees sought to harmonize the two central paradoxes of education. Drawing freely from social science conceptualizations of Lester Frank Ward,[39] the prototype program of the 1913–1916 Committee on Social Studies was rooted in a delicate balance between competing social theories. Deeply indebted to the new discipline of sociology,[40] the Social Studies conferees sought, on the one hand, to attend to the needs of society, while, on the other hand, to demonstrate an earnest interest in addressing the needs of individuals.

The program of the 1916 Social Studies did not reflect either a conspicuous or a hidden allegiance to the so-called corporate or monied interests of the state. Instead the 1916 document was imbued with a sense of social purpose that fostered traditional democratic principles and challenged students to question, experiment, or test the institutions and ideas of the status quo. Nonetheless, the full extent of the social studies conferees challenge of the status quo—especially the notion of questioning political decisions—will never be known, because politics and attitudes resulting from World War I quickly closed the door to free inquiry into several sensitive areas.[41]

The division between social studies advocates and traditional historians, as will be discussed later, was not centered on the supposed dilemma between social control and social service, although this was a voiced concern of the social studies conferees. Instead, the dispute was focused on the differing philosophical views as to what purpose and by what method citizens, or individuals, should be educated in society. Put simply, Where on the freedom-conformity/ individual-society continuum would the line be drawn? To benefit society through the individual, or to benefit the individual directly?

It is here that the Spencerian line of thought entered into the educational debate between the traditional history advocates and the social studies insurgents as each group argued their position from a different perspective. The traditional curriculum historians used a mixture of Spencerian social theory and their own Emersonian view of the individual. In contrast, the social studies insurgents made use of sociological ideas from Ward and the more pedagogically appealing arguments of Albion Small, George Vincent, Charles Horton Cooley, Edward Ross, and Franklin Giddings.[42]

SOCIAL EDUCATION

As education became a major issue of social reformers in the 1890s, the notion of social reform as education emerged under a common term. By the end of nineteenth century, the name for this type of development shifted from social science to social education and social studies. That the move to social education came slightly in advance of the first use of the term "social studies" or "social study" should not be interpreted as significant. More or less, the initial deviation between the terms amounted to a difference in scope: social education was viewed as a generic term for a socially centered school curricula that constituted *all* of what went as courses or subject fields. History, geography, or the social sciences in this view of social education were not purposely collected or emphasized under any common umbrella term. What cemented curricula together was a sociological outlook toward education, an outlook that held that the purpose of education was to prepare students in and for social life.

Social studies as a conceptualization had a more narrow agenda: to prepare and serve citizens with "democratic" skills through the specific course/topical areas as found in the social sciences, history, and geography. In essence, social education represented a broad view of education based on social science, whereas social studies, although sharing the purpose of education based on social science, was defined as a specific field of study within the general school curricula given over entirely to citizen preparation.

In 1896 Conway MacMillan, an education professor at the University of Minnesota, presented one of the earliest suggestions for "social education" in schools.[43] Although MacMillan treated popular Hegelian and Herbartian educational themes, his "thought [was] dominated by Spencerianism." MacMillan presented to his readers the concepts of the social and nonsocial individual: the social individual was an individual cognizant of the needs of the group/society. By contrast, the nonsocial individual thought only in terms of the self.[44]

MacMillan believed that a reconciliation of the two competing natures would be an individual; to be a member of a group was possible with "social education." Rather than looking at the paradox between individual and society from the societal standpoint, as social reformers did, MacMillan presented this paradox from the individual's perspective. He reasoned:

> Education of the schools—social education—[in the broad interpretation] has therefore not only the duty of stimulating the individual to do his best as an individual, but more fundamentally it must from its very nature so mould him that he will be the best as a member of society.[45]

Here MacMillan sought to rally educational leaders against what he called the "conservatism of society" and "formalism." He argued that the future of education would not be found in educating the individual apart from social considerations. MacMillan claimed that "the next great step in educational reform and progress" would be taken "from a basis of sociological and thoroughly scientific enquiry into the characteristic of the modern citizen."[46] Although MacMillan was arguing for social education from a broad perspective, ultimately the social studies insurgents fashioned the sociological perspective as the foundation in a more limited program.

Notwithstanding MacMillan's call for a "social education," the notion of presenting an educational perspective apart from the individual as supreme was troublesome to educators. In the *Third Yearbook* of the National Herbart Society (1897), Charles DeGarmo, a noted teacher-educator, explained to the cautious that the education of the social individual was founded in a "social," not a "socialistic," concept of society. DeGarmo's view, drawn heavily from William James, was that the socialistic version was too "unwieldy and highly mechanical" and unsuited to a nation like the United States. Speaking from a Spencerian position, DeGarmo argued:

[A "true" social concept] permit[ed] the agencies of production to remain in private hands, and eschewing all artificial schemes of distribution, [was] marked by its freedom of association, by its permission of individual initiative in every department of life, and by its division of authority between large and small bodies. It [was] permeated by the Anglo-Saxon idea of local control of local affairs.[47]

According to DeGarmo the new socialized or social-centered education would not be a threat to individual freedom or laissez-faire attitudes; it was in actuality a boon to freedom. "The non-social individual," wrote DeGarmo, "centers all his thoughts and activity in himself. The social individual, on the contrary, expands his personality."[48] To DeGarmo, borrowing from Dewey, the new socially tuned education would focus upon how schools would educate social individuals.

DeGarmo's proposal was founded on three bases: the "formation of right social ideals," the "cultivation of adequate social disposition," and the "formation of efficient social habits."[49] These "ideals" were to be developed through "school studies"; the "dispositions" were to be cultivated by "awakening of an abiding interest in the social ideals"; and the "habits" were to be formed "with respect to regularity, punctuality, silence and industry also with respect to punishments and to play." Thus, in the educational setting socially centered education guided the social individual to greater freedom, thereby addressing the paradox of freedom versus conformity.

DeGarmo's theme, originating in William James and John Dewey, became quite familiar to educational readers before 1913. In 1906 William Owen of the University of Chicago High School changed the emphasis from social education as simply helpful, to social education as necessary. Owen reasoned that the school as a "social institution," like other social institutions, needed to "be tested by its fitness to perform social service."[50] Here, in an attempt to argue that a "unified view of the world" was required to make "individual effort rational and social aims intelligible," Owen addressed the paradox of the social versus nonsocial individual (society versus the individual).

Nonetheless, Owen's concept of social education, like that of DeGarmo and MacMillan, was still a general call to socializing the entire school system under a uniform curriculum. Similarly, Colin Scott also wrote extensively about "social education" in the early

1900s.[51] Scott attempted to detail what such a socialized curriculum would look like. However, as did other social education writers, he did not single out the social sciences or history for special curricular attention. These writers, in the spirit of the Social Education Congress that sought to further the cause of social service,[52] essentially worked to bring social service and social control ideas into the overall school system.

David Snedden

Within a decade of MacMillan, the call for a unified social education, opposed to a broad theoretical interpretation of social education, was refined and focused. In 1907 David Snedden, one of the most prolific educational writers of his day, argued that there existed "an awkward tendency in present discussion to use the term social education too broadly or inclusively."[53] To Snedden, although all subjects in the school curricula had social significance, not all subjects were social-centered. Given this foundation, Snedden separated school curricula into five divisions: "(a) physical education; (b) vocational education; (c) cultural education; (d) social education; and (e) the education which aims at general mental discipline."[54] In Snedden's treatment of social education—which he also called "social study" here—we find several important bridges or conceptual links between theory and practice. First, Snedden placed an idea of social education in the school. Then he positioned social science with history as complimentary elements of the same curriculum. Next he explained that in using this "social education" or "social study," the newer developmental approach to pedagogy was necessary to counteract the "intrusion of the adult standard into the affairs of children's education."[55] Later, Snedden's three conceptual links were incorporated in the 1913–1916 social studies proposal.[56]

Although others articulated the need for socializing education or placing the social sciences in the schools before him, Snedden presented the first argument that called for a focused or more defined social education, together with an attack on the traditional history curriculum. Snedden explained:

> The educator is asked in his mission of taking the child from where he is physically, vocationally, socially, and intellectually, to where he ought to be in these regards at early maturity, to teach so many subjects . . . that he is obliged to make numerous choices, and he feels that he has the right to call

upon the proponent of any special subject to justify its inclusion in the curriculum. So he asks, why teach history to children?[57]

With this "simple" question Snedden advanced the social education/studies movement from a theoretical base within social theory to the arena of school curricular politics. His question attacked the entrenched traditional history curriculum, which to its proponents was a given. Snedden did not wish to displace history per se; however, he did argue for a different type of history to be taught. To historians Snedden's suggestion that history instruction be adjusted to fit social needs and considerations was tantamount to a declaration of war against the field of history itself. Snedden argued strongly that the preservation of "chronological continuity" was "both cruel and futile," that such instruction produced "little more than verbal knowledge and a feeling of repression towards the subject."[58] It would seem that historians would bristle as their rock of "chronological continuity," the foundation of history instruction, was laid to siege by Snedden. Still, initially Snedden's question attracted little attention among historians. However, other social-centered educators picked up Snedden's attack.

In a refinement of Snedden's position, Charles Ellwood offered that in "some cases" history should be taught from "the sociological point of view."[59] Although a modification of Snedden's attack, Ellwood's position acknowledged the shifting sands of school curricula. To the social education insurgents, the traditional history curriculum was not impervious to change. The notion that educators could question and adjust traditional history curriculum opened the argument for social studies to enter the school curriculum.

By sharing slogans, the social studies insurgents symbolically joined the forces for social efficiency in the 1910s. Snedden's potent appeal that questioned the validity of the traditional history curriculum rallied many educators against the history camp. Moreover, Snedden's clarification of history's place in the curriculum combined with his argument for social education/studies provided the spark that launched the movement to place social studies into the schools at the expense of the traditional history curriculum. In sum, Snedden's writing moved the concept of social education from simply a vague orientation of the curriculum to a specific concept of citizenship education.

One year after the Social Studies Committee reported, Henry Johnson, then dean of the entrenched traditional history camp, recognized the serious nature of Snedden's charge.[60] For Johnson and the traditional historians, however, it was too late; the social studies foot was already solidly in the school door.

SOCIAL STUDIES

In a title revealing its philosophical origins, the Committee on Social Science was formed in 1912 as part of the National Education Association report on the Reorganization of Secondary School Studies.[61] The term "social studies" itself had to wait another year before it entered the mainstream educational vocabulary with the publication of the preliminary report of the retitled Committee on Social Studies in 1913.[62]

Although the popularity of social studies did not rise appreciably until the decades of the 1920s and into the 30s, the term did have a limited but significant history before 1913. Beginning in 1905 "social studies" was used by Thomas Jesse Jones, who later became chair of the Committee on Social Studies, as the title of a course of study for blacks and Amerindians at Hampton Institute in Virginia.[63] In this setting, Jones, as an "Instructor in Social Studies," presented a curriculum that included political, sociological, and economic work, but clearly excluded any formal instruction in history and geography. In the spirit of Booker T. Washington, Jones taught social study that accepted at face value second-class citizenship for blacks and Amerindians, and sought through the study of social science the gradual improvement of both.

Education for Jones appeared to attend to both social service, defined as the helping of blacks and Amerindians to survive in the world, and social control, conceived as the explaining to blacks and Amerindians their role in American society. Although there were parallels to the education advocated by social reformers of the American Social Science Association, education for the Hampton social studies, at least the practical application, was decidedly directed at social control. Under Jones, students at Hampton were not instructed or inspired to political activism. Instead, students were taught to accept the political and economic status quo as well as Anglo-Saxon values. This type of educational system was not radical. Schools, in the main, accepted the political and economic status quo and were essentially immersed in Anglo-Saxon values. In view of the social conditions at the time, what made the Hampton social studies unusual was that blacks and Amerindians were given the opportunity for an advanced or higher education.

The sense of social education as a means of reconstructing society (implied in the 1916 Social Studies program) was missing at Hampton, and, indeed, would hardly have been acceptable to the sponsors of this institution. Jones's Hampton social studies is an example of theory clashing with social reality. On the one hand, the Hampton program sought to educate students outside the prevailing practice of history instruction (thus linking it to the emerging social studies movement); while on the other hand, the Hampton program remained strictly within the bounds of the status quo limits to educating blacks and Amerindians (thus linking it to the status quo itself). This contradiction in the Hampton social studies (being both liberal and repressive) was, however, worked out by the 1916 Social Studies. With the later social studies program, limits where not suggested or implied for any group of children; active participation and skepticism were encouraged with all children.

Contrary to conventional mythology on the origins of social studies,[64] the 1916 Social Studies Committee did not coin the term "social studies." The inaugural use of the term "social studies" in the United States can be found in the title of an 1887 book on the conditions and prospects of urban workers.[65] Drawing heavily from his membership in the American Social Science Association, author Heber Newton spoke of social study that was specifically selected from the social sciences for the purpose of improving the lot of the poor and suffering urban workers. Newton was reacting to problems he perceived to be caused by or related to the rapid urbanization and industrialization of the nation. Again, like Jones's "social studies," the contents of Newton's book centered on data generated largely from the emerging fields of political science, sociology, and economics. History and geography were not considered in Newton's vision of social study and reform.

From Newton and Jones we find that the initial use and shaping of the term "social studies" was directly tied to the utilization of social science data as a force in the improvement of human welfare. In Newton's case, the new-age urban industrial worker was the target for uplifting; for Jones, blacks and Amerindians were instructed to "improve" themselves by learning and accepting their role in society. In reference to Newton's and Jones's base in social science, there was a strong association between the message given in Newton's book and Jones's work at Hampton. Furthermore, Newton specifically noted the contribution of Hampton Institute in the cause of "industrial education,"[66] a cause that Jones later came to champion at Hampton and as the chair of the 1913–1916 Social Studies Committee. Both the Newton and Jones concepts illustrate an evolutionary shift in the use of the term "social studies." Beginning with social studies as rooted in the social sciences for the purpose of attending to social welfare, the term evolved into social studies grounded in the social sciences for the purpose of directly educating future citizens.

Beyond Newton's book, two other texts used the term "social studies" in their titles before 1913, *Social Studies in England* by Sarah Bolton (1883)[67] and *Social Studies* by Lady Jane Wilde (1893).[68] Both Bolton and Wilde were members of the British National Association for the Promotion of Social Science. The subject matter of each text, however, did not address schools or schooling specifically. Bolton, like Newton and Jones, sought to promote the use of the social sciences to serve urban workers—that is, for social welfare. Wilde also argued, in a much broader manner, for the "elimination" of the human evils of "poverty and degradation and misery." Yet, in this effort she chose to emphasize the value of all sciences (without stressing the social sciences).[69] Taken as a whole, writers on both sides of the Atlantic worked to fashion an educational program that drew upon the social sciences for their content and purpose.

The phrase "social studies" or "social study" did make appearances in other forms of print prior to 1913, along with a seemingly never-ending list of words prefaced by the term "social" that connected social education to citizenship education. The first outline of "a programme for social study" was published by sociologist Ira Howerth in May 1897.[70] Howerth claimed, however, that the work was "practically adapted from [Albion] Small and [George] Vincent's *Introduction to the Study of Society*."[71] Howerth presented a "Constitution" for the development of "Social Study Club[s]," where, according to the constitution, the expressed object was for members to conduct "actual investigations of social conditions and institutions . . . and the study of social questions, with a view to the improvement of local conditions and the advancement of the members of the club in the knowledge and art of true social life."[72]

Howerth suggested to his colleagues that in the effort to attend to the "present widespread discontent in regard to social conditions" (ca. 1890s), interested parties drawn from the public at large should organize themselves into "study clubs to pursue local social investigations."[73] Howerth's invitation that any citizen could and should study "social life" was to sociology what Carl Becker's suggestion that "every man be his own historian" was to the discipline of history of the next generation. Howerth's notion, credited to Small and Vincent, that individual citizens should organize and become active participants in social welfare issues, although not aimed specifically for the public schools, did become a central tenet of the 1913–1916 social studies program in "community civics."

Howerth via Small and Vincent offered a general program of social study for society. The earliest use of utilizing the term "social study" as a field derived specifically from the social sciences for pedagogical purposes can be found in a paper by Edmund James. Then president of the American Academy of Political and Social Sciences, he delivered a paper to the membership of the National Herbart Society one month after Howerth's "social study" plan in June 1897.[74] James had made his plea for the entrance of social studies (without using the expression) into the public schools earlier in 1897 in a paper to the membership of the American Academy of Political and Social Science. Here James declared, in the spirit of Newton, Bolton, and Wilde before him, that the social sciences reduced in some pedagogical form were to be used for the promotion of "the welfare of modern society in general, and especially to the welfare of modern free societies."[75]

In his Herbart Society paper James made the point, perhaps his major contribution to the history of the social studies, that the natural sciences consisting of "geology, mineralogy, biology, etc." were successfully introduced in schools under the generic rubric of "nature studies." The political and social sciences could also be introduced under a common title. James noted:

> Of course that does not mean necessarily that we shall put into the primary grades a subject which we shall call politics, and which we shall call economics, and which we shall call sociology. . . . [But rather, as with the use of the] term "nature study," which is simple, intelligible, and comprehensive, and which may include all that is possible or feasible to utilize for the purposes of instruction in the lower schools, gives us a hint of what may be accomplished under the head of "social study," if we choose to use such a term, or indeed of what may be done without the use of any term at all, to delimit the work in which we are engaged from other useful work in the schools.[76]

Thus, "social study," according to James, was purely an expedient term, a way to "delimit" curricular matter. Simply put, social study was a helpful, descriptive phrase like "nature study," employed to describe the use of the social sciences in the schools for the development and nurturing of young citizens. James's definition of social study compares more favorably to the 1913–1916 Social Studies use of the term than does Howerth's broad definition of "social study." Howerth's broad definition was later given a different perspective by his two mentors, Small and Vincent, indicating the maturation of the notion of educational perspective in regard to social theory.

In fact, George Vincent in 1901, although not giving the idea any particular title, made a similar argument to James and not Howerth for a corollary social course for schools comparable to the collection of fields under "nature study."[77] Vincent wrote:

> Those who cultivate history, economics, politics, anthropology, and sociology, and who believe that social science in a large sense has an all-important role to play in education, are naturally concerned to know what relation these studies may sustain to the elementary and secondary schools. . . . This process [the nature study concept from the natural sciences] may well serve as a model to those who are anxious to see the social sciences influence the earlier years of the school.[78]

Arthur W. Dunn

In 1905 Arthur W. Dunn, a former student of Small and Vincent as well as the future chief secretary and compiler of the 1913–1916 Social Studies program, continued the line of reason begun by James and called for a course in "social study" in the manner of the sciences.[79] Then, in 1907, again using the James analogy, David Snedden of Columbia University, a former student of sociologist Edward Ross, suggested, "just as we have 'nature study' so should we have 'social study' or 'society study.'"[80] Earlier, in 1896, Small himself articulated a call for a generic "study of society" for schools that suggested a restricted and reduced use of social science.[81]

Small's advocacy of a "study of society" should not be interpreted as an endorsement for formal sociology study in schools. Despite Small's sociological grounding, he strongly opposed the formal study of sociology below the "senior year in college."[82] Small's distinction between the formal study of a subject field as sociology at an institution of higher education and an introductory study in public schools constituted an important step in the development of social studies theory. It also signaled the beginning of the notion that academic subjects could be "watered down" for use in public schools.

Moreover, this separation of study between university and school study was a departure from what the insurgents claimed was the traditional history curriculum's attempt to make what amounted to "little historians" out of school children. Small's classification was an early example of viewing subject matter and process/application in developmental terms. The 1913–1916 Social Studies program clearly reflected Small and Vincent's philosophical position that children were not merely physically different but possessed varying degrees of conceptual and perceptual capacities that required a curriculum attuned to their needs. This developmental distinction, of course, did not necessarily rule out history instruction. Historians, in general, shared the notion that "professional history," too, could be successfully graded for schools.[83]

Edmund James, however, was the first to propose a course in social study for schools and was also the first to predict that this type of curricular approach to social science in schools was "possibly another generation or two" away from reality.[84] James was remarkably accurate. Twenty years later, the social sciences through "social studies" (which incidently was the title accepted by the social education insurgents) entered the American educational scene with the 1916 Social Studies Committee report. If any claim to be the "father of social studies" could be made based upon the use of the term "social study" in the context of citizenship education, Edmund J. James is the most likely candidate for this honor.

Given these examples of the earliest uses of social studies, it is clear that the term as a general rubric did not appear haphazardly or as an afterthought in the 1913–1916 Social Studies report. Long before the 1916 Committee on Social Studies publication utilized the terms "social study" and "social studies," the conception of a specific curriculum offering distilled from the social sciences was in the air. The fact that Social Studies conferees like Dunn and Jones, as well as the influential Snedden, all used the term well in advance of the committee's deliberations offers insight into the origins of how the term was used to describe the 1913–1916 Committee's prototype program.

The significance of the introduction of social study defined as delimiting the social sciences for pedagogical use can be discovered in the National Herbart Society papers of 1896 and 1897. These publications reveal the philosophical groundwork for the social studies movement as a whole. To test this supposition we look at Arthur W. Dunn's textbook *The Community and the Citizen* (first published in 1906). The common thread of education as a means to further social welfare can be found in it. Dunn, who later became the driving force behind the 1913–1916 Committee on Social Studies as its chief secretary and compiler, established a connection between one of the earliest uses of the term "social study" as the future name of the Social Studies Committee. But more importantly with his *Community* text, he also drew the connection between the Herbart papers of 1897 and the social studies program of the 1913–1916 Committee.

In this influential civics text, Dunn credited John Dewey's essay "Ethical Principles Underlaying Education,"[85] that appeared as the lead paper in the 1897 Herbart yearbook, as providing the "aim and spirit" for his work. Moreover, Dunn expressed his "indebtedness to Albion Small and George Vincent" for suggesting the methodology used in his text. The notion of using social science and, in particular, sociology as a basis for a new approach to civic instruction—which Dunn called "community civics"—served to illustrate the first meaningful movement from theory to practice in emerging social studies literature.

In the 1923 yearbook of the Herbart group (renamed in 1900 the National Society for the Scientific Study of Education), Earle Rugg explained that Dunn's "epoch-making" book accomplished three important feats:

> (1) It widened the concept of what civics courses should teach. . . . (2) It stimulated many other communities to work out courses adapted to their own particular city. . . . (3) It led to the creation of a very influential committee, the N.E.A. Committee on the Social Studies.[86]

In addition, Henry Johnson also commented:

> The whole framework set up by the Committee for the social studies was in fact an application of the spirit and point of view of community civics, the special field of the compiler of the *Report* [Arthur William Dunn].[87]

The fact that Dunn was instrumental in the deliberations of the 1913–1916 Social Studies is unquestionably true. Given Rugg's and Johnson's later comments, Dunn should not be construed as the "creator" of social studies. Rather, Dunn should be credited with activating the notion of community civics. What was significant for the history of the social studies was the connection between Dunn's sociological outlook and Dewey's views as expressed in his "Ethical Principles" article. Dewey's interest in and energy toward social reform and progress, as Ellen Condliffe Lagemann has developed,[88] was firmly rooted in a sociological approach to education. This, of course, was an approach shaped and influenced by the same two sociologists (Small and Vincent) that Dunn mentioned as being influential to him.

Highlighting the importance of Dunn's sociological foundations is necessary because in the same issue where James discussed the possibility of "social study" and Dewey introduced the "social individual," the theoretical roots of the 1913–1916 social studies model can be found. Additionally, two other important articles published in the 1897 yearbook contributed to the philosophy that the study of society (social study) was the means toward achieving the twin goals of social efficiency and social progress. Articles by Charles DeGarmo, who differentiated between the "non-social individual and the social individual,"[89] and C.C. Van Liew, who discussed how educators should go about the preparation of "children for better, more perfect and efficient participation in the social life of the future,"[90] articulated a favored position of the Herbartians: to serve the human community. Collectively these papers from the 1897 Herbart yearbook on citizenship education make this work an important early milestone in the history of social studies.

Three Revolutions

Henry Suzzallo of Columbia University is the ninth illustration of the educational use of the term "social studies" or "social study" prior to 1913 presented here. He illustrates that the term had matured from a crude introductory approach to social science materials and data (in Newton) to the conception of an organized body of instruction firmly rooted in social philosophy. Suzzallo noted that this movement of "education as social study" represented the "third revolution" that ushered in the new education.[91] The first was that the teacher was freed from the constraints of convention and "institutional habits," and, incidentally, freed from the domination of church or religious authority in curricular matters. The second was that the new education called for "more effective ways" to teach students; ways that signaled the "growing professional consciousness that the child or youth [was] a pertinent factor in education to whom some adjustment must be made."

In practice, the third revolution dictated that the school be recognized as a social institution, that students be recognized as social individuals, that education in general be recognized as a social enterprise. "The greatest single need," Suzzalo wrote, "of the educational profession today, both for its efficiency and its respectability, is that it shall possess itself of a sound social point of view."[92]

Suzzalo illustrates an important theoretical turning point in the social studies movement: the introduction of "social efficiency" into the argument for social studies. Social efficiency's entrance into the argument for educational reform indicated another stage of social studies thought. Raymond Callahan's classic study, *Education and the Cult of Efficiency*, found that social efficiency entered the educational mainstream in the early 1900s.[93] Barbara Berman, on the contrary, has claimed that social efficiency and its businesslike orientation appeared well before 1900 in three "identifiable" periods of "developmental phases."[94] For the social studies movement, however, social efficiency as a guiding concept first had to clear the theoretical hurdle erected by Spencer and Sumner, which held that social change could not be altered directly by individuals.[95] For this movement at least, social efficiency could not be used as an argument for social studies unless meaningful social change was a viable possibility. By the early 1900s, just as Callahan had found, the decks had been cleared of Spencerian domination, thereby making social efficiency a powerful argument for the introduction of a new, less traditional subject as well as for progressive pedagogical methodologies.

In this context Suzzalo made clear that the old style of educational thought was dying. Suzzalo declared:

> For American society and its schools, the implication is plain. The school is the largest and most enduring force for social unification under free governmental institutions. Along with other agencies which educate through the transmission and diffusion of common sentiment and belief, home and church and vocation, the school creates that common social consciousness which leads men toward political cooperation, and prevents that "over-class consciousness" and that "over-individualization" which are dangers to the common weal. . . . The liberalizing power of education creates unity among men

by implanting ethical ideas that control men from within. Truly educated men are free in their own eyes because the fundamental ideas with which they are equipped make individual desire and its ensuing acts such that the state need not subject them to restraint.[96]

Social Efficiency

Explanations notwithstanding, Suzzalo's contention that education made "men and women efficient and free," that education "liberalized" men and women, formed the battle cry of the social studies insurgents: "education for social efficiency!" Suzzalo also addressed the paradox of freedom versus conformity. He noted:

Two things seem to be in opposition here. One is the idea of common culture and general social training; the other is the idea of personal competitive efficiency and specialized vocational training.[97]

To approach the paradox, Suzzalo believed that culture and efficiency required definition. His resolution, like that of Dewey and Colonel Francis Parker before him, was founded in the education of the child in the "whole social life," where culture was "always relative to social conditions, and efficiency [was] always determined by social needs."[98] Therefore, to both Suzzalo and the social studies movement, "social education" was the indicated future of education. The school was "created by social necessity," and thus required special attention to the shifting social conditions and needs of citizens. The 1913–1916 Social Studies Committee made good use of the social efficiency arguments that Suzzalo and David Snedden articulated for placing social study/social education in schools. Berman's treatment of social efficiency offers a possible explanation (which will be treated more fully in the following chapters) as to why the fully entrenched traditional history curriculum mind-set among superintendents faded so quickly once the social studies movement embraced social efficiency as its battle cry.

At the 1921 Columbia University "Conference Upon Desirable Adjustments Between History and Other Social Studies," the "friends of social studies" and the "unionists" who wished to merge history and social studies were viewed as having the upper hand against the "out of date" historians.[99] Although social studies programs had made considerable progress with school curricula—in opposition to and presumedly at the expense of the traditional history curriculum—in states like North Dakota, New Jersey, New York, and Iowa, and cities like Philadelphia, the unionist position was largely unsuccessful.[100] Nonetheless, school administrators were very receptive to social studies considerations. Administrators appeared to hold a predisposition, gained through a long tradition, of being receptive to arguments for a particular curricular approach when social efficiency was used as a foundation.[101] But the receptiveness of social studies conceptualizations was not the major reason why social studies entered mainstream curricula.[102]

Nonetheless, as education became a formalized institution with political clout,[103] educators did not take long to realize the importance of utilizing historical and geographical formulations with social science conceptualizations. As early as 1885 Mary Sheldon Barnes was producing textual materials that incorporated a new design of history study for elementary and secondary schools. They integrated the social sciences with history and geography.[104] The inclusion of history in the social studies model, or as Barnes put it, the inclusion of social science in teaching history, represented a significant shift in defining social studies content.

Much later, in 1899, Paul Hanus, in his appeal for a general education for all students, outlined a conceptualization of education that called for the use of "social studies." He defined this term along the lines of the program outlined by the 1892 Madison Conference as history, civics, and economics.[105] Hanus's plea for "social studies," couched in Spencerian terms, was directed at the common history curriculum. Hanus argued:

> We ask that our meager and inadequate courses in history really comprise an elementary descriptive sociology, and the account of the development of institutions of modern society. Instead of consisting chiefly of accounts of war, dynasties, and court intrigue, it will deal by preference with the arts and occupations of peace, with the history of industry, of commerce, of scientific inventions . . . with the history of art, education, and philanthropy.[106]

In 1901 Frank W. Blackmar of the University of Kansas, who had pedagogical connections to both sociology and history, also suggested the notion of the teaching of social science and history in schools. Blackmar correctly predicted that the joining of social science and historical studies was "destined to occupy [a place in the] future" of schooling.[107] Blackmar, however, did not advocate the fusion or integration of social science and history within a program. Instead, he proposed the teaching of social science and history as *subjects* within a course of study.

In 1903 Charles McMurry, a strong advocate of Herbartian moralist pedagogy, also hinted at the prospect of placing social sciences under the history umbrella. McMurry's version, however, emphasized "history [more as a] moral and social study" than history with as a scientific study.[108]

As with Barnes, the curricula that Hanus, Blackmar, and McMurry proposed served to illustrate the earliest theoretical arguments for a course of "social studies" that included both history and social science by name and by implication. These, however, were more a reaction within the traditional history curriculum than part of the social studies movement. Nonetheless, the contributions of Barnes, Hanus, Blackmar, and McMurry are significant to the history of the social studies. They illustrate that educators were thinking in terms of merging foundational studies with the social sciences in advance of the deliberations of the 1913–1916 Social Studies conferees.

With the exception of Barnes, Hanus, and Blackmar, the conception of social studies presented thus far has expressly excluded historical and geographical considerations in favor of the exclusive use of the social sciences. The revolutionary notion, proposed in theory by Hanus and Blackmar, and outlined in practice by Barnes, that history and social science not only could contribute on an equal basis in the same curricular model, but were eminently necessary in elementary and secondary education, came to characterize the later social studies proposal. This hybrid consensus made the social studies prototype program of the 1913–1916 Committee unique.

The merging of curricular ideas as found in the conflict between the notion of the nonsocial and the social individual exposed the distinction between the two conceptualizations of social service and social control. As a result, this action came to dictate educational purpose for social efficiency.[109] The question of how this merging of ideas was accomplished will be discussed in more detail in the following chapters.

2. BEGINNINGS OF TRADITIONAL HISTORY

FOUR HUNDRED YEARS after Columbus landed in the Americas, Chicago, that great new metropolis by Lake Michigan, held a world's fair to celebrate the event. Millions of people attending the fair marveled at the exhibits of machinery, art, and architecture. Honoring the triumph of bringing the Old World to the New World and the new to the old, the fair's planners devised a somewhat pretentious theme: to display and demonstrate the new technologies of American industry in an atmosphere of Old World art and architecture. The 1893 World's Columbian Exposition was both a bold statement of New World mastery over the Old World as well as a milestone in America's rise to industrial preeminence.

Educational footnotes were also being written that summer in Chicago. At the fair's height a brash young historian from the University of Wisconsin named Frederick Jackson Turner delivered a speech at a meeting of the newly formed American Historical Association (founded in 1884). Turner recounted a simple message, "the superintendent of the census for the 1890 reports . . . that the settlements of the West lie so scattered over the region that there can no longer be said to be a frontier line."[1]

Turner argued that the frontier was not only instrumental in the "promotion of democracy," but it also rooted American civilization in the spirit of "frontier individualism." To Turner it followed that "so long as free land exist[ed]," individualism would triumph.[2] The passing of the frontier, however, "closed the first period of American history" and opened a new era of great uncertainty, danger, and perhaps even decay. To Turner, therefore, it was ironic that just as America was rapidly becoming a premier industrial power of the world, it was decaying from within.[3] If cultural decay was to be prevented, intellectuals needed to mount a defense. The promotion of historical studies in the schools was one aspect of this defense.

The program of foundational studies that emerged in the 1890s has become known as the traditional history curriculum.[4] Turner, as did many important historians, made contributions to bring history into the schools. Although chapters 2 and 3 discuss the contributions of historians to the development of the traditional history curriculum in schools, the intention of these chapters is not so much to examine the roots and rationale of the infusion of history into the schools as to identify the traditional history curriculum itself.[5] In this chapter two of the earliest history teaching textbooks are examined as well as the reports of the Committee of Ten, Subcommittee on History, Civil Government, and Political Economy, hereafter referred to as the Madison Conference, specifically to distinguish the substance and methodology of this new curriculum.

The rationale for the examination of these particular committees (including the Committee of Seven report that will be outlined in the following chapter) is that school leaders of the period were readily influenced by university and college scholars of history, as were textbook authors, curriculum writers, and their respective publishers. As Arthur Schlesinger, Sr., a dean of American historians during the first half of the twentieth century, later wrote: "whether we like it or not, the textbook, not the teacher teaches the course." Good textbooks, therefore, were the basis of good teaching, and the good textbook, in order to be published, prudently followed the guidance of two preeminent national history committees. For textbooks at the turn of the century this meant attending to the recommendations and suggestions of the Madison Conference and the later Committee of Seven.

INTRODUCTION OF TRADITIONAL HISTORY

The development of "scientifically based" history instruction was in its infancy during the 1890s when the German trained Ph.D.s teaching at Johns Hopkins, Harvard, Michigan, and the University of

Chicago began the quest for historical truths.[6] Until this time history in the schools largely meant the study of myths and legends from ancient Greece and Rome, heroes of the American Revolution, discoveries of the New World, and other stories designed to inspire patriotism and moral certitude. Under the control of various religious groups, concern for historical mindedness or scientific searches for truth were often looked upon as undermining the church; schools were to teach proper respect for the church not challenge its authority. Notwithstanding the powerful effect of church ethics and morality, history instruction was in a state of flux. Like the later Committee on Social Studies, these early national history committees sought to bring order to the confusion over what ought be taught and why.

The origins of what unfolded as the traditional history curriculum can be traced to young historians from Michigan, Harvard, and Johns Hopkins such as Andrew White, Herbert B. Adams, Charles K. Adams, and others. These men believed in the value of historical knowledge to strengthen the individual, sharpen the mind, broaden the horizon, and give depth to the soul. These men believed that history had great pedagogical value for school students beyond standardizing courses for university admission. These historians and those like-minded sought to emphasize history's values to educators not only for its mental discipline but also as a source of useful facts. To its developers, the discipline of history was directed by a scientifically coherent method of inquiry that provided a comprehensive or holistic view of the world. They believed that this new way to treat history had the ultimate civic and social values required by the modern age. To these pioneers, history was a window to the past and a door to the future, and anyone who studied it properly could apply its lessons to everyday life. Simply put, history had the potential to be the premier discipline of the school.

The concept of the past as a vital link to the present was a common theme of the period. As N. Ray Hiner concluded, "the study of history satisfied an almost compelling psychic need of nineteenth century Americans to reexperience time, to analyze it, to capture it conceptually, and thereby in a personal way control it."[7] The Madison Conference membership sought to capitalize on the emerging popularity of history by formalizing its introduction into the secondary school as part of a required "modernized" curriculum. To these writers, any introduction of the discipline, however, was predicated on the expectation that history credits, as well as those from the other "modern" practical studies, be accepted as legitimate courses for college matriculation.

The movement toward promoting what was known as the traditional history had its beginnings among university historians near the time of the advent of the American Historical Association (1884). Although academic historians as the accepted experts of the field dictated the substance and methods of collegiate history, a psychologist and an academic educator introduced secondary teachers to traditional history. Moreover, the shape of the traditional history curriculum was principally influenced by the alliance of two socially founded movements, psychology and scientific objectivity. The former was the primary focus of the emerging professionally trained educators, the latter was the primary focus of historians.

G. Stanley Hall

G. Stanley Hall, although more noted for his work in the new field of child-centered psychology, edited one of the first "textbooks" for history instructors. Several prominent historians of the day, including Andrew D. White, Charles K. Adams, Albert Bushnell Hart, and Herbert B. Adams, contributed essays to the text on various teaching methods in history, political economy, political science, geography, and archeology. In addition, they offered "advice" concerning teaching historical studies, topical history, special methods of historical study, and the "philosophy and state of history teaching." The book apparently was popular with history teachers and went through two printings before it was replaced at the turn of the century with popular texts by Edward Channing and Hart, Mary Sheldon Barnes, Burton A. Hinsdale, William Mace, Frederick M. Fling and Howard Caldwell, and Henry Bourne.[8]

In its introduction Hall outlined the need for the text and why it was selected as the first teaching aid in the D. C. Heath Pedagogical Series. That history was the subject of the first textbook in the series illustrates the unsettled nature of what passed for history instruction in the 1880s and earlier. As Hall wrote:

> History was chosen for the subject of the first volume of this educational library because, after much observation in the schoolrooms of many larger cities in the eastern part of our country, the editor, without having a hobby about its relative importance or being in any sense an expert in history, is con-

vinced that no subject so widely taught is, on the whole, taught so poorly.[9]

Hall offered his readers a bibliography of "historical literature and other sources of authority" that covered nearly a third of the text's 391 pages, most of which were given over to the new German methods of teaching and studying history. These new German methods centered on the scientific search for truths in order to tell the whole story, or as much as practical, of the history of humankind. In the college classroom, students were to pour over original sources in weekly seminars, discussing with their mentors and colleagues possible interpretations. Eventually they were to produce written records of their efforts.

Neither Hall nor the authors of the text's essays, however, advocated duplicating the "German research methods" in the high school. Instead, they proposed to prospective instructors of history to give their future charges the semblance of such research by passing on the central concept of historicism. Teaching about this idea involved inculcating students with the essence of history—that is, the movement or sweep of time, or in a word, chronology. Although not necessarily involved in actual historical research, of the university variety, secondary students were to learn *about* history, not write history. The task was to read, recite, review, and remember the personages, events, and dates that composed the history of humankind. In addition, the mighty empires and their monarchs, the annals of their exploits, and all the details in between were to be learned.

No one "method" of teaching was to be favored over another, and as Hall cautioned, "no rules can be laid down . . . in pedagogy to be followed blindly."[10] Hall felt that it was "essential that the teacher shall know and ponder many good methods, so that he may have a wide repertory of means from which to choose the best for the attainment of his ends."[11] Hall noted several of the major problems of teaching history: that "text-books were dry compilations; [that] teachers of history generally [gave] instruction also in several other often unrelated branches; and worst of all, perhaps, history [was] crowded into a single term or year."[12] In response to these problems Hall emphasized the need for "two radical changes in secondary education:"

First, there should be . . . special teachers, who go from room to room, or from one school house to another, and give instruction in history alone. . . . The teacher's mind must be kept saturated with [history's] spirit, stored with copious illustrations of varied lessons, be wide and diligent reading, or history can not be taught effectively to the young. The high educational value of history is too great to be left to teachers who merely hear recitations, keeping their finger on the place in the textbook, and only asking the questions conveniently printed for them in the margins or in the back of the book. . . . Nowhere is so much of the time spent on text-books by pupils lost on school artifacts, mistaken for the perplexities inherent in the subject itself.[13]

At this point Hall shows his concern that those who teach history must: (a) teach or specialize only in that subject; (b) be thoroughly immersed in the new methods of historical study; (c) be highly motivated to prepare and present their lessons; and (d) place most of their energies in presenting the subject apart from relying on texts. In this context, "When we reflect that what men think of the world depends on what they know of it, it is not surprising that the wider altruistic and ethical interests" of history, that to Hall gave history its special function, can be made to "control [the] narrower and more isolated and selfish aims [of] life."[14] Thus, to Hall, history had three valuable uses: as a tool for self-control; to broaden the experiences of the individual; and to redirect or channel the individual's "natural" tendency toward selfishness.

The second "radical change" that Hall advocated was that in order to accomplish the first change "the time devoted to historical study in public schools should be increased."[15] Hall reasoned that since "historical comprehension" is "so slow . . . that even the time now given to history would probably be more advantageously used if distributed over more months or years."[16] The notion that the "childish mind" requires more time to absorb historical truths points to Hall's concern for grading the curriculum to fit the psychological needs of the student. Apparently historians could lay out the material to be studied, but Hall saw the need to adapt this material to the psychological abilities of the student by presenting it when the child was ready for it or presenting it very slowly so as not to overwhelm the child.[17]

The distinction between the historian and the psychologist is crucial at this point. Although many historians at least tacitly agreed with Hall on the issue of readiness, the decision as to what was to be taught and how was clearly in the domain of the historians. Nonetheless, psychologists like Hall made it their role to voice their concerns that the timing or amount of history to be presented at each developing stage of the student's growth needed to be carefully monitored.

The Madison Conference's focus on teaching the subject was later turned about by child psychologists who supported the notion that the child, not the subject, should occupy the center of the curriculum. This early conflict came to the surface during the first decades of the twentieth century when historians and social studies educators did battle over control of the history curriculum. Hall's text, where historians and educators shared the promotion of school history, represents the first collaboration of these later bitter adversaries.[18] Nonetheless, despite the arguments of psychologists during the 1880s through the turn of the century, historians, holding the dominant position, were able to convince educators to accept the traditional history curriculum virtually in full.

Burton A. Hinsdale

Ten years after Hall's text, the notion of a modified education value of scientific objectivity[19] was introduced to many school teachers with the publication of Burton A. Hinsdale's *How to Study and Teach History*. Like Hall's text, Hinsdale's book was part of an "International Educational Series," edited by William T. Harris, devoted exclusively to pedagogical concerns. Hinsdale, who, at the time of publication was listed as a "Professor of the Science and Art of Teaching" at the University of Michigan, offered the first history methods textbook written by a professional educator and nonhistorian.

In the editor's preface Harris wrote that the historian had two tasks: to "inventory the environment" of humankind, and to "inventory . . . people."[20] Although the notion of preparing an "inventory" appeared to be far removed from the classic German-style scientific history, Harris claimed that historians could assist young people in it:

> The study of our own national history . . . [including] the great European movements that led to the discovery and colonization of America . . . [the study of] medieval and modern European history . . . [and finally] the investigation of the three peoples—Greeks, Romans, and Hebrews—that furnish the three strands which combine to make modern civilization.[21]

Here Harris was clearly advocating what would become more familiar later as the "four blocks" of school history: ancient, medieval, modern, and American history. Hinsdale, too, applauded the new interest in history as a school subject. As did Hall a decade earlier, Hinsdale felt that history was "poorly taught." Unlike Hall, however, Hinsdale offered several explanations for the regrettable condition of history teaching:

> The reasons for this [poor state of history teaching] appear to be that only a short time has elapsed since the new emphasis was placed upon the subject, that it is commonly taught by teachers who are not prepared for the work (on the theory that almost anybody can teach history), and that history presents some peculiar difficulties for the teacher.[22]

It was these "peculiar difficulties" that ostensibly led Hinsdale to write his teaching textbook. Because of the newness of the field in schools and the lack of qualified/trained teachers to present history either in content or methodology, Hinsdale's text served to meet a very real need. Yet, Hinsdale was not willing to put all his faith in methods. Although he championed historical methodology derived from scientific inquiry as well as pedagogical helps, Hinsdale was careful to avoid overreliance on methods to teach the subject. Hall's text, by contrast, stressed the need for a variety of methods to present history, and downplayed the need for the teacher to be grounded in the subject first. Notwithstanding the value of methods, Hinsdale was careful to point out:

> There is reason to fear that the normal schools and the institutes are leading some teachers to think that the requisite is not knowledge, but methods. No greater mistake could possibly be made. Methods can not be understood until subject matter has been mastered, and even, if they could be, they would prove empty and useless. . . . The most monstrous error in the history of pedagogy is the dogma that a man can teach what he does not know. . . . Without [knowledge] the insight, the interest, and the enthusiasm so necessary to success are impossible.[23]

The aims of Hinsdale's text were modest. He reasoned that although many teachers in the field were untrained and thus unqualified to teach history, they could with diligence better prepare themselves by reading heavily in history, presumedly guided by the wealth of citations offered in his text. Hinsdale intended his text to be practical. He made no effort to "tell the teacher *just* what to teach or *just* how he shall teach it," but rather to define history and its possible uses in "concrete" terms with "concrete illustrations."[24] Specifically, Hinsdale's concept of pedagogical aid for the untrained history teacher included detailing the necessary abilities required to function in the classroom. The prospective teacher needed a thorough grounding in the ability to

> present and to illustrate criteria for the choice of facts, to emphasize the organization of facts with reference to the three principles of association [time, place, and cause/effect], to indicate sources of information . . . and finally, to illustrate causation and the grouping of facts.[25]

In presenting the facts of history, however, Hinsdale did not mean for the teacher to "crowd as many facts as possible into the child's mind."[26] Those teachers who regrettably forced facts upon children were, according to Hinsdale, simply wrong. Once the "meaning of facts [was lost], the stream of thought, the life of the action, [and] the interest of the story" were lost as well. "Such teaching is unspeakably dry and uninteresting," continued Hinsdale, "and is worse than no teaching at all. It is far better to leave the child to such spontaneous interest in history as may spring up within him, than to blunt the edge of his mind with mere tables of dates and other indigestible material."[27] For Hinsdale, then, it was possible for the teacher to present history but only from a position of understanding and knowledge that consciously worked to build that same connected understanding and knowledge with his students. Chronology (the first lesson), geography (the second), and cause and effect (the third), comprised the lessons of history to be presented.

Hinsdale's text, although limited to American history for exemplification, was the first teaching textbook in the field to recognize the educative value of historical presentations. Although at the time of its publication, faculty psychology was falling into disrepute as the prevailing educational theory, the training of the representative powers of the mind to remember, to imagine, and to judge or compare the data of history were still held to be important. To Hinsdale, however, the teaching of history could offer other practical benefits as well. The thinking faculties could also be cultivated through careful analysis of historical data. The ability to shift through the "complex facts" of history and "resolve [them] into simple ones" was just as valuable as training the memory. Hinsdale wrote:

> Many facts called simple are really complex, and must be ana-lyzed before they can be understood. Arnold's treason is a fact, but composed of many minor facts. Our Civil War is a fact, but one that sums up volumes of history. History makes an equally strong appeal to the faculty of comparison or judgement. Events and characters are a constant challenge to the balancing power of the mind. . . . Then judgement passes into reasoning or thinking proper. Here the characteristic mental act is in-ference, or the drawing of conclusions from premises. If the study consists of mere committing to memory of facts, it will do little for any of the logical powers; but studied philosophi-cally, due to attention paid to the discovery of relations and criticism of method, it becomes a noble exercise of thought. . . . To observe chronological connections and geographical condi-tions, carefully to search out causes, is thinking no less than solving mathematical problems.[28]

The connection to mathematics and scientific studies is im-portant at this point. As William Harris had attempted delicately to balance the relationship between history as a scientifically ordered study and history as a philosophical endeavor, Hinsdale also worked to clarify this subtle distinction:

> In historical matters the process of making up one's mind is a kind of moral book-keeping: some items are entered on the credit side and some on the debit side of the ledger, and the balance is struck between them. . . . In fact, soundness of judgement and clearness of perception in collecting and arrang-ing these premises is a large part of each man's or woman's work. . . . [Although], mathematical and scientific discipline enables the mind to deal with those subjects, both numerous and important . . . [it] does not necessarily enable it to handle the elements of probability, or human questions. . . . Conse-quently, it is possible to be a great mathematician indeed [working with exact numbers and exact answers perceived from axioms] and be at the same time a very ordinary person in most other fields of mental activity.[29]

"Hence," said Hinsdale, "we must resort to some other source than mathematical or science for . . . moral knowledge." The sciences might be useful to explain our environment and even physical humankind, but they were inadequate to shed much light on the mental state of humankind. "Historical knowledge" was "moral knowledge" for Hinsdale, knowledge that claimed as its "subject matter the doings of human beings."[30] It was this moral knowledge that entailed the systematic study of history. The ability to understand the environment (from the sciences) and to exercise our mental abilities (from historical investigation) were the ultimate educative goals of schooling. The capacity to identify familiar features, as well as to explain and to interpret data enabled the student to "proceed from the known to the unknown, and make new acquisitions," thereby furthering knowledge.[31] The contributions of science were important to Harris and Hinsdale in terms of material understanding. The comprehension of and exercise in mental faculties beyond mere memory, that were found in the study of history, provided the mind with the intellectual skills that gave humankind its human qualities.

Beyond the great educative values of history for the intellectual skills, Hinsdale also credited history for cultivating cultural enrichment and furnishing "motive power as well as guidance." Although spending less time and space outlining the values of cultural attainments and patriotic sentiment, which was listed as a form of motive power, than on the intellectual virtues of history, Hinsdale made the case for all three. Cultural attainment, being necessary for the continuity of civilization, was easily made available from the study of historical data. Hinsdale felt that "argument wasn't necessary to show that history enriches and adorns the mind with noble ideas."[32] Continuing, Hinsdale described patriotism or love of country as being equally valuable for the advancement of national or political goals, "and it is mainly at the altar of history that patriotism feeds her fires."[33] But, "far more than anything else," asserted Hinsdale, "is the stress laid on the national history as the means of forming youthful character."

In sum, Hinsdale presented the case for intellectual values and for training the faculties of memory, imagination, and judgment. Moreover, other values were important for the young student, including cultural attainment, patriotism, and character development. To Hinsdale, history was to present and provide equivalent practice in each over the course of the student's stay in school. Those teachers who unfortunately stressed selectively one value or another from the list, stunted the intellectual growth of their charges. For example, noted Hinsdale:

> If the facts of history are taught simply or mainly to be remembered, if the student's sole ambition is "to know" a great deal of history—then the powers of analysis, comparison, and inference will be feebly developed. Nay, more; the mind will take on a conservative cast, facing backward rather than forward, and so be unfitted for useful initiative in practical affairs. Rightly studied, history has a strongly sobering effect upon the mind, in which fact consists much of its value; taught as a mnemonic exercise, it becomes a burden and obstacle to progress. . . . The results are all the worse if history is regarded as a necessary evolution, in which the individual will counts for nothing, because history becomes then a bar to free individual and social movement.[34]

Although others had made a case for citizenship education as a primary concern, neither Hall nor Harris nor Hinsdale followed suit. The development of the individual mind through the study of history may have collaterally produced "good citizens," but the specific growth of citizenship was not a primary goal for traditional history.

FORMALIZING THE INTRODUCTION OF HISTORY

At the request of the National Education Association's Committee of Ten, a gathering of prominent historians convened at the University of Wisconsin-Madison during the last days of December 1892, to discuss the nature and scope of history in American schools. Among the list of notable conferees present were historians Charles Kendall Adams, Albert Bushnell Hart, James Harvey Robinson, and political economist and future president, Woodrow Wilson.[35] This influential group, led by the historians, were to devote themselves to a study of "history, civil government, and political economy" for the secondary school and develop appropriate recommendations in the effort. The governing concept for the Madison Conference, as well as the Committee of Ten itself, was that "the preparation of a few pupils for college or scientific school in the ordinary secondary school be the incidental, not the principal object [of the secondary school] . . . at the same time, it is obviously desirable that colleges and scientific schools should be accessible to all boys and girls who have completed creditably the secondary school course."[36]

While the committee conceded that some recommendations were of a "radical nature," they made it a point to ask their readers to notice that "on a careful reading of the appended reports it will appear the spirit of the Conferences was distinctly conservative and moderate."[37] In effect, the radical suggestions were the new modern studies, while the conservative and moderate statements were reaffirmations of the study of classical languages. Ultimately the compromise represented the transition of the "classically minded" education toward a new focus in secondary education. In the report nonclassical studies, by design, received the most attention. The "scientific approach" or the "modernized curriculum" that was already established in many colleges and universities was now being recognized and legitimized in the nation's secondary schools. The modern age was beginning in secondary education. The era of the elite, narrowly focused curriculum, as represented by Latin and Greek language studies, seen as a characteristic leftover from the time when religious dogma dominated most public school systems, was giving way to what was to become the democratic centerpiece of one of America's premier egalitarian institutions.

The Committee of Ten intended to "modernize" the secondary curriculum with a proposed program of standardized courses that would in effect expedite college and university admissions. Given the sixty plus different "history" or "civics" subjects reportedly offered by prospective students at matriculation before 1892, it was shown that there was little, if any, continuity between existing secondary history programs and their college or university counterparts.[38] It was little wonder that colleges and universities had to start from "the ground up" with their diversely "trained" charges.

In the development of their report the conferees recognized the established orthodoxy of "American individualism" as the foundation of their efforts. Nonetheless, as the encroaching force of social efficiency was beginning to invade the philosophy of university and lay intellectuals, including historians, an eventual accommodation was indicated. The Committee of Ten sought to forge a compromise between individualism and social responsibility; between intrinsic values of the mind and public order. In sum, this effort revealed the historians' response to the twin paradoxes of liberal-democratic education.

Curiously, given the beginnings of the call for the public reform of rampant economic individualism, in adopting the "one education for all theory," the conferees retained the concept of intellectual enlightenment. Notwithstanding the notion of egalitarian democratic ideals, the resolutions of the Madison Conference for secondary schools appeared beyond the reach of the average student. Clearly, they were aimed at a very select clientele—that is, those few who planned to further their formal education in an institution of higher education. Individualism for the Madison conferees was not so much a celebration of the pioneering spirit of self-sufficiency as it was a call for the recognition of individual interests.

The Madison Conference resolutions, although couched in democratic theory, were quite aristocratic in practice. Nonetheless, unlike the works of Hall and Hinsdale that preceded the publication of the overall findings of the Committee of Ten, the Madison Conference report constituted the formalization of history as a legitimate discipline for the emerging secondary school.

OPERATION AND RESOLVES OF
THE MADISON CONFERENCE

If change in the broadest sense is a "constant" in a modern society, then it would appear that the so-called status quo is at best a transitory entity, ever adapting, altering, or giving over political, economic, or social power to other entities through time. Nevertheless the political and economic status quo is capable of self-preservation by controlling or "stabilizing" change through its institutions, principally education and law. Education supposedly transmits the cultural heritage—that is, the prevailing system—to the young; law is given the task of preserving it. But in the American democratic experience, preservation of the status quo—that is, the dominance of the political, economic, and social elite—was dependent upon the successful efforts of both education and law.

If educators were unsuccessful in reproducing the governmental and economic institutions for the nation's youth to mirror, or if youth rejected the teachings of their mentors, then the "established society" changed. The greater the disparity between youth and their elders, the greater the potential for change and chaos. Conversely, the closer the similarities between youth and their elders, the greater the chance for the perpetuation of the status quo. In times of great technological change, formal education becomes essential for the maintenance of the status quo. Here the outward appearance of society may be altered, and altered for the better, but the underlying institutions that support it remain relatively unchanged. The means of regulating change via education results in a system based on social control—that is, the preservation of the ruling political and economic powers and institutions. The sort of curriculum offered by historians was decidedly placed on the conformity side of the freedom-conformity continuum. A curriculum openly critical of the existing society (leaning toward the freedom side of the continuum), as later advocated by John Dewey and the social studies insurgents, was the antithesis of the program devised by the Madison Conference and the later Committee of Seven.

The "resolves" of the NEA Subcommittee on History, Civil Government, and Political Economy as set down at the Madison Conference in 1892 were popular with educators as well as the public. The Madison Conference membership was managed by university historians led by Charles Kendall Adams, who was then president of the University of Wisconsin. Other prominent leaders included Albert Bushnell Hart, Jesse Macy, Edward G. Bourne, James Harvey Robinson, Ray Greene Huling, and future President Woodrow Wilson. They were to answer, as were the other nine subcommittees of the Committee of Ten, eleven basic questions. The collective subcommittee responses were then to form the basis of the final overall report of the Committee of Ten.

Specifically each subcommittee was asked a series of basic educational questions. The more relevant questions asked were: "At what age should the subject be introduced? How many hours per week for how many years? What topics should be covered? How was the subject related to college admission requirements? Should the same course be given for all? What were the best methods of teaching the subjects? and What were the best methods of testing students' attainment of the material for college admission purposes?"[39] The Madison Conference answered the basic questions with diligence and thoroughness, placing summaries of their answers in the appendix of their report, together with cross-references for both their answers and resolutions.

With few exceptions the nine conferences of the various subjects held on December 28, 1892, met at several locations throughout the country with their full memberships present. The meetings continued for three days with fairly typical business to attend to: selecting the chair and secretary, discussion of the questions, and writing the first drafts of their respective reports. The conference reports were due by April 1, 1893, in order to give the Committee of Ten time to prepare the final report for presentation of the Education Congress in July, which, coincidentally, was held in Chicago during the great fair. Yet unforeseen delays occurred and the final revised proofs were not printed until early December, nearly a year after the first conferences were held.

The Madison conferees had a "different task" to accomplish than the more established subjects, such as Greek and Latin, grammar, and mathematics, which comprised the core of the prevailing curriculum. History was an upstart, or in the words of the Committee of Ten, "still very imperfectly apprehended." The members of the Madison Conference sought to correct this situation by proposing and justifying a comprehensive plan for history instruction in the secondary school.

The conferees took great "pains to declare their belief, in the efficiency of these studies in training judgement, and in preparing children for intellectual enjoyments in after years, and for the exercise at maturity of a salutary influence upon national affairs."[40] History instruction was presumed to have value to the developing student, but significance as well for the mature citizen.

Reporting that their resolutions were not merely based upon considered thoughts and opinions, the conferees grounded their report in a variety of methods and topics currently in practice "in the best and most carefully taught [secondary] schools."[41] It was fairly clear that the conferees wanted to improve the nature and scope of secondary history instruction as well as history instruction in the grades. Coordination between the two schools was essential for the Madison program to be effective, and conversely, its effectiveness, as perceived by the conferees, would result in improved relations between the high school and colleges.

In his review of the period, Henry Johnson found that early cooperative efforts between the secondary schools and colleges, although properly concerned with "increasing the amount" of history being taught in the secondary school (as was the intention of the Madison Conference), failed in "specifying the kind of history [to be taught]."[42] The result was:

[That history courses] had developed in response to local opinion and local practice and were now becoming somewhat unmanageable. Most high schools had to consider a variety of college requirements and taught in consequence, not a carefully arranged course in history, but, as of old, merely subjects in history. Most colleges had to consider a variety of preparation for college work in history and prescribed in consequence college courses that were themselves preparatory. It would clearly be to the advantage both of high schools and of colleges to encourage at least some degree of uniformity.[43]

To Johnson, the schools, the colleges, the students of each, and their teachers and professors, required some sort of cohesiveness. Later, Earle Rugg also cast the actions of the historians of the Madison Conference and the later Committee of Seven together with the needs of the schools:

American high schools increasingly became preparatory schools for our colleges. When the higher institutions of learning demanded that students desiring a college education should show evidence of scholarship in their high school courses, the secondary schools were forced to devote much of their instruction to subject matter that would meet these conditions. In the field of history college professors were "alarmed" at the little knowledge of their subject that high school pupils, entering their classes for advanced study, exhibited. Hence, they met together as "committees" and outlined courses that elementary and secondary schools should follow.[44]

As Rugg put it, the "professors" had taken control of the history curriculum away from "teachers, clergymen, and professional textbook writers" and attempted to influence "what should be taught in school history and indirectly in how history teaching, itself, in the schools should be improved."[45] The mutual interests of secondary schools and universities required some sort of "harmonious resolves." On the one hand, the universities of the period much like today influenced secondary schools in a variety of ways. Higher education provided schools not only future teachers and administrators, models of the most effective methods for instruction as well as the "modernized curriculum," they often set the university admission requirements that determined the nature and scope of secondary offerings. On the other hand, as Charles Eliot pointed out, improved instruction in the secondary school would enhance the quality of the university program.[46] It was simple logic that the two coordinate their efforts.

In a critique of the prevalent nature of all studies in the public secondary school, the conferees remarked:

The college teacher of history finds in like manner that his subject has never taken any serious hold on the minds of pupils fresh from the secondary school. He finds that they have devoted astonishingly little time to the subject; and that they have acquired no habit of historical investigation, or of the comparative examination of different historical narratives concerning the same periods of events.[47]

Upon reaching college the "fresh-from-the-secondary-school" student often betrayed the source of these shortcomings, suggesting that instruction in the common secondary school needed improvement. Moreover, students needed to spend more time exploring history than memorizing it, to learn the concept of historical investigation, and to use more sources than an antiquated textbook. These were the needs of the student as perceived by the conferees. Essentially, these needs became the resolutions of the Madison Conference. It was felt that if these needs could be met, the entire education system would be strengthened.

The thirty-five resolutions offered by the Madison conferees were guided by two basic objectives:

One object of historical study is the acquirement of useful facts; but the chief [second] object is the training of judgement, in selecting the grounds of an opinion, in accumulating materials for an opinion, in putting things together, in generalizing upon facts, in estimating character, in applying the lessons of history to current events, and in accustoming children to state their conclusions in their own words.[48]

The challenge for educators was to fulfil these objectives, especially to accommodate fact acquisition and judgment skills, such as the ability to select, accumulate, construct, generalize, estimate, apply, assimilate, and accommodate historical knowledge. Given the focus on fact accumulation and the training of what presently might be called critical thinking skills, history instruction had other advantages as well:

History has long been commended as a part of the education of a good citizen. . . . "History," says an English writer, "furnishes the best training in patriotism, and enlarges the sympathies and interests" [of citizens toward their country]. . . . [Moreover] a significant advantage of history is that, intelligently taught, it might be a medium for the literary expression of the pupils.[49]

Four Fundamental Questions

In the presentation of their report the Madison conferees divided their thirty-five resolutions into seven units: length of time for studies (one resolution); subjects (nine resolutions); programs (seven resolutions); methods in history (ten resolutions); civil government and political economy (three resolutions); relations with colleges (four resolutions); and a resolution of thanks (one resolution). Although the Madison Committee specifically addressed each of the basic eleven questions asked by the Committee of Ten in the appendix of their report, they chose to concentrate their efforts on what they called the four fundamental questions. According to the Madison conferees:

> They were how far they should make recommendations which could be applied only in favored parts of the country; whether they should recommend an ideal program, or a simpler program practicable in good schools with their present means and apparatus; how far they should insist on a uniformed program; and what relations they should suggest between the schools and the colleges.[50]

These fundamental statements outlined the introductory nature of the Madison conferees' attempt to define the limits of history for schools to a common core. The answer to the first question set the stage for the others. "The recommendations should be the same for all," was the foundation of the report. This "sameness" implied the presentation of an ideal program; however, the conferees insisted that their program was not anything beyond what was "already being done by some good schools."[51] The resolutions were an attempt to raise the standard of quality in the presentation of history to a level allegedly achieved "by some good schools." The assumption was that if some schools could produce the results aimed for in the resolutions, then any school could.

In answering the third question the conferees stressed that it was not their purpose "to reduce the teaching of history to one uniform program to be carried out on a uniform method."[52] Much like the later 1916 Social Studies Committee, the Madison conferees emphasized that it would be counterproductive for the various suggestions to effect a reduction of history study to a single plan for all. A national plan for history instruction would contradict the stated intellectual goals of the Madison Conference (the development of judgment) by taking away the opportunity for local schools to adjust the Madison program "according to local necessities and difficulties."[53] Consequently, they expressly believed that the time presently devoted to history and allied subjects be increased, that subjects beyond American history be presented, and "that the dry and lifeless system of instruction by text-book should give way to a more rational kind of work."[54] By suppressing the individuality of local schools to make decisions for themselves, the conferees reasoned that the development of a specific national program would make the realization of these objectives an impossibility. Moreover, a rigid national plan ignorant of and insensitive to local conditions would perhaps appear less attractive and, therefore, impractical to school boards. Nonetheless, in practice, many schools worked diligently to follow the suggestions of the history experts.

Given the contemporaneous critics of traditional history, in answering the fourth question concerning the relationship of the public school to the college, the conferees asserted:

> The colleges can take care of themselves; our interest is in the school children who have no expectation of going to college, the larger number of whom will not enter even a high school. This feeling is strengthened by the consideration that proportionally a much smaller number of girls go to college than of the boys, and it is important that both sexes shall be well grounded on these subjects. An additional responsibility is thrown upon the American system of education by the great number of children of foreigners, children who must depend on the schools for their notions of American institutions, or of anything outside their contracted circle. Hence our recommendations are in no way directed to building up the colleges, increasing the number of college students, or taking out of the hands of the colleges the historical work which they are especially fitted to do.[55]

After establishing the egalitarian nature of the committee resolves, the conferees outlined their program. The Madison program provided two levels "for a proper historical course" (one eight years, the other six), dependent upon the resources of the local school. The first program began in the fifth grade with an emphasis on biography and mythology. This format then continued into the sixth grade. The seventh and eighth grades were to teach American history, with elements of civil government and ancient history, respectively. For the great majority of students during the 1890s this was the limit of their experience in history. To those few continuing on in high school, the ninth and tenth grades were devoted to French and English histories, respectively, "to be so taught as to elucidate the general movement of medieval and modern history."[56] Finally, the eleventh grade was to be devoted to a more thorough examination of American history, with the last year of high school designed to encompass a special period of intensive study in a selected historical topic. The balance of class time was to be given over to studies in civil government.

The alternate program of six years, suggested to begin when applicable, included a two-year study of biography and mythology, to be followed, if practical, by a year's study of American history and civil government in the common school. Additionally, the last three years of the high school program were to include a year of ancient history, a year of English history, to present medieval and modern movements and connections, and finally another year of American history and civil government.

Aside from the titles of subjects in history (ancient, medieval, and modern French, English, and American histories) little by way of explanation was offered as to what topics or facts should be presented to students. Notwithstanding the one grouping of helps provided in the list of suitable topics for the year of intensive study, it appeared that the history suggested was a complete entity—that is, a discipline already known and understood by educators. Although condemning the notion of a general history taught in a single year, "because it is almost impossible to carry them on without degenerating into a mere assemblage of dates and names,"[57] the conferees' suggestion of an eight-year program without specific explanations appeared to yield the same results.

In a curious contradiction to their objection to general histories, the conferees admitted "the advantage of a broad outlook," and that "the history of any great country is so extensive that the schools can hardly expect to teach more than an outline."[58] If the suggestions of the Madison program amounted to no more than a list of subjects to be presented over a period of eight years, then what were schools to make of the report?

To historians, that history should have a place in the schools was taken as a given. However, the focus of the conferees' rather loose and unspecified resolutions was less clear. Apparently the committee was not interested in outlining a specific program, for this would have been usurping the intellectual faculties of discrimination and judgment from educators. The conferees clearly articulated that history was to be part of the school experience and that such exposure was to lead directly to the development of the intellectual faculties. The question of what history and what particular topics should be taught was avoided. In its place an explanation of the values of history was emphasized. Ostensibly, educators were to chart their own course, each according to their own needs and interests. Educators, however, largely ignored this suggestion and solidified the traditional history curriculum. Curiously, later, when social studies insurgents argued for curricular innovation and decentralized curricula, historians quickly rejected the notion.

Unintentionally, the conferees may have endorsed a fixed program by providing two rather strong bits of advice: (a) schools should pay particular attention to the topics and substance of college entrance examinations; and (b) schools should pay good salaries to teachers and insist that the teacher of history should have "a knowledge of illuminating methods of teaching history."[59] Methodologically, the conferees suggested that few, if any, lectures be offered and instead more "informal talks which will explain cause and effect of events, and which may add interesting illustrations and comparisons to the lesson of the day."[60] Moreover, they agreed "that a practice be established in the schools of using two, three, or four parallel text-books at a time . . . to be supplemented by other methods."[61]

Concerning the use of textbooks, the conferees stressed the need to utilize the "open text-book recitation" over the "old fashioned way" of "setting pupils painfully to reproduce the words of a textbook, without comment or suggestion on the teacher's part. . . . It would be better to omit history altogether than to teach it [this way]."[62] Continuing with textbooks the conferees suggested:

> The first duty of the teacher is to emphasize the essential points of the book, to show, if possible, what is the main thing worth remembering in the lesson that day. It is also a duty to point out the things which the writer of the text-book has inserted, but which, in the teacher's judgement, may safely be neglected. . . . The questions in a recitation ought not to demand from the pupils a bald repetition of the phrases or ideas of the book, but ought to call for comparison and comment. . . . Here is the place where the teacher's superior knowledge and training tells; here is the place also for stirring up the minds of the pupils.[63]

In spite of the value of recitations, the conferees warned that "recitations alone . . . cannot possibly make up proper teaching of history. It is absolutely necessary . . . that these should be parallel reading of some kind . . . [from] historical literature bearing immediately on the subject in hand; and, secondly the use of miscellaneous literature, poems, historical novels, and biographies."[64] With extensive reading in history and related subjects, students were expected to devote a considerable amount of time and effort on written projects that develop "both the power of expression, and the power of dealing with historical material."[65]

Taken as a whole the specific and general suggestions of the Madison Conference provided the structural framework for the introduction of history into the schools, and in particular the high schools. Largely couched in vague language and generalities, the apparent problem with the Madison resolves was the lack of commitment to a particular program. On the one hand, educators may have appreciated their respect for their own judgment concerning the history curriculum; on the other hand, educators may have been dismayed and unsure as to what curricular path they should follow. Nonetheless, this lack of guidance, whether good or ill, led directly to the forming of the Committee of Seven whose task it was to examine the schools and offer a complete history curriculum. The Madison Conference, therefore, was perceived as a first step toward this goal as well as the formal introduction of history into secondary schools. The Committee of Seven report (the subject of chapter 3) has been viewed as the second and "final step" toward the realization of a viable curriculum for history in the schools.

3. SCHOOL REFORM AND THE COMMITTEE OF SEVEN

THE INTRODUCTION AND justification of history as a new "core" subject was a celebration of individualism. In practice, implementing the aims and objectives of the Madison Conference resolves, however, proved to be beyond the realities of the average school in the 1890s. At that time, those education systems that championed individualism were being undermined by forces that would eventually reshape the definitions of education under a banner of social efficiency. Several significant trends and themes emerged during the last decades of the nineteenth century.[1] The trends that affected public schools appear to be quite eclectic and often unrelated; yet when taken as a whole, they portray a society in transition.

While a semblance of laissez-faire thought sponsored in part by Spencer was maintained as the status quo in educational thought through the 1890s, Lester Frank Ward, Spencer's chief critic, was advocating the overthrow of such theories in favor of a "dynamic" welfare state.[2] The overriding theme and driving force of nearly all societal change was the shift from a rural, agriculturally based society to an urban, industrial society. This shift, fueled by the massive influx of immigrants from southern and eastern Europe, appeared to threaten the established English-German-American domination over finance, commerce, culture, and government.

In the public schools as well as universities, professional educators displaced lay and church "educators." This shift led the way for a more secular, liberal curriculum founded in the scientific method and infused with Darwinism.[3] Here the classical education centered in the study of Greek and Latin, ideal for divinity students, was giving way to the more practical, modern courses of mathematics, natural science, history, social science, and English.

As for the new studies, historians like Andrew White at Cornell saw the social sciences as compatible, as complementary studies to history, and for the most part *sponsored* them to address the changes in the status quo. Nonetheless, when the pressures to unburden the country of society's "ills" became overwhelming, historians as a group were unable to extricate themselves from associations with the distant past. Problems and conflicts existed in the present, and the present was the domain of the new social sciences of sociology and political science (political economy). Taken somewhat unawares and often being labeled part of the status quo—that is, part of the problem—historians eventually would have to reconceptualize the part history was to hold in the secondary curriculum.

The Madison Conference resolutions appeared at a time when history in the school curriculum in terms of textbook production was largely in control of nonprofessional historians. These authors often viewed the business of history as an exercise in patriotism and moralistic virtues, a mode of thinking that persisted throughout the nineteenth and twentieth centuries. The more secular approach of the scientifically orientated Madison conferees worked to negate the influence of these writers by pointing out the "modernized" methods and values of history as well as the need for competent, scholarly, academically produced history. In effect, the Madison historians of the scientific school sought to disassociate themselves from lay historians. Regardless of the turf fight, times and conditions were changing so rapidly that the Madison resolutions soon appeared to educators as unmanageable and without any real value. Public schools simply did not have adequate financial and physical resources to enact many, if any, of the suggestions. While the Madison Conference report, at least in its rhetoric, instituted traditional history as an integral subject, its resolution appeared oblivious to the realities of the schools.

The pervading social and cultural change in the school population, combined with its rapid growth in sheer numbers, dictated another fundamental reorganization.[4] Not to mention the lack of resources, these changes, the resolutions of the Madison Conference as well as the overall report of the Committee of Ten also appeared too intellectual for the emerging egalitarian schools. Simply put, these proposals were considered to be obsolete when faced by existing conditions. As one modern writer observed, "there was a wide gap between the schools and the society, and the reformers [who sought] to repair their society through education."[5]

The social concerns of society, however, would have to wait for another period of reform, because the individual members, who were steeped in the intellectual tradition of mental discipline, wrote their outlook and interests into the report. In spite of the many emerging problems in the schools, according to Henry Johnson, the main objection to the problems of school history as diagnosed by the Madison Conference was that schools "had to consider a variety of college requirements, and taught in consequence, not a carefully arranged course in history, but, as of old, merely subjects in history. It would clearly be to the advantage both of high schools and of colleges to encourage at least some degree of uniformity."[6]

Regardless of the mounting problems of the mid-to-late 1890s, many schools were not prepared to consider a radical reform of their programs beyond the implementation of the Committee of Ten plans. Apparently educators did not anticipate having to react to unavoidable societal upheaval. Rather, administrators and teachers wanted clarity, unity, and more history based upon intellectual development, but not at the expense of the individual. Despite the feeling that times were changing and that social change implied the need for school change, historians ignored the suggestions of the new social scientists for the schools to make a more relevant and meaningful contribution in attending to social problems. Additionally, historians also ignored other critics of school programs, such as Joseph Rice, who conducted the first major general survey critical of public education in the United States.[7] Nonetheless, despite the call for action by Rice and the social reformers, historians continued to argue for the development of the individual's intellectual capacities, not the individual's sense of social awareness. Whether this distinction was a rhetorical issue or not, historians displayed neither symbolically nor in reality any interest in placing current or developing social, cultural, and political problems, questions, concerns, or issues within the scope of history study.

NEW DIRECTIONS

In answer to the admittedly intellectual and nonspecific resolutions of the Madison Committee, August F. Nightingale, chair-

man of the Nation Education Association's Committee on College
Entrance Requirements, "asked the historians [at an AHA meeting
in 1896] to provide a report on the scope and place of history in the
secondary schools, with model courses for the same."[8] Eagerly historians complied and the most influential committee for history
reform, known as the Committee of Seven, was formed. Two years
later the Committee released its report, *The Study of History in
Schools.*[9]

Henry Johnson, Rolla Tryon, and Edgar Bruce Wesley, the principal early historians of the field, found this new committee to be
the best and most important of its kind. In describing the committee, Johnson wrote forty years afterward:

> [It] found the question of college entrance so bound up with the
> larger question of why history should be taught in schools and
> what history should be taught as to call for a study of the entire
> field. The *Report*, written by the chairman, Andrew C. Mc-
> Laughlin, was the ablest document relating to history for
> schools ever produced in America.[10]

Tryon and Wesley both echoed Johnson's praise of the Committee report and mentioned its pervasive influence. Tryon noted that
the Committee report was "without parallel in its field."[11] Wesley
related that the document "was the most influential ever prepared
in the field."[12] Specifically, wrote Tryon:

> For at least two decades after its appearance, high school
> courses in history in the United States were almost 100 per
> cent dictated by it. In fact even today [1935], more than a gener-
> ation after the publication of the report, its influence is domi-
> nating in probably one-third of the high schools of the coun-
> try. . . . With respect to textbooks, they became as they
> appeared in rapid succession after 1900 imposing monuments
> to the Committee's efforts. . . . The fact of the matter is that a
> textbook intended for high school use in history published be-
> tween 1900 and 1915 had hard "sledding" if it failed to claim
> that it conformed to the report of the Committee of Seven.[13]

Wesley, two years later, continued the applause:

> In spite of the quaintness of some aspects of the report it is
> even yet a vigorous and persuasive document. Its timeliness,

its specificity, and its completeness within the area treated led to its immediate acceptance.[14]

Clearly the plaudits of later historians of social studies indicated the power of the Committee of Seven's suggestions for secondary history. Notwithstanding these praises, the report was only one segment of legitimation for traditional history. The report carried the inertia of the traditional history movement from the university into secondary schools and soon came to be considered the definitive statement on traditional history, despite other articulate voices. The Madison Conference, the teaching textbooks of Hall and Hinsdale, and a variety of history textbooks for secondary schools had earlier made the case for traditional history. But the Committee of Seven's national visibility remained a beacon to those in need of direction, and, unfortunately for historians, a beacon to those who came to criticize traditional history.

The Rationale of the Committee of Seven

In their preliminary comments, McLaughlin and the other six committee members (Herbert B. Adams, H. Morse Stephens, Albert Bushnell Hart, Charles Haskins, George Fox, and Lucy Salmon) outlined the rationale for their investigation:

> Before this work was undertaken, there had not been any systematic attempt of this kind; nor had there been any prolonged effort of any national association to present the claims of history, or to set before the educators a statement of what might be considered the value of historical study and the place which it should occupy in the school programme. We do not leave out of consideration the work of the Committee of Ten, nor do we underestimate the value or the effect of the able and highly interesting report of the Madison Conference on History, Civil Government, and Political Economics; and we do not lose sight of the fact that historical instruction in the secondary schools had often been discussed in pedagogical conferences and teachers' associations. Before we began our work, it was plain that there was all awakening interest in this whole subject, and the time seemed to be at hand when a systematic effort would meet with response and produce results. . . . In spite of this awakened interest, there was no recognized consensus of opinion in the country at large, not one generally accepted judge-

ment, not even one well-known point of agreement, which would serve as a beginning for a consideration of the place of history in the high-school curriculum. . . . The task before the committee was, therefore, to discover the actual situation, to see what was doing and what was the prevailing sentiment, to localize and establish a modicum of practices and principles, however small and limited it might be; and apprehend what was best and most helpful in spirit and tendency among teachers of the country, to seek to give that spirit expression in a report that would be helpful and suggestive, and that would be of service in widening the field of agreement and go in laying the foundations for a common understanding.[15]

This statement reflects what might be considered a textbook example of how a committee defines its work. Proceeding logically from point to point, the seven committee members: (a) identified that a problem existed; (b) distinguished that an investigation of this phenomenon had never been attempted before; (c) established that ample interest existed to warrant a thorough study; and (d) explained that action now would produce results. This last qualifier established the importance of the investigation to educators and gained their immediate attention.

Given the nature of the problem, the conferees outlined their working procedures by explaining that since no common agreement was found to establish a reference point as to what place history should hold in secondary schools, the Committee wanted to "discover the actual situation." Ostensibly the seven conferees were not offering anything radically different to educators or breaking new ground with their suggestions. They were, however, (a) polling schools as to what history was being presented and how it was being presented; (b) culling from this data the best and most promising ideas and concepts in regards to content and methods; (c) organizing the data into a viable and coherent form; and then (d) disseminating it to educators for implementation. The general aim of the conferees was, therefore, not to pull a completed curriculum "out of a hat," but to present what they considered to be a practical consensus curriculum for secondary history based on considerable data that would ultimately widen the "field of agreement . . . for a common understanding."

Utilizing the careful scholarship of the new "scientific/systematic historical method" that sought truth over fiction, empirical research over "unauthentic research," discovery of motives/cause and effect over mere chronicles, and a global view of a study over inaccurate and incomplete accounts, the Committee of Seven agenda went far beyond that of the earlier Madison Conference. In coming to grips with the work of their Madison colleagues, the seven conferees did not dispute the Madison Conference's contribution to the introduction of history into the secondary school. The seven outlined the need for a more systematic and unified approach toward a national history curriculum that was still unanswered and unattended. Philosophically, this is the principal disparity between the two committees, albeit a subtle one.

Nevertheless, the commonalities between the committees were numerous. Both reports acclaimed that (a) history should be required in the secondary curriculum; (b) each student should follow the same course of study regardless of age, sex, or ability; (c) history should be divided into four general areas (ancient, medieval, modern, and American); (d) general histories should be avoided as counterproductive; (e) the development of intellectual abilities should be the chief aim and purpose of instruction; and (f) qualified teachers armed with effective pedagogical methods should be employed at all costs. In contrast, the Madison Conference illustrated that it would be presumptuous, if not contradictory, to call for intellectual exploration and expression in schools on the one hand, while at the same time dictating a national curriculum on the other. Rather, they believed that the actual curriculum should be ultimately decided at the local level.

Despite philosophical agreement on this point, the Committee of Seven held that this was precisely why the history curriculum was in such a state of amorphic confusion. What was needed (in the opinion of the Committee) was a viable, coherent guide or plan of what they considered to be the ideal curriculum for secondary history, a guide that the Madison Conference unfortunately did not provide. The agenda of the Madison program was to define the importance of history, not to detail an ideal curriculum or to rationalize whatever the local school held was the ideal. The Committee of Seven, by contrast, determined their suggestions democratically. That is, they ascertained what the majority of the schools were doing in history, detailed that for educators, and struck that as the ideal. In doing so, the Committee of Seven was providing schools an ideal history curriculum for *selected* adoption dependent, of course, upon prevailing local conditions. The committee explained:

> We have sought chiefly to discuss, in an argumentative way, the general subject submitted for consideration, to offer suggestions as to methods of historical teaching and the place of

history on the school programme, being fully aware that, when all is said and done, only so much will be adopted as appeals to the sense and judgement of secondary teachers and superintendents; and that any rigid list of requirements, or any body of peremptory demands, however judiciously framed, not only would, but should be, discarded in schools whose local conditions make it unwise to accept them.[16]

The Program of the Committee of Seven

The program outlined by the Committee of Seven was based upon an extensive survey of 300 secondary schools (260 were returned, and of those 210 were complete). To assist those educators who may not have had the opportunity to answer the inquiry, a detailed explanation of the survey, including a summary of details on each question was printed in the appendix of the report. With the questions and results in hand, the interested secondary teacher, principal, or superintendent could compare their school curriculum with that of schools across the country as well as against the highly lauded European programs.

Seemingly such a comparison would encourage the nonconformists to adapt to what was being touted as *the* modern program for school history. In relating their findings to educators, the principal topics for discussion were to (a) establish the values of historical study; (b) explain the continuity of historical study and its relationship to collateral subjects; (c) outline the four blocks of history (ancient, medieval, modern, and American); (d) detail methods of instruction and sources; (e) dramatize the need for trained teachers; and (f) identify the relationship between high schools and colleges in terms of entrance requirements.

The thesis of the study centered on what the conferees believed was the axiomatic purpose of education: to provide students with an understanding of their environment. To the conferees historical instruction held an important place in the curriculum. They underlined:

Secondary education ought to fit boys and girls to become not scholastics, but men and women who know their surroundings and have come to a sympathetic knowledge of their environment. . . . The most essential result of secondary education is acquaintance with political and social environment, some appreciation of the nature of state and society, some sense of the duties and responsibilities of citizenship, some capacity in dealing with political and governmental questions, something of the broad and tolerant spirit which is bred by the study of past times and conditions.[17]

In establishing the place of history in the secondary school curriculum, the Committee found it necessary to compare the treatment of history to other studies in the curriculum in regard to generating knowledge of the environment:

> If it is desirable that the high-school pupil should know the physical world, that he should know the habits of ants and bees, the laws of floral growth, the simple reactions in the chemical retort, it is certainly even more desirable that he should be led to see the steps in the development of the human race, and should have some dim perception of his own place and of his own country's place, in the movement of men.[18]

Essentially, the argument was that history was at least equal to any other subject in the school, and subsequently, should be made available to every student. To solidify their argument for traditional history the conferees recognized and described the various values history offered students. The following is the Committee's list of the particular values and benefits derived from historical exploration.

Global Values:
1. The student who is taught to consider political subjects in school, who is led to look at matters historically, has some mental equipment for a comprehension of the political and social problems that will confront him in everyday life, and has received practical preparation for social adaptation and for forceful participation in civic activities.
2. While we believe that it is the imperative duty of every high school and academy to teach boys and girls the elementary knowledge of the political machinery which they will be called upon to manage as citizens of a free state, we insist also that should have the broader knowledge, the more intelligent spirit, that comes from a study of other men and of other times.

Specific Values:
3. History cultivates the judgement by leading the pupil to see the relation between cause and effect, as cause and effect appear in human affairs. . . . History has to do with the becoming of past

events,—not simply with what was, but with what came to be,— and in studying the simplest forms of historical narrative even the average pupil comes to see that one thing leads to another; he begins quite unconsciously to see that events do not simply succeed each other in time, but that one grows out of another, or rather out of a combination of many others.

4. The study of history gives training not only in acquiring facts, but in arranging and systematizing them and in putting forth individual products. . . . If a pupil is taught to get ideas and facts from various books, and to put those facts together into a new form, his ability to make use of knowledge is increased and strengthened.

5. History is also helpful in developing what is sometimes called the scientific habit of mind and thought. . . . The scientific habit of mind in a broader sense means a recognition of the fact that sound conclusions do not rest only on somebody's patient investigations; that, although we must accept the work of others, everybody is required to study and think and examine before he positively asserts; that every question should be approached without prejudice; that open-mindedness, candor, honesty, are requisites for the attainment of scientific knowledge.

6. By the study of history the pupil acquires a knowledge of facts that is to him a source of pleasure and gratification in his after life. . . . Many a teacher has found that, in dealing with the great and noble acts and struggles of bygone men, he has succeeded in reaching the inner nature of the real boys and girls of his classes, and has given them impulses and honorable prejudices that are the surest sources of permanent and worthy refinement.

7. A no less important result of historical study is the training which pupils receive in the handling of books. History, more than any other subject in the secondary curriculum, demands for effective work a library and the ability to use it.

8. With these results of historical study two other of decided value may in conclusion be briefly mentioned: by the reading of good books, and by constant efforts to recreate the real past and make it live again, the pupil's imagination is at once quickened, strengthened, and disciplined.

9. And by means of the ordinary oral recitation, if properly conducted, he might express himself in well chosen words. . . . In the study of history, while [the student] must speak truthfully and accurately, he must seek to find apt words of his own with which to describe past conditions and to clothe his ideas, in a broad field of work which has no technical method of expression and no peculiar phraseology.[19]

In sum, the values of historical exploration for the Committee of Seven were presented primarily to inculcate intellectual skills. History instruction had the power to train the young intellect to adopt to everyday life; to broaden knowledge; to cultivate judgment; to sharpen the ability to actualize knowledge; to develop the scientific habit of mind (critical inquiry); to build character; to teach effective library and book use; to fire the imagination; and to provide equivalent practice toward the improvement of expression skills. Certainly this was a formidable list by any standard. As Tryon noted:

> Their [the listed values] influence on history in schools has been tremendous. They have been accepted by thousands of history teachers as goals of their endeavors. It would be difficult to overstate the good that has resulted from them.[20]

The overt intellectual nature of the Committee's stated values of history consistently carried over to their proposed curriculum. The chronologically based ninth-grade program began with "Ancient History, with special reference to Greek and Roman history, but included a short introductory study of the more ancient nations . . . [to include, at the discretion of the teacher, either the] establishment of the Holy Roman Empire (800), or with the death of Charlemagne (814), or with the treaty of Verdun (832)."[21]

Followed by a full year of "Medieval and Modern History, from the close of the first period to the present time" in the tenth year, "English History" in the eleventh year, and "American History" in the last year of high school.[22] Rather dogmatically the conferees stressed the presentation of *all* four blocks of history without variation. They wrote:

> As a thorough and systematic course of study, we recommend four years of work, beginning with ancient history and ending with American history . . . and recommend that they be studied in the order in which they are here set down, which in large measure accords with the natural order of events, and shows the sequence of historical facts. . . . No one of these fields can be omitted without leaving serious *lacunae* in the pupil's knowledge of history. Each department has its special value and teaches its special lesson.[23]

"The history of the human race is one subject," reasoned the conferees, and a four-year course appeared the most suitable for secondary students. It was the Committee's considered opinion that history brought unity to other school subjects. Ancient history was related to Greek and Latin, medieval and modern history to the humanities, and American history to our common culture. Continuing, the conferees declared:

> History has a central position among the subjects of the curriculum. . . . It belongs to the humanities, for its essential purpose is to disclose human life; but it also searches for data, groups them, and builds generalizations from them. Though it is not a science itself, its methods are similar to scientific methods, and are valuable in inculcating in the pupil a regard for accuracy and a reverence for truth.[24]

History: Humanities and Science

History, therefore, encompassed a dual role as part humanities, part science: a uniqueness unmatched by any other subject in the secondary curriculum. To the conferees history was the most important subject in the school. History bridged the gap between the incipient urban industrial state that degraded the individual and reduced the human being to a mere cog in the machinery of capital and finance, and the human spirit that gave each human a special quality. By utilizing the methods of science with the eloquence of literature, history took the hard edges off the sciences while celebrating humanity, a justifiable compromise.

Admittedly, and despite the criticism against their presentation, Ancient, Medieval, and Modern Histories were defended as within the mental and intellectual abilities of students. "Pupils should pass from the known to the unknown," responded the conferees. That is, difficult material inspired the student, allowing and providing for growth. Thus history was not only to be offered, but was also to be made available to every student. Whether the student was or was not able to digest historical content and methodologies did not matter, the strength of the discipline presented with a sound pedagogy would transform any child. Knowledge *and* intellectual skills would be the end results.

Reluctantly conceding to the criticism that some schools could not "devote so much time to history," the Committee countered that just because some schools could not offer as much history as they were proposing, did not mean that they should not report what the better schools were doing, or further, present "an adequate course" in history. The conferees stated:

We are not seeking to induce schools to give history a great amount of attention at the expense of other subjects; but a course altogether complete and adequate needs to be outlined before one can rightly discuss the availability of anything else. An approach to an ideal course, in order of subjects, methods, treatment, and time, is better than one that is constructed without reference to the best and most symmetrical system.[25]

Acting from their comprehensive data base, this willingness to take a position was the strength of the Committee of Seven. Educators could accept or reject the program in part or in total, but the proposal itself would remain sound. The program of traditional history could thus serve the schools as a point of common understanding, as a benchmark and guide to assist educators to address the many needs and interests of their students. As earlier mentioned, the survivability of the program was a testament to its appeal and practicality. Nonetheless, it appeared the report was not needed for the better high schools, for they already had the program, nor was it practical for the least able, poorest, and rural, for they could not possibly follow it. Instead it was targeted for the rapidly growing urban high schools across the nation. The leadership of these schools were willing and eager to follow the dictates of the history experts in order to modernize and upgrade their secondary curricula.

The conferees, unlike their Madison Conference counterparts, offered more than "titles" of the prospective courses. With the bulk of the report of the Committee of Seven given over to a discussion of "how the different blocks or periods may be treated" and what "methods of instruction" would be most helpful, educators, as noted by Tryon, Johnson, and Wesley, adopted the program nearly in toto.

The foundation of their program was Ancient History. Owing to the fact that the average student would most likely (if he or she managed to enter high school at all) leave school sometime during the tenth year, educators felt the best option for those having just one full year of high school before dropping out was to study Ancient History. Some schools, reported the conferees, offered no other branch of history, a leftover to the days when Greek and Latin language studies dominated the secondary curriculum. In breaking with that tradition, the Committee argued that "the time has come when ancient history may be studied independently" from the classics.

A thorough study of the histories of ancient Greece and Rome formed the core of the offering with a special introductory section devoted to our oriental heritage. This introductory section was to include a survey of the length and reach of recorded history and an outline of the "definitive knowledge of the names, location, and chronological succession of the early Oriental nations." In addition, the seven conferees suggested providing a description of the distinguishing features of these civilizations as concretely as possible and an accurate depiction of the recognizable lines of their influence upon later times.[26]

The most important lesson of the full year course in ancient history was the inculcation of the sweep of time: that a nation's life was not lived in isolation from its neighbors, that the acts of men have great and grave influences on their own times and for the future, and that the thread of life beginning in ancient times extends to the present.[27] In suggesting that the details of the Peloponnesian war might be omitted for other areas of study, the committee implied that they did not wish to inundate students in a sea of history.[28] It is important to note that the committee was not advocating the whole of history be taught in a lockstep chronology, as found in many textbooks of the period, but rather that teachers should exercise a measure of selectivity and present the "chief events" of history as they saw fit.

The one thousand years of European history between 800, 814, or 832 A.D. and the present was suggested to be studied as Medieval and Modern History, in the tenth grade. With so much history to present, the question for the teacher, wrote the conferees, was whether to treat the whole field "superficially" or "only the main lines"? In any event, the seven conferees stressed that "some unity be discovered if possible, or that there should be some central line with which events or movements could be correlated."[29] Continuing the lessons of Ancient History, the teacher was apparently to focus increasingly on the lesson of unity and continuity.

Admittedly, the seven committee members suggested that the teacher may wish to present the sweep of history by either presenting "the broad field of European history with special reference to movements or epochs [alone]" or to present these movements or epochs by isolating the history of a single nation, preferably France. The suggestion was that this might be all the student "should be asked to acquire," that by focusing on the history of one nation, by studying and understanding its "chief transitions," students would be able to secure the lesson of the "central thread."[30] With France as the central focus, all the principal topics suggested for Medieval and Modern History—for example, growth of the Church, feudalism, and the rise of present democracies—might be adequately covered. The conferees wrote, however:

> If neither of the two methods here suggested appeals to the teacher, he must seemingly do one of two things: he must endeavor to get a very general view of the field, give all the main facts and dates, and follow the histories of the nations in parallel lines; or he must omit large portions of the historical field altogether, and content himself with the study of a few important epochs.[31]

Nevertheless, the Committee cautioned that the use of either of the secondary methods mentioned above—"all the main facts" or "omit large portions"—could produce several unhappy results. First, to use either meant giving up the lesson of unity. Secondly, the study of "all the main facts and dates" commonly led to "cramming the memory with indigestible facts and in mental confusion." Finally, the study of "important epochs only," although successful in some schools, was not appropriate for high school students because of their inability "in comprehending general tendencies" without first a solid understanding of these movements.[32] Although it was clear that the Committee of Seven advocated French history as the central focus of the tenth-grade offering, as had the Madison Committee before them, they left the door open for educators to adopt other variations.

During the eleventh year English history was to be presented, concluding the European survey. English history provided "some measure of review" of Continental history and most importantly served as a "preparation for American history in the last year of high school." The close connections between American institutions and their historic roots in England stood paramount during this year of study. In fact, wrote the Committee.

> Without a knowledge of how the English people developed and English principles matured, [students] can have slight appreciation of what America means. Even the Revolution, for example, if studied as an isolated phenomenon, is bereft of half its meaning, to say the least, because the movement that ended in the separation of the colonies from the mother country and in the adoption of the Federal Constitution, began long before the colonies were founded.[33]

The importance of American links to English soil for the conferees cannot be overstated. England was the "taproot" of democratic ideals and therefore required the most careful scrutiny. The Committee concluded that "considerable, if not chief attention be paid to the gradual development of English political institutions."[34] They did not suggest that the entire length and breadth of the English political situation and intrigue be presented, "simply the main features." They noted that "the fundamental principles and practices of constitutional government should be studied, and that the steps in its development should be marked." Although the Committee neglected to point out exactly what those "fundamental principles and practices" were, they did stress the social aspects of this history. Specifically, "how the state grew in power, how the government developed, and how it became more and more responsive to the popular will and watchful of individual interests" were the important questions that the proposed course was to address and study. Here the conferees placed the emphasis on how individuals claimed their rights in the process of democratic government.

For all practical purposes the Committee saw English history as a study of political institutions. The important lesson to be learned from this study was that English history was not confined to the environs of England. The history of the English was a case study of how one nation interacted not only with its immediate neighbors in spreading knowledge and the English language, but also with the world.[35] The connection between England's interactions and reactions within and outside its realm to the teeming cosmopolitan composition of America's urban centers was not lost on the Committee. America's "melting pot" image required a model to boost its faith in a democratic, pluralistic society and English history filled this role quite well. Again, the emphasis was not on a complete historical study from Saxon days to the present, detailing each battle, king, and political intrigue; but rather to select those vital and connective facts, personalities, and events that led to the development of America's democratic form of government.

For the final year of high school the Committee recommended that the study of American history "be taken up as an advanced subject, with the purpose of getting a clear idea of the course of events in the building of the American Republic."[36] The Committee argued that since many schools placed a survey of American history in the eighth year, even with three successive years of European history following it, it was unnecessary to repeat another survey of

American history in the ninth grade. The conferees recommended the advanced American history course in the final year:

> [Its] chief aim should be to give the pupil knowledge of the progress of political institutions, ideas, and tendencies. We believe also that he should know the economic phases of life; that whenever possible, attention should be directed not merely to economic and social conditions, but to economic and social developments; and that those economic, industrial, or social modifications should receive chief attention which have permanently altered social organizations, or have become embedded in institutions, ideas, or governmental forms. . . . We should see, if we can, how such things influenced human progress and had effect on the nature, organization, and destinies of the American people.[37]

While it was thought not possible or practical in the opinion of the Committee to teach or present a careful study of American life in the grades, it was feasible to do so in the high school and in particular the last year of school:

> [Special attention] must be paid to movements, and an effort must be made to cultivate the faculty of drawing truthful generalizations, for seeing and comprehending tendencies. . . . Since there is so much to be done in a single year, there is not time for the study of such past industrial and social conditions . . . as stand unrelated, isolated, and hence meaningless, and perhaps are without real historical value.[38]

American history was to provide students with as complete a picture of their present life as possible. Economic or social facts, as important as they may be, or political and governmental facts, as important as they may be, were not to overwhelm students by overreaching one another. Instead a balance was to be struck between the two. Noted the conferees:

> The greatest aim of education is to impress upon the learner a sense of duty and responsibility, and an acquaintance with his human obligations; and that a manifest function of the historical instruction in the school is to give the pupil a sense of duty as a responsible member of the organized society of which he is

a part, and some appreciation of its principles and its fundamental character.[39]

The culmination of historical studies with American history
was the production of the responsible citizen. Although much play
had been given over to intellectual processes, the end result for the
Committee of Seven was that the student would become a fully
functioning member of society, cognizant of one's own civil responsibilities. To emphasize this point the conferees suggested that civil
government be offered in conjunction with the final year of history.
Feeling that both subjects should be integrated, the Committee recommended that students be exposed to the study of our country's
laws, political theories, and practices in the course of learning about
American institutions. The federal system, our colonial heritage,
the interworkings of local and state governments, and our constitution itself were to be interwoven: they were the nation's history. The
abstracts of political theory, reasoned the Committee, could be applied to concrete situations (and vice versa), making American history and civil government compatible partners in the educative
process.

METHODS OF INSTRUCTION AND TEACHER PREPARATION

If the Committee of Seven paid any homage to the Madison
Conference for that committee's contribution to history, it was with
the methods of teaching history. The Committee of Seven credited
the "widely read and used" Madison report for bringing "some measure of agreement" among teachers concerning classroom methods.
Moreover, the Committee of Seven cautioned that "this committee
will perhaps be no wiser in its recommendations and suggestions;
and . . . the best plan may be to leave well enough alone."[40] In spite
of the value of methods in teaching, the conferees stressed that
"more important than method, is object," a point to which the
earlier committee gave little attention. "Means are valueless," continued the conferees, "to one who has no end to be attained."[41]
Therefore, during the teaching process, the teacher, not the subject
matter, established the ends before instruction began.

The stated values of history, as previously outlined, were found
in its educational ends, yet it was necessary for the teacher to place
those values in order and be "sure that he knows what he wishes to
accomplish." Nonetheless, to the Committee, this action appeared

axiomatic; competent teachers would know and understand their educational goals. The key to success in "bringing out the educational value of the study" was to identify the more useful methods directed toward that end. To accomplish the most modest aims of history, the conferees suggested six basic methods: use of textbooks, collateral readings, written work, written recitations or tests, student notebooks, and extensive map-geography work, as a supplement to historical expositions.

The conferees considered the textbook a valuable tool for those teachers without "wide training, long experience, and, in addition, daily opportunity carefully to examine the field and to search out the nature of the problems that he is called upon to discuss."[42] Indeed, this qualification was apparent to many prospective history teachers, given a catalog of their own qualifications. To such teachers the textbook was an absolutely essential teaching aid. "Without the use of the text," emphasized the conferees, "it is difficult to hold the pupils to a definite line of work."[43] Additionally, "within the covers of one book, however, it is impossible to bring together one hundredth part of the material which any careful historical writer would examine for himself before coming to a conclusion."[44] On the one hand, the textbook brought unity, continuity, and historical mindedness; on the other hand, the textbook was incomplete, prone to lead students to accept generalizations as facts, and, by the unwitting teacher's erroneous emphasis on fact accumulation, foster an unhealthy dulling of historical appreciation.

The conferees "strongly advise[d] the use of material outside the text." However, the teacher should not let students "lose sight of the main current [chronological flow]," advising instead that "it is the current and not the eddies" that students should watch.[45] Nevertheless, the conferees suggested that multiple texts would perhaps be better placed in the "more advanced grades." Again, the conferees, alluding to the probable inadequate preparation of the teacher, suggested that "unless [the teacher] has the time and opportunity to master all the texts himself and to examine outside material with care," the teacher would find "many practical difficulties" with the use of multiple texts.[46] The Committee concluded that supplementary texts, as useful as they may be, were perhaps better placed in the hands of the competent teacher to illustrate comparisons as opposed to student dissection and analysis. Material outside the text, however, was a different matter.

Sources collateral to the study of history, such as great works of literature, were especially recommended for "all branches of historical study and in every year of the secondary course."[47] Outside reading was encouraged because of its capacity to heighten the interest of the student in history and more importantly, to the Committee, to teach the student "the power of using books." Outside readings combined with textbook use provided the necessary base for the successful exploitation of written work, recitations, and notebook keeping, without which the educative process would prove fruitless. To utilize the written recitation, for example, the student would be required to possess some notion of the historical topic. Wide readings and close attention to the text narrative would, therefore, supply the student with the requisite information to prepare and present considered opinions and criticisms.

The historical process hinged upon the proper habit of book use. "The library," declared the conferees, "should be the center and soul of all study in history and literature; no vital work can be carried on without books to which pupils may have ready and constant access."[48] It was evident, however, that the methods recommended for history study were decidedly single-minded. Popular college methods, such as working with original sources and individual topics, lecture-discussions, and intensive historical study were not advised for use below the university, unless, of course, the schools were staffed, outfitted, and prepared to provide that level of service. Moreover, the oral recitation, the staple of many secondary school classrooms, was similarly discounted. Yet despite their cautions, schools more able to provide advance methods, like the source and topic methods, were encouraged to do so. Schools of lesser means were to use whatever appeared to work best, which was typically textbook recitation.

In any event, the conferees were not suggesting a definitive plan for training new historians, but rather a means of guiding students to think historically, to the end that they would attain a proper historical perspective on life. In contrast to the Madison program, the Committee of Seven saw the ability to think historically of greater value than the acquisition of the skills necessary to write history.

In spite of the completeness of the Committee program in theory, without proper implementation the report would hold little value. "If history is to take and hold its proper place in the school curriculum," wrote the conferees, "it must be in the hands of teachers who are thoroughly equipped for the task of bringing out its educational value."[49]

It is still not very unusual to find that history is taught, if such a word is appropriate, by those who have made no preparation, and that classes are sometimes managed—we hesitate to say instructed—by persons who do not profess either to be prepared or to take interest in the subject. . . . As long as other subjects in the course are given to specialists, while history is distributed here and there to fill up interstices, there can be no great hope for its advancement.[50]

The teacher, according to the Committee, needed three broad qualities to successfully prepare and present the lessons of history. First, knowledge of history and its relative importance to other things. Second, the teacher should have a complete understanding and competence with the "tools of the trade," which included a thorough understanding of methods, and skill in the handling of books. And lastly:

A successful teacher must have more than mere accurate information and professional knowledge. He needs to have a living sympathy with the tale which he tells. He must know how to bring out the dramatic aspects of the story. He must know how to awaken the interest and attention of his pupils. . . . He must have had his own imagination fired and his enthusiasm kindled; he must know the sources of historical knowledge and the springs of historical inspiration; he must know the literature of history and be able to direct his pupils to stirring passages in the great historical masters; he must know how to illuminate and brighten the page by reading from literature and by illustrations from art.[51]

These later ideal attributes, however, were difficult if not impossible to obtain from a university education. "Much depends upon the personality of the teacher," the conferees agreed, "upon his force, insight, tact, sympathy, upon qualities that cannot be imparted by the university courses or by prolonged research."[52] Despite the inability to "teach" these indispensable characteristics, prospective history teachers could at least receive instruction in teaching methods and learn the "essentials of history study and historical thinking." Apparently, for the conferees, this was simply the best that could be done.

COLLEGE ENTRANCE
REQUIREMENTS AND EXAMINATIONS

The last section of the Committee report was given over to a discussion of college entrance requirements and their relationship to the preparation of secondary students. Initially the Committee of Seven was called into being specifically to "report a scheme of uniform requirements" for secondary history, so that students would arrive at the university with a common understanding and knowledge of history. The Committee wrote:

> Probably no field of work offers greater problems [with developing standards for college] than does that of history, because the schools have no common understanding as to the amount of history that should be offered in the curriculum, and because universities differ materially in their requirements.[53]

During the investigation, however, the focus of the report shifted from the narrow task of recommending a college preparatory course to providing a course for all students. Admittedly the report of the seven conferees and the Committee on College Entrance Requirements outlined similar objectives for secondary schools, yet the seven conferees found those phenomena to be merely coincidental. The problem with designing the secondary curriculum to fit university needs ignored the fact "that a very large percentage of secondary students (greater than eighty per cent) do not go to college."[54] Given this situation, educators were not designing *their* curricula to match university needs; rather they saw the need to adapt their courses "primarily for the pupils who finish their study with the secondary school." Prudently, the seven conferees' program was an outgrowth of existing conditions, a creation that accepted the premise of a scheme for college entrance requirements, but acknowledged of far greater importance the need to address the majority. On the one hand, the Committee on College Entrance Requirements emphasized portions of the report that "were developed with that purpose in mind." But on the other hand, the Committee of Seven stressed:

> The curriculum [secondary] must be prepared with the purpose of developing boys and girls into young men and women, not with the purpose of fitting them to meet entrance examinations or of filling them with information which some faculty

thinks desirable as a forerunner of college work. . . . [Because universities vary so widely in requirements], it is an almost impossible task so to arrange the programme that pupils can be fitted for more than one institution. . . . For this reason we welcome the efforts of the committee of the National Education Association to simplify and unify college entrance requirements. We believe, however, that the first requisite of a successful accomplishment of this task is a recognition of the fact that the great majority of schools are not fitting-schools for college; and it seems to us that any rigid and inelastic *regime*, which does not take into consideration the fact that schools are subject to different environments and are subject to different limitations and conditions, cannot be very widely accepted or prove useful for any length of time.[55]

Here, the distinction between a body of recommendations conceived as a rigid program and as a proposal for an ideal course of study needs to made. To later critics the "four block system" was a fixed curriculum; to its framers, however, it was especially, and directly, a flexible plan given to educators for *their* disposal. The seven conferees were charged with the task of developing a college preparatory program for secondary schools and in realizing the futility of such a creature, instead prepared a terminal program in history specifically designed for secondary students. In explanation of their actions the committee stated:

We feel justified, therefore, as students and teachers, in marking out what we think is the best curriculum in history, in discussing the educational value of the study, in emphasizing the thought that history is peculiarly appropriate in a secondary course, which is fashioned with the thought of preparing boys and girls for the duties of daily life and intelligent citizenship, and in dwelling upon methods for bringing out the pedagogical effect of historical work. . . . We do not feel that we should seek to lay down hard-and-fast entrance requirements in history and ask colleges or the committee of the National Education Association to declare in favor of an inflexible *regime*.[56]

As with the earlier report of the Madison Conference, the Committee of Seven ultimately decided against the presentation of a fixed curriculum. Ironically, many educators and educational critics perceived their program to be fixed nonetheless. Their rationale, however, differed from the Madison Conference. The Madison conferees believed the ideal curriculum should not be set by a national committee, because of the possibility of usurping decision-making at the local level. The Committee of Seven, equally dismissing the notion of a rigid program, despite being called upon to develop one, reasoned that a common program for all was simply impractical. Pragmatically, educators were ultimately going to select their own program to match their own needs. Therefore, the best plan was an ideal plan that provided enough flexibility to be implemented by local educators as needed.

Taking into consideration their reservations against "college entrance requirements for history," the Committee of Seven did concede to outline a series of *suggestions* for students in the four prevalent secondary curricula: college preparatory program or classical, Latin, scientific, or the new English course of studies. "The general recommendations" the conferees distinguished were "summed up as follows:" for the classical course and Latin course, one unit of history selected from the four blocks; the scientific course, any two units from the four blocks; and the English course, at least three units from the four, with a strong recommendation to include all four.[57] Essentially, the Committee of Seven implied that the individual school, if it must, should select the appropriate units from the four blocks according to the needs and interests of its students. Although they naturally favored the full course, all four blocks, realistically they understood the importance of maintaining a neutral stance. That is, they knew that if the report were to yield any measure of success, they had to steadfastly hold to the notion of an ideal program, acceptable first as a terminal secondary program, and second, if needed, as a college preparatory plan.

In addressing the problem of correlating a student's secondary program in history to facilitate a passing score on any college entrance examination, the Committee of Seven simply stated the "present system of entrance examination" needed revamping. "It is time," declared the conferees, "to consider how [the system of examinations] may be changed."[58] The suggestions they offered were not directed at preparing the prospective college student; but rather they were aimed to assist colleges to "bring about a more just and adequate system of examinations in history." The Committee of Seven recommended that educators design their history curriculum along three primary guidelines: (a) make no distinction between terminal high school students and those preparing for college; (b) teachers should be more concerned with teaching "what history is and how it should be studied" than covering a particular field or topic of history; and (c) educators should set a length of time and the number of periods each "block" of history should meet for each term. Correspondingly, according to the Committee of Seven, if the student carefully followed the four blocks of history, college entrance examinations or credit conditions would not pose a barrier to matriculation.

With increasing pride during the 1890s, America's emerging path toward industrial preeminence began to tact a new course. The passing of the frontier fostered many new apprehensions concerning the future of the nation. Americans, perhaps optimistically, turned introspective to mark their achievements, calling for a place among the modern urban industrial powers. The great World's Columbia Exposition exemplified the evolving American character that favored industrial strength, cultural pride, and intellectual hope. No nation rightfully can be considered great without a past complete with a chart provided by history studies of its wanderings and discoveries, joys and triumphs, tragedies and failures, and heroes and villains. It was history and history alone that supplied a nation this chart. Early American practitioners of the late 1890s eagerly welcomed the opportunity to translate their faith in historical studies to the teaching of history in public schools, not simply for the sake of posterity but also for the sake of our younger citizens. America needed a sense of past amid all the progress; it was vital to the nation's well-being to teach the American heritage to its youth.

Beginning with the thoughts of individual thinkers such as Andrew D. White, Albert Bushnell Hart, Francis W. Parker, G. Stanley Hall, Mary Sheldon Barnes, and Burton Aaron Hinsdale, who all identified the need for a traditional history approach in the emerging secondary school, and culminating in the increased devotion to history studies by national committees, history made its entrance into the nation's schools. This chapter as well as chapter 2 discussed the appearance of the traditional history curriculum that emerged in the last decades of the nineteenth century. The spread of this new gospel to the secondary level was initially voiced through the works of its early practitioners, such as Hall and Hinsdale, whose texts found an audience for these new ideas by illustrating the values of history study.

The making of the traditional history curriculum as described in Hall and Hinsdale as well as the reports of the Madison Conference and the Committee of Seven was founded upon a felt need and the belief that history had value. Consequently, although these individuals and committees acknowledged that history was indeed a part of many school curricula prior to 1892, the poor quality of this teaching warranted a coherent plan or guide. Hall and Hinsdale attempted to introduce these ideas, offering suggestions for teachers as well as school administrators. Eventually the importance of teaching history garnered the attention of educators at the national level and led to the formation of the Madison Conference and the Committee of Seven. Although both committees were called upon to investigate history studies for secondary schools, they also addressed the implementation of history in the grade school. The Madison Conference and the Committee of Seven were not the only committees that met to discuss history in the schools, and Hall and Hinsdale were not the only individuals that delineated the traditional history curriculum, but they were the most influential.

4. TOWARD SOCIAL EDUCATION REFORM

"WE ARE IN THE PRESENCE of a new organization of society," proclaimed Woodrow Wilson during his successful 1912 presidential election. He continued:

> The life of America is not the life that it was twenty years ago; it is not the life that it was ten years ago. We have changed our economic conditions, absolutely, from top to bottom; and, with our economic society, the organization of our life. . . . We are facing the necessity of fitting a new social organization, as we did once fit the old organization, to the happiness and prosperity of the great body of citizens; for we are conscious that the new order of society has not been made to fit and provide the convenience or prosperity of the average man. The life of the nation had grown infinitely varied. . . . To-day, the every-day relationships of men are largely with great impersonal concerns, with organizations, not with other individual men. Now this is nothing short of a new social age, a new era of human relationships, a new stage-setting for the drama of life.[1]

The 1912 presidential election exemplified a shift in political power from the conservative William Howard Taft to the progressive Wilson. Despite labeling himself a "progressive" in the 1908 presidential campaign, once elected president, Taft encountered difficulties in his relations with progressive leaders. Historians of the era found that Taft's relationship with his political allies was at best strained. For example, Arthur Link characterized Taft as a "philosophical progressive" and his cronies as "too sweeping in their denunciations, too impatient, too willing to experiment with untried measures."[2] Taft slowly alienated himself from progressive insurgents who came to believe that he had realigned himself with mainline conservative interests. The fallout of his political dealings hinged on tariff revision legislation (Payne-Alrich Law 1909), and the Ballinger Affair (Taft's defense of Richard Ballinger, secretary of the interior who sought the quick disposition of lands remaining in the public domain against the wishes of progressive conservation forces). These involvements exposed Taft to the public as a conservative wrapped in progressive clothes.

In spite of the earlier successes of the progressive Theodore Roosevelt, many citizens, by 1912, were uneasy and restless over the failure of the Taft administration to make much headway with statutory controls over big business trusts, Wall Street bankers, and railroad interests. They clearly welcomed the return of another, more dedicated progressive in Wilson. Wilson pledged that he would devote himself to working for the "general interests" of the nation, not the "special interests."[3] Twenty years before he became president of the United States, Wilson, as a member of the Madison Conference, helped draft the first traditional history reform statement for the nation's public schools. Now, twenty years later, he had been elected to initiate, foster, and institute reform on an even grander scale.

With his "New Freedom" program, Wilson set out to tackle such problems as the banking system, tariffs, income tax, direct election of senators, opening the Panama Canal, and curbing big business abuses. Later, reversing his earlier views and traditional Democratic Party positions as well, Wilson sponsored social reforms such as farm bills, child labor legislation, standardization of the eight-hour workday, workers' compensation bills, and other social issues under a revamped program called the "New Nationalism." In effect, these actions widened Wilson's social program to include the whole Progressive Party platform of 1912.[4] What Wilson had begun in 1912 as a modest program of political and economic reform, eventually became a plan of sweeping social betterment as well.

The Commission on the Reorganization of Secondary Schools was chartered to initiate socially responsible and efficient programs in this climate of "reforming" government and big business abuse.

The beginning of the Commission and the beginning of Wilson's tenure as president were not coincidental; both were an outgrowth of the era that Arthur Link called the "flowering of the progressive movement."[5] The concept of radical reform in American society was not, of course, original to Wilson or the new Commission. Nevertheless, the political power to enact meaningful change provided by widespread public support was novel.

Considering the great strides made during the last decade of the nineteenth century toward providing that free education be available to nearly every citizen, reforms in education, as with nearly every other segment of society, were still demanded. According to one writer, the history of the nature, substance, and extent of school change in the period revealed two very different interpretations. On the one hand, turn-of-the-century progressive educators sought genuine reform to enact two broad interconnected results, social control or social service. On the other hand, it was claimed that so-called progressive educators, while seeking these results in rhetoric, were actually quite conservative in practice, and in fact their actions "inhibited rather than fostered social change and reform."[6] Understanding this anomaly, during this reform period, is vital.

With reference to the conservatism of the social studies insurgents of the period, Michael Lybarger argues that the 1916 Social Studies report was seriously flawed. Lybarger claimed that despite the feeling of the conferees that social problems should function as content for the new social studies, students were not encouraged to define or identify problems or consider criticisms made quite widely by muckrakers of the period. In sum, Lybarger found that the social studies of the 1916 report was "drained of critical content in order to pursue piecemeal improvement of social, economic, and political conditions while at the same time obscuring the causes of poor conditions."[7] To Lybarger, this draining of "critical content" by the conferees illustrated a shallow commitment to social concerns and problem-solving. The conferees were not, however, striving to hide or diminish critical content. On the contrary, the document expressly suggested that teachers encourage students to be critical of traditions and accepted practice, thereby making the report highly controversial.

The report broke new ground in education and called upon educators to experiment and cut new ground themselves. On the one hand, Lybarger was half-right, the report was a symbolic curriculum guide—that is, something that attended to popular progressive concerns without really getting down to the nitty-gritty on solving, discussing, or exploring such problems. On the other hand, the report went beyond symbolism by expressly fostering a healthy critical attitude toward society and its institutions. Part of historian Henry Johnson's early bitter criticism of social studies made clear that the social studies insurgents were indeed merging symbolism and action. Johnson thought the notion of preparing a curriculum before instruction was axiomatic, yet the social studies curriculum, as he pointed out, defied preparation; How was one to know current events and problems before they happened?[8]

Although the nature of present-based instruction, a la the social studies model, did make preplanning difficult, there was another reason that the conferees were vague about social problems. They were hopeful that educators would accept and implement their suggestions, yet they did not wish to alienate educators, or worse, prescribe a detailed "fixed" program. In the hopes of making a more appealing reform package, exact details or prescriptions were omitted; the reformers simply wanted educators to make their own curricular decisions.

In practice there was a great difference between muckraker literature and social studies insurgents as well as historians. As Samuel S. Shermis noted, "the Muckrakers, most of whom also wrote for liberal journals, identified social problems for the purpose of persuading the public to identify the same problems."[9] Despite the focus upon social problems in rhetoric, students, in the classroom, were rarely engaged in any analysis of popular muckraker topics, such as exploitation of immigrants in the work force or quality of canned foods.[10] Sadly, although the 1916 Social Studies report called for such examinations to be made, the curricular materials that followed the report did not generally include nor advocate students to investigate social concerns/problems. In essence, there was "much talk about problems, [however] there was no substance . . . in the curriculum."[11]

What is important for our purposes is that the period's curricular reform was not an isolated phenomena specific only to the history curriculum; *every* curricular offering *and* every social, political, and economic institution was under the scrutiny of a host of critics from "malicious muckrakers" to sincere social reformers like Jane Addams. The pivotal questions at this point are what criterion was used to support the inclusion or exclusion of a particular subject or discipline in the secondary curriculum? And, given that answer, What case was made against the subject in question?

Social Efficiency versus Intellectual Focus

Two "tests," both aiming at social progress as the end result, were utilized to make the determination for inclusion or exclusion: Was the subject socially efficient—that is, did it contribute to social progress? Did the subject answer a present need and interest, or solve a present problem? Although the difference between the two was subtle, it was distinct. Parenthetically, the older "test" of intellectual focus, used by traditional historians, was almost entirely discounted to a secondary role by the socially motivated reformers. These reformers argued that judging each discipline according to its contribution in shaping the individual's mental functions was more than outdated, it was wrong; social efficiency was to guide the school curriculum.

The source of the "social efficiency" test may be traced conceptually to one of the pioneers of sociology, Lester Frank Ward. In his influential, yet initially unrecognized, masterwork *Dynamic Sociology* (1883), Ward revealed that through education humans were capable of shaping the future. For Ward (as discussed in chapter 1) "the object of education [was] social improvement."[12] The concept of man-made "social improvement"—that is, that change could be self-directed and was not something preordained by God or evolution—was integral to later progressive ideology. Remarkably, the notion and application of social efficiency for public schools came not from the reaches of higher education but from the most pervasive force in American society, business-industrial executives.

According to Raymond E. Callahan in his *Education and the Cult of Efficiency*, the school efficiency movement that reached "mania" proportions by the early 1910s derived its ideology and techniques from the "Taylor system" of business management and its impetus from the constant battering of critics who wanted to ensure that schools were properly fitting young people for their roles in the world of work.[13] The test that sought to measure school operations and results was the test of social efficiency. In effect, this test was an example of social control. Typically, the school offered those subjects that would provide the greatest amount of return for the least amount expended. Superfluous studies that offered no immediate results were not viewed as cost-effective and were therefore expendable.

Specifically, three models or variants of efficiency testing emerged at the turn of the century. (a) The investment model, which viewed the school as a conservative institution designed to serve society and, in particular, the business sector in an investment for predictable returns relationship. (b) The production model, which viewed the school as strictly a business operation of determining costs of production—materials, personnel, and physical plant—per product student. (c) The management-accounting model, which studied costs versus benefits ratio, established need for long-range planning, and set budgets accordingly.[14] Notwithstanding these variants, the application rationale remained consistent. Initially each course was suspected of being inefficient and, as such, every course of study or subject was held accountable to the doctrine of social efficiency that directed each "school subject to prove [its] right to exist."[15] To be viable, education had to produce tangible results, and this meant adhering to the doctrine of social efficiency.

The second test "administered" during the period was that of meeting the present needs and interests of students, or, at least, working toward a reconciliation of a particular *real* social problem. The primary source of this second test was, of course, John Dewey.[16] The questions asked were complex: Were the school's offerings prepared and presented according to and in view of the student's needs or interests? Did the offering tackle a real social problem in the hope of exploring a viable solution? If schools did not attend to these issues and continued without consulting student needs and interests, they were inviting disaster upon democracy as well as delaying or destroying any hope for social progress.

Although the goal of social progress remained consistent, the difference between the two tests was revealed in how they were administered, as well as in how the results were scored. Social efficiency was a management-based evaluative procedure that put the measure of its operation and eventual effectiveness not under the control of the teacher and his or her students, but in the hands of the managers of the school—namely, the principal, superintendent, and school board. The managers of the school, then, generated and read the statistical data that "proved" the school's accountability— that is, its social efficiency. Moreover, it was the managers who devised the measurement instruments to "test" that their employees were or were not productive. The Deweyan test checked its results from the progress of the student and measured the advancement of the individual student within the context of the social whole. In application, this illustrated an approach to the paradox of the individual and society. The Deweyan test attempted to account for individual as well as social progress. The major contrast between the two tests was that the former viewed the student not as an individual but as a single entity—namely, the collective student body—whereas the latter viewed the student as a vital element of the whole of society.

Regardless of which of the two tests were applied to schools, both essentially called the subject offered into question and debated its intrinsic and extrinsic worth relative to social progress, often defined as the advancement of the nation or democracy. Given the challenge of socially progressive reform and considering the changes in society as well as public schools that had taken place since the inaugural secondary report of the Committee of Ten, this chapter presents a review of the criticisms of and arguments made against the traditional history curriculum. These critiques emerged in the early 1900s after the dissemination of the seminal Committee of Seven report.

From 1902 to 1916 the battle lines were drawn between the three camps concerned with history in secondary schools: (a) those who accepted and sought the maintenance of the traditional history curriculum as written by the Committee of Seven; (b) those who criticized the program and called for revision, yet chose to remain within the general guidelines of the program; and (c) those who rejected outright and argued for the complete reformation of the discipline. This chapter addresses each of these groups, but it will concentrate on the latter two.

As criticism of the traditional history curriculum became widespread by the 1910s, this examination will be confined only to the principal criticisms and arguments. In addition, the arguments for social education as determined from literature in the field and supported by its leading early historians Henry Johnson, Edgar Dawson, Edgar Bruce Wesley, and Rolla Tryon are also treated.

Those groups who articulated the principal criticisms and remained chiefly within the history camp included the New England History Teachers' Association, the Association of History Teachers of the Middle States and Maryland, and the American Historical Association's Committee of Five. Those critics that argued for a complete reformation of history for the secondary school were headed by David Samuel Snedden and Clarence Darwin Kingsley. Although John Dewey did not specifically aim to dislodge the traditional history curriculum, in that he voiced no direct attacks on the program, his arguments did imply a need for its reformation and greatly influenced contemporary critics. Snedden's, Dewey's, and Kingsley's arguments are outlined in the following chapters.

In addition, the principal critiques of the major history teacher associations as well as those of the American Historical Association will be presented. Furthermore, those individuals who revolted from the status quo, as well as other influential voices of dissent will also be recognized.

Essentially, the bulk of the criticism against the traditional history curriculum centered on the findings and recommendations of the Committee of Seven, a point that would appear to confirm the contention of later historians that the Committee of Seven was the focus of attention as well as the most influential and pervasive history curriculum devised for secondary schools in the period.[17] Consequently, the following section concentrates on the principal criticisms of the proposed Committee of Seven program. This chapter discusses the decisive criticisms of traditional history, identifies the critics in favor of maintenance and modification, and highlights those who advocated complete reformation.

INITIAL REACTIONS AMONG THE ADVOCATES OF TRADITIONAL HISTORY

The first significant remarks against the Committee of Seven's report were voiced in 1902 at a conference of secondary school principals and deans affiliated or cooperating with the University of Chicago. These educators were concerned with the Committee's recommendation that general history should not be offered in the secondary school.[18] At this meeting they maintained that a course in general history should be given "preference to the history of any isolated period, where there is time for only one."[19] That this point was raised may have been anticipated and in fact should have been expected, given the statistical data generated by the Committee. This data revealed general history or the "short course" in history was (a) the most frequent course in the schools at the time of their survey, and (b) being offered "in almost exactly half the schools."[20]

Despite this data, the Committee of Seven's argument against such a course was explicit:

> We do not recommend a short course in general history, because such a course necessitates one of two modes of treatment, nei-

ther of which is sound and reasonable. By one method, energy is devoted to the dreary, and perhaps profitless, task of memorizing facts, dates, names of kings and queens, and the rise and fall of dynasties; there is no opportunity to see how facts arose or what they effected, or to study the material properly. . . . By the second method, pupils are led to deal with large and general ideas which are often quite beyond their comprehension, ideas which are general inferences by the learned historian. . . . They are taught to accept unquestioningly broad generalizations, the foundation of which they cannot possibly examine. . . . The first method is apt to heap meaningless data together . . . the second alternative . . . is all order and system.[21]

The Chicago educators' point stressed practicality; not all schools could follow the program of the Committee of Seven, and in reality many schools could offer just one and, at most, two courses in history. Although the Chicago educators "most cordially" supported the overall program, their practical concern was for those schools that for one reason or another could not closely adhere to the Committee's recommendations of the course of study and instead should offer general history. There was no other recommendation or argument made by the Committee that was so poorly understood or so little agreed to by educators.

Whether conscious or not, substituting general history for the four block system violated two basic tenets of history: the illustration of cause and effect, and the questioning of historical data. That general history, later retitled world history or world civilizations, *increased* throughout the period and beyond illustrated either arrogance of the status quo or ignorance of the Committee of Seven's argument.[22] Later criticisms of the traditional history program, including those of education critics today, were centered on the belief that traditional history championed rote memorization of unrelated or disconnected facts, and relied heavily on uncontested generalizations. This cannot be further from an explanation of the Committee's true conception of history. That educators ignored or misunderstood its objection to general history was to persistently plague followers of the Committee of Seven.

The next blow that undermined the Committee's program was voiced at the 1904 American Historical Association Convention. "At this meeting," history professor John Bach McMaster "sounded the first faint echo of the distant thunder of pedagogical strife."[23] McMaster suggested that in the "process of Americanizing the foreigners we must fill their minds with the facts of American History which they may not understand, but which they must take as so much medicine."[24] The recommendation that scientifically derived history should be subverted for the indoctrination of newly arrived immigrants was a reversal of the Committee's position that history was a tool to sharpen the intellectual skills of the individual, not a processing agent that amounted to what contemporaneous writers referred to as social control. Later, educators, particularly urban educators who had to contend with the problem of assimilating young immigrants, appraised history in light of its ability to secure social control through direct patriotic and nationalistic overtures.

Similarly, at the annual meeting of the North Central History Teachers' Association in 1907 the influence of immigration upon the teaching of history was discussed. As one of four respondents to this theme, Jane Addams argued that "our formal attempts to teach patriotism to [the immigrant], and his children . . . assume[s] that experience and tradition have no value."[25] Continuing, Addams asserted:

> How far a certain cosmopolitan humanitarianism, ignoring national differences, is either possible or desirable, it is difficult to state; but certain it is that old type of patriotism, founded upon a common national history and land occupation, becomes to many of the immigrants who bring it with them a veritable stumbling block and impediment. . . . The usual effort to found a new patriotism upon American history is often an absurd undertaking; for instance, on the night of one Thanksgiving Day, I spent some time and zeal in a description of the Pilgrim Fathers, and the motive which had driven them across the sea. . . . The Greeks listened respectfully, although I was uneasily conscious of a somewhat feeble attempt to boast of Anglo-Saxon achievement in hardihood and privation, to men whose powers of admiration were absorbed in their Greek background of philosophy and beauty. At any rate, after the lecture was over, one of the Greeks said to me quite simply, "I wish I could describe my ancestors to you."[26]

What Jane Addams described as the "cruelly widen[ing] gulf between immigrant fathers and their children who are 'Americans in process'"[27] and McMaster's suggestion that administering American history like a "medicine" to purge immigrants of their past, received no attention in the Committee of Seven's program. On the one hand, McMaster envisioned American history as a tool for the "Americanization" of the immigrant, where Addams, understanding and rejecting this subverted use, appealed for a more universal approach to studying history that would include rather than "allow this valuable human experience [the immigrant's cultural baggage] to go to waste."[28]

Both McMaster's and Addams's selected use of history served social goals. Addams's notion of presenting a more representative picture of human achievement would not have been inconsistent with the Committee of Seven's definition of history. However, Addams's use of history struck a dissonant chord with the Committee's aversion to using history as a tool primarily for social purpose. Although McMaster's and Addams's concepts of history differed—McMaster to relieve social pressure and conflict, and Addams to ease assimilation and to recognize the potential contribution and ultimate worth of all Americans—these educators had both argued that the true value of history was not seated in its intellectual attributes but in its social specific aspects of manipulation.

Between 1902 and 1909, arguments that either ignored the foundation of history as promulgated by the traditional historians or proposed a truncated application of history were not treated seriously by those interested in and in control of school history. The Committee of Seven report, however, was given serious consideration by traditionally minded historians at the 1904 meeting of the Association of History Teachers of the Middle States and Maryland, at a 1909 meeting of the New England Teacher's Association, and more formally at the annual convention of the American Historical Association itself in 1908. At the AHA meeting, a special "Conference of History" was held to discuss the Committee of Seven's report in light of the recent criticisms concerning its heavy emphasis on ancient history and lack of attention to civil government. The conference members, under the chairmanship of Andrew C. McLaughlin, who was named to chair the newly appointed American Historical Association's Committee of Five, were to reconsider the Committee of Seven's report and to offer any corrections or other suggestions to the Committee of Five.

At the earlier meeting (Association of History Teachers of the Middle States and Maryland) four "defects" were cited: (a) "an immoderate amount of work" was required in the first year (Ancient History); (b) "slight reference" was made to practical secondary methods, with too much emphasis placed on "university methods"; (c) insufficient time was allowed for "modern history"; and (d) the

Committee made more of the connection between secondary schools and higher education institutions than was warranted.[29]

Similarly, at the 1909 meeting of the special committee headed by Blanche Evans Hazard, a future conferee of the 1916 Committee of Social Studies, found three areas of the Committee of Seven's report that needed "modification." First, in regard to Ancient History "more definite recommendations" were desirable, because the Committee's vague selection of topics led some educators to present far too much material to students to ensure proper coverage for college entrance board examinations. Secondly, concerning Medieval, Modern, and English Histories, "more definite divisions and limitations of courses might be outlined," as many schools favored one at the expense of the other, and "often omitted English history altogether." And finally, to offer a better presentation of civil government, the "Association favors the separation of American history and of American civil government."[30] A fourth concern was also raised by the New England Committee that was not foreseen by the Committee of Seven. "Since the report of the Committee of Seven was drafted, a new type of school," wrote the New England teachers, had "come to the front." Given this new condition, they asked, "What history should be given in such schools?"[31]

Outside the perennial "Why should history be taught at all?," no other question created more dissension and conflict among history teachers than to suggest that something other than traditional history should be offered in the new industrially minded (vocational) high schools. This troublesome condition led James Harvey Robinson to modify his initial thoughts on traditional history that stemmed from his work on the earlier Madison Conference to a reconceptualization of school history that was often labeled the "new history."[32]

This new history, which Robinson described as the selection "from the annals of mankind those facts that seem to have a particular bearing on the matters it [the age or period in time] has at heart," was presented to educators at a National Education Association meeting in 1910.[33] Although given specifically in the context of answering what history was suitable for industrial education, educators came to believe, as did Robinson, that the new history should be *the* history presented in all public schools, a point Robinson himself made while serving on the 1916 Committee of Social Studies.[34]

The third important meeting relative to the revision of the Committee of Seven report, held prior to the completion of the review of traditional history by the Committee of Five, was the "Conference on History in Secondary Schools" that met during the

1908 AHA Convention. Called expressly to reconsider the recommendation of the Committee of Seven, as was the aforementioned 1909 New England History Teachers' meeting, the conferees debated two of the three major areas of disagreement with the Committee report: ancient history and civil government. The third, not investigated here, but addressed by the Committee of Five, concerned the lack of emphasis on modern history.[35] Many members of the conference believed the ancient history program, as written by the Committee of Seven, was plainly "too difficult for high school consumption."[36] In addition, the conference membership was greatly distressed over the dearth of civic instruction in the schools to counterbalance the "growing problem of juvenile delinquency."[37]

Collectively the various history conferences, reports, and committees provided much food for thought for the Committee of Five to consider. In addition to these, William MacDonald's status report on secondary history in 1907 provided two other important constructive criticisms of the Committee of Seven's report that warranted the attention of the Committee of Five.

MacDonald, a history professor from Brown University, reported that although the Committee of Seven recommendations "were regarded as standard" by secondary schools, the College Entrance Examination Board and colleges and universities, there were two "serious criticisms" that required the immediate attention of the American Historical Association. First, given the "excessively crowded curriculum of the average school," declared MacDonald, "it has not yet been proved generally possible to secure from a class any considerable use of books other than the textbook." Secondly, "there is a striking lack of orderly and exact knowledge, even of elementary matters, and a pervading reliance upon the general and the vague."[38] Here MacDonald noted:

> Examination questions have often tended to become general rather than specific, and to demand a breath of knowledge and maturity of judgment beyond what most young people possess. The colleges having insisted that the schools shall not teach dates exclusively, many schools have responded by not teaching dates at all. As a consequence, it not seldom happens that an answer in an examination book contains little specific error, and yet fails entirely to show whether or not the writer really knows anything about the subject.[39]

Although giving value to "developed collateral reading that presupposes library facilities," in practical terms, many schools were simply unable to provide history books, let alone duplicates for student research. Given the economy of running a school, all that could be expected in most cases was the provision of a set of classroom textbooks. To suggest a program based upon wide collateral reading and library use was apparently beyond the means of the average secondary school. MacDonald called for the AHA to simplify and scale down its history recommendations to meet the actual conditions in public schools. The Committee of Seven, in seeking to raise the standards of history teaching, perhaps unwittingly set the mark too high for all but a few schools.

Paradoxically, MacDonald's second concern implied that the lack of collateral materials directly contributed to continued reliance on a single textbook as the sole source of history presented in secondary schools. The singular use of textbooks exacerbated the acceptance of textbook generalizations as fact and tacitly rejected the importance of historical criticism. MacDonald argued that unless the Committee of Five modified the Committee of Seven's guidelines, the bulk of the secondary schools would certainly be left behind. Perhaps, more importantly, if the Committee of Five did not reemphasize the need to balance the textbook with collateral and source readings, the effort of the Committee of Seven and its supporters would have been in vain. MacDonald's attentions were not entirely selfless, however, for he edited four of the five Macmillan source textbooks on the textbook market.[40] If schools were to buy into the need to go beyond a single textbook, MacDonald and his publisher were clearly in position to capitalize on the shift.

MacDonald presented an interesting dilemma. If the AHA neglected to support the employment of collateral materials as the backbone of the curriculum, it would be disavowing the very essence of the traditional program. If, on the other hand, it failed to modify the existing plan, not recognizing the inability of some schools to afford research materials, the fate of traditional history would be sealed. Exhibiting a healthy respect for the authority of the American Historical Association, MacDonald as well as the other history committees and conferences put this crucial issue into the hands of the Committee of Five to resolve.

RECONSIDERING HISTORY'S PLACE IN THE SCHOOLS

The Report of the Committee of Five

On Wednesday, December 28, 1910, Professor Frederick Jackson Turner, then of Harvard, delivered the annual presidential address, entitled "Social Forces in American History," to the general membership of the American Historical Association in Indianapolis, Indiana.[41] In his speech Turner outlined the pervading theme of the period: rapid change. He duly noted the "influence upon national history" of the "recent industrial revolution in the United States," by which he meant within the past twenty-five years. In words later echoed by Woodrow Wilson, Turner cautioned:

> Old theories of equality and rights of man must be reconsidered and restated; the old American democracy had been invaded by many factors foreign to its earlier principles. Among these new features were the vast army of immigrants arriving each year, the passage of arable national domain into private hands, the extension of financial and banking interests with their centre in New York, and the attainment of self-confidence by American labor. To-day vested interests and trusts occupy the strange position of insisting upon the old individualistic democracy, while the insurgency is demanding new democratic functions in the control of trusts and new democratic safeguards to take the place of the former safeguard—the free lands of the republic.[42]

Turner presented an interesting predicament. Historians of the 1890s had acknowledged the accelerated growth of America's social, political, and economic institutions, and theorized about relative cause and effect. However, they had rejected or ignored how these changes affected schools. Historians continued to insist that the best education for all was one that centered upon the growth and development of the individual. By 1910 it became abundantly clear that such a static position was simply not practical, given the emerging pluralistic-egalitarian American democracy and the heavy criticism of the politically potent progressives. The growth of the pluralistic egalitarian movement, reflected in the extensive number of political, ethnic, religious, and other special interest groups, was *gaining* political power and public attention at the expense of the "old guard."

Turner's speech gave considerable attention to the need for reexamination and restatement: to maintain the old order in light of the seemingly uncontrollable conditions or to reshape old guard values into a new dynamic definition of democracy. Debates over the use of source material, that historians wanted to include, against single-use textbooks, because that was what the public preferred or was all that schools could afford, appeared petty and insignificant compared to the larger question of whether to maintain the status quo or follow the emerging pluralistic dynamic democracy. In a concluding plea to the convention for adaptation to changing conditions, James Harvey Robinson encouraged his fellow historians to integrate into their historical research data from the new social sciences:

> The scientific organization of history had interfered with its progress. The concept of history had changed through the centuries, but in recent years it had not kept in touch with its sister sciences nor used their product to improve its own work. Evolution, the great theory of biology, has not yet been adopted by the historians; the work of archaeology, anthropology, of animal and social psychology needs to be assimilated by the historian.[43]

To Robinson, who had accepted a holistic view of history—at least this can be inferred—the fixed definition of history that Turner alluded to had to be refashioned or more seriously reformulated to include the scientific data derived from the emerging social sciences. Questions concerning historical interpretations and status quo maintenance made the disposition of source materials appear unimportant. All three, however, were directly related. Despite the philosophical necessity to remain consistent with the tenets of historical research, if, on the one hand, historians preserved the recommendations of the Committee of Seven, in effect, they would be viewed as confirming the old guard and an antiquated version of provincial democracy that championed individual effort and intellectual abilities while excluding social science data. If, on the other hand, they readapted the Committee of Seven's program to fit the present needs, interests, and capacities of secondary schools, they would then be betraying the old guard attitudes and values that had shaped the nation as well as the American history profession. To historians, neither direction appeared appealing. At this point compromise was the only viable course of action.

The formal call to reconsider the findings and recommendations of the report of the Committee of Seven had come earlier, at the 1907 annual meeting of the American Historical Association. A Committee of Five was "appointed to determine what modifications, if any, were needed in the recommendations" of the Committee of Seven.[44] The Committee of Five's original membership included University of Chicago historian Andrew C. McLaughlin, chairman; Charles H. Haskins, Harvard; Charles W. Mann, Lewis Institute, Chicago, who died in 1909 and was not replaced; James Sullivan, Boy's High School, Brooklyn, New York; and James Harvey Robinson, Columbia University.

Major writers on the early social studies did not hold a very high opinion of the work, or rather, the results of the Committee of Five.[45] In his exhaustive study of the beginnings of history and social studies, Rolla Tryon remarked simply that the Committee of Five "need not detain us long."[46] Although some recommendations were made, noted Tryon, "so far as the writer knows there is no statistical proof that the Committee of Five wielded any significant influence."[47] Nearly thirty years after the revision committee, Edgar Bruce Wesley spent a scant page on the Committee report, commenting that it was only "an argument for the report of 1899 [Committee of Seven], and so had little discernable effect upon the curriculum."[48] Earlier, Henry Johnson, writing in 1915, had reached the same conclusion, finding that the report was "essentially a re-argument of the case presented by the Committee of Seven." Johnson disparaged its significance because "the majority of schools apparently still find the plan of the Committee of Seven feasible."[49] Later, in his 1940 text, Johnson viewed the Committee of Five as more or less, too little and too late, because the "reorganization of education had already begun."[50]

Although it may have been true that the Committee of Five confirmed the bulk of the report of the Committee of Seven, and perhaps there was little or no data to support a claim that the Committee of Five made much of a curricular impact, its report was the high-water mark of the traditional history curriculum. Indeed, its value and importance in the history of the traditional history curriculum was due to its ineffectiveness. Simply put, it was not what the Committee of Five did that was memorable, it was what it did not do that is significant. Essentially, the report's adherence to the position of the Committee of Seven cleared the last obstacle for the social studies advocates and in effect ended the locus of curricular control among academic historians.

Despite being largely ignored by contemporaneous educational historians, the Committee of Five report was a remarkable document in its own right. Like the Committee of Seven, it reached its recommendations after a complete survey of history in contemporary secondary schools. Additionally, the Committee of Five called upon each of the major history teacher associations and conferences to supply data. From this body of information they extracted: (a) a picture of the status of history in secondary schools; (b) an appraisal of the effectiveness of the Seven's report; and (c) an inventory of the leading criticisms of the Committee of Seven's report and of history teaching in general. Given these accomplishments, the Committee of Five offered its recommendations. The result was a commendable and candid case study in how to prepare and present a committee report.

The Committee of Five's analysis and review of school history could be divided into two broad areas: curriculum and methods. This review, however, did not question the value or place of history in the secondary school; this was a given. Notwithstanding the committee's general acceptance of traditional history concepts, eleven arguments against the Committee of Seven's report were investigated. These included the following: (a) the report was impractical; (b) the recommended curriculum required too much material to cover; (c) too much emphasis was placed upon comprehensive knowledge and general historical facts; (d) Ancient History was too difficult for the immature first-year high schoolers to comprehend; (e) many schools were not able to offer a full four-year course; (f) the argument against general history was weak; (g) too much memory work was required; (h) Modern History was more important than Medieval; (i) history for commercial high schools was not included in the recommendations; (j) American history should be separated from civil government; and (k) the perennial problem of adequate teacher preparation was not addressed. The committee sought data and provided space for each of the eleven problems.

Based upon data that found that the Committee of Seven's recommendation of four years of study in place in over half the schools polled, the Committee of Five simply denied that the report was impractical.[51] Despite those schools that could not, for reasons of economy and time, provide the full four-year program, the Committee of Five still maintained the need for four years of history. Reluctantly, the Committee conceded that if only three years were available, it was possible to complete the sequence only if the school provided students with a "knowledge of history which will fit them for their work in society and give them a basis for satisfaction in the intellectual life."[52] The general history course, despite its continued popularity among administrators because it helped streamline costs, was again not recommended and two years of European history were considered the minimum. A third year was reserved for American History and civil government. For the newer trade or commercial high school, however, the Committee stated that two years of history were considered the minimum, allotting one year to Modern History and one year to American History.

The Committee of Five argued that if circumstances warranted it, the four-year course could be abridged by omitting Medieval History to provide more time for Modern History. Nonetheless, although they "heartily approve[d] this feeling," the Committee did "not recommend an immediate and universal rearrangement of courses."[53] Yet if the school was inclined to favor Modern History, Medieval History could be relegated to a brief introductory survey as a preface in the Modern History course, or given space at the end of the Ancient History course as part of the summary of ancient history and as a preview for the student's work in Modern History. Moreover, Medieval History could also be surveyed in the English History course. For the American history/government course, the Committee recommended both should be given "sufficient time." This was translated to be two-fifths of the course for separate civil government studies and the balance for American History.[54] In any event, any adjustments to the curriculum required the teacher to be very careful that the important institutions, ideas, and characters were not left out or given inadequate coverage.

The Committee of Five rejected the complaints that the Committee of Seven required too much material, that the material was too difficult, and that it was offered to students too immature to deal with it. The Committee of Five reasoned that it was possible that a teacher making "wise commissions and clever condensations in some portions of the field" could allow "time to plough deeper in other places."[55] With a judicious trimming of details, teachers could easily cover the field in question within a year. To the Committee of Five, the ability to successfully trim history into a body of teachable data, stressing "emphasis and clarification," was part of the "essentials of good teaching."[56]

Some critics argued that Ancient History was in particular too difficult and taught too early. Not finding this issue problematic, the conferees responded:

> Not if Ancient History is made simpler and less abstract: not if more attention is paid to great men, and less to the history of institutions; not if meaningless wars and constitutional details are omitted and time thereby gained for easy, familiar talks upon the great deeds and achievements of antiquity.[57]

That many students were said to be cramming for the college entrance exams did not necessarily reflect upon the recommendations of the Committee of Seven. The Committee of Five placed the blame for too much emphasis of comprehensive knowledge and general facts directly on the universities themselves and the College Entrance Examination Board. The Committee found that only ten percent of the survey respondents agreed that the Committee of Seven was at fault. Many historians at the 1908 AHA annual meeting criticized the College Board, holding them responsible for the problem with comprehensive knowledge, shallow concepts, and test cramming in the final year of high school.[58] Lucy M. Salmon, a member of the Committee of Seven, agreed entirely, declaring that colleges and the College Board were "merely standing on the necks of the secondary schools."[59] Commenting on this connection, Howard Boozer wrote, "it was [Salmon's] opinion that if the colleges would reform, the high schools would measure up to what was expected of them."[60] Clearly an impasse on this issue was reached. The Committee of Five held their pedagogical ground—or rather that of the Committee of Seven's—and refused to concede any responsibility at all. Remarkably the connection between single-use textbooks, the lack of collateral reading, and the synthesizing nature of secondary history were not raised at this point.

Concerning the persistent complaints against memory work and poor teaching, the Committee of Five simply stated if "mere memory work" was adopted, "there is not much to be said in favor of the retention of [history] as an important part of the curriculum."[61] Although the Committee of Seven did acknowledge the value of a good memory, they did not condone rote memorization of facts in any form. The Committee of Five did, however, acknowledge a difficulty:

> Teachers attempted to lead students to the two essential results [of history study:] obtaining a firm grasp of a reasonable quantity of facts; [and] second, a sense of the meaning of historical facts and historical relations, some aptitude in gleaning knowledge from historical books, some appreciation of what history is, some historical imagination, some skill, though it be not great in putting together the facts that one has learned.[62]

Acknowledging difficulty is one thing, but offering a viable solution is quite another. In this light all the Committee could recommend was that the teacher exercise "good judgment and good teaching."[63] Curiously, they neglected to address what either was, or how it could be obtained and exhibited. But the Committee did offer some advice for educators: "the most important factor in the school-room [was] not the curriculum, the text, or even the method but the teacher."[64] Continuing, "the committee strongly assert[ed] the need of better prepared teachers and urge[d] that superintendents and school trustees should give teachers sufficient time to prepare their lessons and seek out illustrative material."[65] The Committee of Five, much like the Committee of Seven, perhaps believing that specific suggestions or guidance on the improvement or standardization of teaching training programs was out of their scope of responsibility, left no details.

As Tryon reported:

> Lest the reader infer that the Committee of Five made no specific recommendations respecting the course in history in the high school, the gist of the scheme proposed is hereby presented in the words of the Committee.[66]

1. Ancient history to 800 A.D. or thereabouts, the events of the last five hundred years to be passed over rapidly. . . .
2. English history, beginning with a brief statement of England's connection with the ancient world . . . as far as is possible or convenient the chief facts of general European history, especially before the 17th century, and give something of the colonial history of America.
3. Modern European history, including such introductory matter concerning later medieval institutions and the beginnings of the modern age as seems wise or desirable, and giving a suitable treatment of English History from 1760.
4. American History and Government, arranged on such a basis that some time may be secured for the separate study of government.[67]

In comparison to the Committee of Seven, three basic differences were evident: English History was transferred from the eleventh grade to the tenth; Medieval History was dropped or subsumed within the Ancient or English History course; and in its place, Modern History was given a full year.

As mentioned at the outset of this section on the Committee of Five, the historians were given the opportunity to bring the traditional history curriculum into the twentieth century and to revise the program to reflect the new demands of education. This included emphasizing social efficiency, social responsibility, and meeting the needs and interests of students. Believing that its report stood on the solid ground of public support as well as teacher-school support, as indicated by school surveys and committee reports, the Committee of Five maintained the intellectual-individually based traditional history program of the Committee of Seven. The Committee of Five presented its preliminary findings and recommendations to the membership of the American Historical Association in early 1910. Its final report was published later that year in the AHA *Annual Report*.[68]

Entrenched in a relatively fixed position and buttressed by the support of the field's practitioners, the traditional historians drew their line in the curricular sand. Concurrently, advocates for social efficiency and responsibility marshaled their forces. Although earlier skirmishes took place, to the insurgents the time was ripe and the opening was recognized for the major battle to begin.

Textbooks and the Traditional History Curriculum

The examination of history textbooks of the turn of the century reveals a close relationship between textbook authors and the Committee of Seven report. One reason the coming battle between historians and the social studies insurgents favored the history camp was that so many of the teachers being asked to change banners were accustomed to textbooks based upon the four-block model of the Committee of Seven. Given the training of history instructors, which even the historians admitted was poor, the classroom textbook became absolutely indispensable to teachers.

In the forty years prior to the writing of the Committee of Seven report and in the twenty years following its dissemination, the textbook was—as Rolla Tryon put it—the "King of Kings" and "Lord of Lords" of the traditional history curriculum.[69] Although this critique of history texts prior to the Committee of Seven, and several others like it, validates that history was indeed in the schools, between 1860 and 1900 history classroom textbooks were "frequently" the product of "a literary hack." The New England History Teachers' Association's Standing Committee on Textbooks of 1898 wrote:

> [Such an author was] ready to compile a dictionary, annotate a classical text, or write an algebra, as occasion offered. Of spe-

cial training he had none; but he had read a good deal, had a number of apt stories at his command, and made up for his limited knowledge by a vivid and pliable imagination.[70]

Such was the standard criticism of history textbook authors prior to the dissemination of the report of Committee of Seven. The standing committee's report, despite the unfortunate prior situation, noted that textbooks were improving:

> One no longer expects, arbitrary outlines, or dry and formal statements, much less the biased emphasis so often mistaken for patriotism. Our text-book writers, as a rule, now tell only the truth, and tell as much of it as the immature mind can assimilate; they arrive after solidity of substance as well as attractiveness of form. . . . It may frankly be said that recent writers show many intimations of approaching perfection. The extent to which they fall short is the measure of the teachers disadvantage.[71]

To the Textbook Committee, the contemporaneous American textbook circa 1898 represented not only the curriculum but did so to near "perfection." Accordingly, any failure in the learning process was leveled not on the textbook-as-curriculum, but on the inability of the teacher for whatever reason to present the textbook properly. Textbook authors Hinsdale, Barnes, Edward Channing, Albert Bushnell Hart, and Henry Bourne commented on the necessity of a good narrative textbook but declined to go so far as to label the textbook-as-curriculum (see chapter 2). Moreover, as much as the national committee reports and popular teaching textbooks downplayed the restrictive and excessive use of classroom textbooks, many teachers persisted in maintaining a single narrative history textbook.

In filling out the definition of traditional history, history textbooks published after the Committee of Seven report seemed to be entirely under the spell of the report's recommendations. Tryon characterized the association between the Committee of Seven and textbook companies and authors succinctly:

> The fact of the matter is that a textbook intended for high school use in history published between 1900 and 1915 had hard "sledding" if it failed to claim that it conformed to the report of the Committee of Seven.[72]

Tryon's examination of history textbooks suggested that the six major book companies of the era each commissioned textbooks to match the four blocks of the Committee report.[73] Among the authors of these secondary texts were some of the leading historians of the day. If the textbook was the curriculum, and we have every reason to believe it was, it would not be an understatement to say that the academic historians had taken control of the history program by literally cornering the history textbook market. Although the textbooks reflected the content of the Committee of Seven, which included Ancient, Medieval, Modern, and American History topics, it did not necessarily follow that teachers were willing or able to follow the recommended methodological guidelines as well. In this view, the textbook may have provided the material for class, but it did not dictate how the material would or should be dispensed.

The ideal textbook, much like the ideal history program, was later defined by Henry Bourne in his teaching/methods text. "The good text-book," he noted, had to be written by a "competent scholar" who understood the "problems of instruction." In specifics:

> [the textbook] should not be overloaded with many details. . . .
> Its pages should not be sprinkled with dates. A distinction
> should be made between those which are inserted for the sake
> of precision and others which are to be committed to memory.
> There must be abundant maps . . . instructive illustrations . . .
> [and] genealogical tables, chronological summaries, topical
> outlines, questions for further study [providing of course these
> elements rested upon "sound scholarship"].[74]

The typical traditional history textbook followed these suggestions. Texts[75] such as George Willis Botsford's *A History of the Orient, Greece, and Rome,* for ancient history,[76] Edward P. Cheyney's *A Short History of England,* for English history,[77] James Harvey Robinson's *An Introduction to the History of Western Europe,* for medieval and modern history,[78] John Fiske's *A History of the United States*[79] and John Bach McMaster's *A School History of the United States* for American history,[80] followed most if not all of these suggestions to the letter.

Notwithstanding that many texts held true to this line, one suggestion of the Committee of Seven's report was clearly ignored. One of the primary criticisms of the history curriculum, defined as classroom textbooks, as it existed prior to the Madison Conference and Committee of Seven reports was that it contained an over-balance of material on military and political events and personalities. Even worse, in most cases the material was almost completely given over to such topics. The traditional history advocates emphatically denied that these topics should be the center of the curriculum to the exclusion of cultural, social, or economic matters. Instead, they preferred a balanced curriculum that included all the above topics.

Although a cursory examination of the five texts revealed the content to be largely political and military accounts of (a) the founding of Greece and Rome (Botsford); (b) Europe, particularly France and England (Robinson); (c) England (Cheyney); and (d) the beginnings of the United States (McMaster and Fiske), each of these texts did provide a healthy dose of cultural, social, and economic information. Botsford and Robinson particularly stressed that the importance of history was to reveal the whole character of a people, not merely their military and political exploits and endeavors.

The Botsford text, a combined volume of his separate Greek and Roman texts, of nearly 800 pages was perhaps among the most complete textbook of the traditional history period. In terms of teaching aids, Botsford included 215 maps and illustrations, 20 in color; abundant sources and collateral readings; a full index of terms, personalities, events, titles, all cross-referenced; a full list of dates and events in chronological order with important events and persons in bold face, 584 events and persons correlated with over 400 dates; the popular "skeletal style" margin notes throughout the text; and 319 chapter questions and suggestions for further class projects. In addition, sample topical outlines and chapter summaries, suggested bibliographic materials for the class, and selected source materials were reproduced to follow the text narration.

Beyond the typical military and political topics, Botsford depicted the Greeks and Romans as a people, a gifted people true, but still a people like any other group with fears, hopes, dreams, achievements, and failures. Consequently, topics such as literature, art, religion, philosophy, and other social aspects were treated in some detail. Botsford's text may be considered a classic example of a traditional history textbook.

In spite of the efforts of Botsford and other traditional history authors, the shift in textbook formats from strict military/political histories to a more balanced accounting—despite the rhetoric of committee reports and other voices—was far from complete. Even Botsford and Robinson, who characterized their works as progressive in social, economic, and cultural content, gave comparatively little space to such concerns. In fact only three chapters of sixteen from Botsford's Greek section and four chapters of forty-one from Robinson were devoted specifically to nonmilitary/nonpolitical topics.

Nonetheless, the so-called traditional history textbooks, contrary to the rhetoric, remained devoted to military and political topics. William C. Bagley and Harold O. Rugg's analysis of "typical school textbooks" reached substantially the same conclusion.[81] In Bagley and Rugg's 1916 study of American textbooks, the authors found that while military topics received ample coverage, "political developments" constituted the "essential core" of history teaching.[82] From this finding, Bagley and Rugg concluded that the content of the traditional history textbook, regardless of "individual characteristics and specific differences of emphasis," was, as a rule, deeply rooted in nationalism.

Whether or not textbooks "tended" to "engender nationalism or patriotism," Bagley and Rugg were not prepared to discuss, but they did believe textbooks "obviously" were moving "toward the promotion of nationalism through giving to all pupils . . . a common stock of information regarding national development."[83] They also raised, but did not answer, the question about the "desirability or undesirability of making [the promotion of] nationalism a primary function" in schools. Clearly nationalist attitudes had a "profound influence upon the collective thought and collective conduct in so far as these are concerned with national problems." However, they asked should not a larger emphasis be placed upon "local history, recent history, and the development of art, literature, science, and industry?"[84] The answer, they believed, could come only from the public.

Although political developments still occupied the bulk of the history textbook, the de-emphasis of military matters was making headway. Bagley and Rugg noted:

> The movement toward a lessening emphasis of wars and especially of the details of battles and campaigns, will doubtless go on; the social and industrial changes that have profoundly modified the course of political events will receive larger and larger emphasis; characters other than those concerned with political and military affairs will receive a more adequate recognition; but the essential organization of events around the unifying thread of political development is probably inevitable.[85]

Given the dominant political/military nature of the tradition-al history textbooks, which were otherwise similar to the sugges-tions of the authors of traditional history, to what extent did the recommendations of the authors of traditional history find a place in secondary schools? From what little data exist, the Committee of Seven and other authors of traditional history did indeed find a place in the classroom through textbooks. What is not clear is whether teachers treated the content of the textbook as the traditional histo-rians intended.

CONTEMPORANEOUS STATUS STUDIES
AND TRADITIONAL HISTORY

This portrayal has presented the legitimate defense of the tradi-tional history curriculum at the time of the First World War. As both a means of reviewing and underlining the successful dissemination of the recommendations, the results of three contemporaneous sta-tus studies with special reference to secondary history (1890s–1912) will also be reviewed. The three include: William MacDonald's "The Situation of History in Secondary Schools" (1907); Hugo H. Gold's "Methods and Content of Courses in History in the High Schools of the United States" (1917); and Leonard V. Koos's "History and Other Social Studies" (1917).[86] This brief examination of these reports will serve to summarize traditional history.

MacDonald began his brief study of secondary history by re-viewing the "essential features" of what he called the "epoch-making report" of the Committee of Seven. These essential features included: "the indication of four historical fields—ancient, medi-eval and modern European, English, and American"; "the repudia-tion of the exclusive devotion to the text-book"; and "the insistence upon the vitalization of historical instruction by enlarged and sys-tematic use of collateral readings, informal lectures, special reports, map drawing, historical pictures and objects, and student note-books."[87] MacDonald held that these features were regarded, by 1907, "as standard" in the secondary history curriculum. However, specifically, what changes did the Committee of Seven work to the benefit of the history curriculum, and what "failures and reverses" occurred as a result of the report?

In MacDonald's words the "substantial gains," in the authors' terms, "of the right sort" were:

1. Methods had undergone fundamental and praiseworthy change. Formal use of text-books . . . [with] verbal repetition and the dry memorization of dates and names, has much declined, and in most of our best schools would not now be tolerated.
2. The content of the subject, too, has changed: less time is spent on military events and incidents of romance or adventure, and more on social, economic, and international aspects of the field.
3. Reference libraries in schools, though still far from adequate, have multiplied and improved.
4. As a direct result of new methods, there has arisen a demand, largely unknown hitherto, for specially trained teachers.[88]

And the "failures and reverses" he cited were:

1. The delimitation of the field of ancient history is strongly, and on the whole increasingly, objected to. [Objectors wanted the field to be confined to history before 476 A.D.]
2. It has not yet been proved generally possible to secure from a class any considerable use of books other than the textbook, without giving to history a disproportionate amount of time. . . . Moreover, the developed use of collateral reading presupposes library facilities, and especially provision of duplicates, such as few schools possess.
3. As for the preparation of student note-books based upon reading or research, that has frankly become a farce.
4. The character of the pupil's attainments in history, too, has changed. . . . There is a striking lack of orderly and exact knowledge, even of elementary matters, and a pervading reliance upon the general and the vague. . . . As a consequence, it seldom happens that an answer in an examination book contains little specific error, and yet fails entirely to show whether or not the writer really knows anything about the subject.[89]

The fact that these "gains" and "failures" were debated at all nine years after the Committee of Seven report suggests the power of the traditional curriculum as espoused by them. Moreover, MacDonald was "convinced" that the cause of the problems cited above was not inherent in the committee report, but rather "that the amount of work involved in the recommendations of the Committee of Seven cannot, as a rule, be satisfactorily accomplished in the time generally available."[90] MacDonald's study thus supports the claims of later "history advocates" that the early history reports were not as wrongheaded as social studies insurgents claimed; but rather something or someone had altered these sound recommendations when they reached the classroom. Speculation aside, MacDonald's suggestions to the American Historical Association, to whom he deferred, was to ask them (a) to reconsider the course of study; (b) to abandon testing of collateral readings and generalized historical knowledge; and (c) to simplify the crowded secondary curriculum.

Gold's and Koos's studies were completed amid an uprising against the traditional history curriculum. In fact, Koos's data, which Rolla Tryon claimed was "in all probability the most nearly accurate information relating to these subjects in the secondary school that has ever been collected,"[91] was gathered for the use of the National Education Association's Committee on the Reorganization of Secondary Schools that in turn generated the Committee on Social Studies report. As MacDonald had found that the traditional history curriculum was still healthy nine years after the report of the Committee of Seven, Gold and Koos reported that the program was not only in good health but quite robust after twenty years. Any noticeable decline in the traditional history curriculum, according to Tryon, was not perceptible until after 1916. Therefore, these reports may be considered to reflect an accurate picture of the traditional history curriculum.

MacDonald's study, although it acknowledged the dissemination of traditional history, does not supply the type of data necessary to assure a firm grasp of the power and sway of traditional history. The survey based studies of Gold and Koos, however, yield a wealth of data on secondary history. These data confirm the strength of the traditional history curriculum that was in effect defined by the Madison Conference and the Committee of Seven some two decades earlier. The results of these studies are summarized below.

Gold—Selected Summary and Conclusions:

I. Administration of courses in history:

1. The aim of history is seldom stated [and] in many cases . . . reflects the reports of committees [the Committee of Seven in particular].
2. More than half the schools offer a four-year course consisting of ancient, medieval and modern, English, and American histories.
3. Only a few schools continue to offer a course in general history

[yet a mixture of ancient, medieval, and modern history later to be known as Western civilization was growing in popularity].

4. The modal number of units of history offered in cities above 5,000 population is four, and in cities of 5,000 population and less there are two modal numbers of three and four units, respectively.

II. As to content of courses in history:

1. The recommendations of the committees that ancient history shall include oriental,[92] Greek, and Roman history have been adopted.
2. The tendency [in accordance with committee recommendations] in ancient history is to spend four or five weeks on oriental history, the remainder of the semester on Greek history, and the second semester on Roman history.
3. The recommendations of the committees that less attention be given to military and constitutional detail apparently have not been adopted.
4. Both the Committee of Seven and the Committee of Five recommend that American history and civics be taught as a single subject. In 103 of 242 schools civics is still taught as a separate course.

III. As to materials and methods:

1. Not half of the high schools have reached the standard minimum requirements of the North Central Association with respect to the number of volumes of supplementary works on history.
2. At any given time approximately half of all high school pupils are taking work in history courses.
3. The prevailing tendency is to recognize the textbook merely as a guide or outline to be supplemented by collateral reading and other materials. The textbook is considered as a standard of minimum requirements, and the pupil is held directly responsible for a mastery of its contents.
4. The most common methods of testing collateral reading are general class reports, oral and written examinations, notebooks, and occasional themes.
5. Most teachers consider collateral reading a very important part of effective history teaching. Many are handicapped by lack of time and improper library facilities.

6. In the United States as a whole, 45 percent of high schools make little or no use of the (original) sources.

IV. As to special aids to teachers:

1. Pictures, postcards, moving pictures, myths and stories, travel reports, industrial exhibits, old relics, and old setters testimony constitute some of the supplements in history teaching.
2. Maps and map drawing were mentioned by 102 teachers as special aids in history work.
3. Chronological charts, outlines and diagrams, drills, reviews, and cross-references are used extensively in locating and correlating events in time.
4. The prevailing practice among teachers seems to be to require the memorizing of only a few of the more important or epoch-making dates and to relate other events to these.[93]

Koos—Selected Summary:

1. Most schools offer 3 or 4 courses in history, exclusive of the courses in civics and economics. The four courses offered are ancient, medieval and modern, English, and American history.
2. With few exceptions ancient history appears in the first and second years, medieval and modern history in the second and third years, English history in the third year, and American history in the fourth.
3. Courses in American history range between two extremes of practice, one typified by such schools as constitute them in no special part of government, and the other by those that divide the time equally between history and government.
4. The textbook is more commonly used as the basis of assignment to be supplemented by required collateral reading, although a considerable proportion of teachers still use it as the main body of the course, with little or no collateral reading.
5. The amount of collateral reading varies somewhat with the place of the course in the history sequence, more of such reading being required for the later than for the earlier courses.
6. The kinds of collateral reading are: other texts, more extended works, source material, biography, historical fiction, poetry, magazines, and newspapers.
7. The methods of checking collateral reading are: oral reports, discussions and quizzes in class, written examinations and tests,

written reports, themes, notebooks, and outlines or digests handed in.[94]

Though available, remarkably, the 1916 Committee did not refer to any of these studies in its report, not even to Koos's, which was a part of its work. For reasons perhaps known only to the conferees, these works were not cited as sources of information. Moreover, in developing their program, the 1916 Social Studies Committee conducted no formal surveys of its own regarding school curricula prior to the release of the report or thereafter. The omission of these data, particularly survey data, ironically casts the 1916 report as more intuitive than scientifically based, and the national history reports as more scientifically based than intuitive. This chapter, together with chapters 2 and 3, presented a conspectus on the tradition history curriculum. The following chapters outline the efforts of this legendary committee[95] that placed the term and concept of social studies into modern public education.

5. SOCIAL STUDIES COMES TO INFLUENCE

DESPITE THE CONFIRMATION of the traditional history model by the Committee of Five, a movement was started by the National Education Association in the early 1910s to reorganize secondary education, in fact, all public education under the socialization banner. In 1911 William Chandler Bagley of the University of Illinois noted that although "[a] new sun of hope dawned upon the educational world," the movement "represent[ed] our first plunge into the wilderness."[1] Clarence D. Kingsley, an educational administrator for the state of Massachusetts, clearly envisioned a similar view for the future of education. Eager to activate the interests of educators, Kingsley circulated a report from the High School Teachers' Association of New York City on the articulation between high schools and colleges. It was distributed among the membership of the National Education Association at the 1910 annual NEA convention in Boston.

This report quickly generated attention. As a consequence, the NEA Department of Secondary Education promptly established the Committee on Articulation of High Schools and Colleges to investigate and report on this topic. It also named Kingsley chairman.[2] Later, the Committee expanded its numbers to include several subcommittees from the various fields of study in the secondary schools. This expanded Committee was reformed in 1913 and renamed the Commission on the Reorganization of Secondary Education. Again Kingsley was named to head this effort as chairman.

One of the original subcommittees of the Commission was the Committee on Social Science. In 1913, after Thomas Jesse Jones was named to chair that subcommittee, the committee's title was changed to the Committee on Social Studies. This subtle but significant alteration symbolically laid the keel for the 1916 launching of the social studies movement into the mainstream of American public schools.

Considering the new committee's charge, if popular opinion supported the actions of the Committee of Five in 1910, that educators endorsed intellectualized-individualized history teaching, something had radically altered that perception by 1913. Tagged as antiquated and unable to meet the new demands of public education by the social studies insurgents, the individual as center approach toward history, as advocated by the Madison Conference, and the Committees of Seven and Five, fell into disrepute among influential members of the NEA. In its place, educational concepts such as socialized education, citizenship training, social efficiency, social responsibility, and social progress had gained favor and currency among educational leaders within the space of a few short years.

This shift from individualism to social centered education was certainly more a symbolic move than real; the traditional history curriculum still dominated the classroom. What was happening to education was that the political control at the top—that is, the policy-making apparatus of the NEA—had turned toward social centered approaches as the new education. Although not articulated by the educational leaders, the shift in fact represented the struggle to attend to the twin paradoxes. Rather than leaning toward freedom, the new leadership was making a move toward conformity. In the second paradox, the shift was clearly toward society over the individual. Simply put, in the effort to reconcile the twin paradoxes of liberalism and democracy, the educational insurgents, including the social studies advocates, altered its focus and direction.

The progressive campaign emerging out of the literature of psychology, the social sciences, and philosophy sought to "reeducate" educators to adopt these newer concepts and to reject what was held to be a narrowly focused program. Given the wide array of subjects to reform, insurgents had already targeted the traditional history curriculum for replacement. Ironically, the insurgents did not call for a new cadre of educators to further the cause. Instead they accepted that the old-style traditional history teachers would carry the social education program into the future.

New Approaches

The voices for school efficiency and school progress, which began to emerge in popular secondary school literature after 1900, reached a "mania" level by 1912. At this time, general education textbooks for school teachers openly discussed the newer approaches to education. For instance, Elmer Ellsworth Brown's text for secondary school teachers, *The Making of Our Middle Schools*, noted that schools in 1901 were promoting a new outlook that included John Dewey's revolutionary concept: "the school is not preparation for life: it is life." This was considered the "keynote of current educational thought."[3] Brown also spoke of the improvement of the "educational efficiency of the secondary schools," as part of the new outlook in secondary education.[4]

Three years later (1904), however, "Charles Scribner's Sons turned down a manuscript entitled "Education for Social Efficiency" on the ground of uncertainty about 'the number of readers to whom the subject will appeal sufficiently to make them wish to possess the book.'"[5] In 1905, though, William C. Bagley wrote:

> Social efficiency is the standard by which the forces of education must select the experiences that are impressed upon the individual. Every subject of instruction, every item of knowledge, every detail of habit, must be measured by this yardstick.[6]

By 1912 preservice teacher education textbooks used in general education courses were given over to the new theories of education and learning. The notion of school efficiency and addressing the needs of students were, at least in the education textbook media, thoroughly entrenched. Writing for new education students, Edward Lee Thorndike of Teachers College, Columbia University, noted:

> One of the most important changes that are taking place in our country's schools is their rapid acceptance of duties other than the mere instruction of children. . . . The school system of a community is becoming an agency ready to act for the community's welfare in almost any way. . . . Its teachers are trying

to cooperate with all forces for betterment; its aims are becoming those of education in the widest sense—to make all men want what is good, and to get for all men the goods they deserve.[7]

Earlier Thorndike produced a statistical monograph for the United States Bureau of Education that emphasized the departure of students from school. Thorndike reported that less than ten percent of those students who entered high school ever graduated. Thorndike stated that "one main cause" for this phenomenon was the "incapacity for and lack of interest in the sort of intellectual work demanded by present courses of study."[8] The data from this monograph inspired other educators as well as Thorndike to reconsider the "present courses of study."

Writing with an increasing assuredness, other authors began to tout the new theories of education. In his 1912 education textbook *New Demands in Education*, James Phinney Monroe, chairman of the National Society for the Promotion of Industrial Education, succinctly stated that "the fundamental demand in education as in everything else, is for efficiency—physical efficiency, mental efficiency, moral efficiency."[9] Charles Hughes Johnston, then dean of the School of Education at the University of Kansas, reported in his 1912 preservice teacher's textbook:

Historic forces in our educational development have forced upon this comparatively young institution [the high school] ideals remote from the common man. Even the most respectable of its courses seem to this aroused and thoughtful public to represent undue and irrationally difficult peculiarities, to be ineffective in attainments which pass counter in the actual moral or industrial world, and be bent upon enforcing unattainable scholastic standards. These standards are thought indeed to smack of intellectual luxury, to be narrow, stereotyped, and undemocratic. There is no considerable prejudice against "unescapable conditions of scholarship and intellectual living." There is, however, coming into vigorous existence a social conscience which will brook no dallying with the likewise unescapable school functions of insuring economic efficiency, sounder moral integrity, and perhaps a measure of aesthetic development.[10]

Although Monroe and Thorndike discussed history only brief-ly, in these discussions one has the sense that history was, as it had been for the twenty years prior to 1912, an acceptable discipline for school study. For example, although Monroe hoped that students would study history as "a living picture of the progress and aims of human society, of the splendid upward sweep of civilization," he claimed that when students were examined they would be tested not for their knowledge of cause and effect or social chronology. Instead students were examined on their supposed knowledge of "the biog-raphy of this king, the plan of that battle, and the chronology of certain outward events which are but the merest froth upon the deep, wide stream of human development!"[11]

Similarly, Thorndike appeared to support traditional history, yet in a different light. He suggested:

The educational value of finding the causes of what is, and then the causes of these causes, is so very much superior to the spurious reasoning which comes from explaining a record al-ready known, or pretending to prophesy what the wisest men of the past could not prophesy, that the arrangement of the first part of the course in history in the inverse temporal order, leaving the forward chronology for later, deserves serious consideration.[12]

Thorndike did not advance the abandonment of history, nor was he implying that history had no place in public schools; rather he was calling for "serious consideration" of a reordering of the teaching of history. Thorndike believed that presenting history in reverse chronological order, teaching students about the present then moving backward, at least initially, was far better than using a strict chronological approach. History as conceived in Thorndike's setting would work toward the benefit of the "community's wel-fare" and thus would clearly take on a socialized accent. Despite Johnston's skepticism of "the attempt to give every subject social significance, as Dewey preached, that "added naturally to the confu-sion" of "curriculum makers," Johnston, too, maintained that cur-riculum developers "should be able to appreciate the social bases" upon which policies and programs rested.[13] Nevertheless, as quoted above, Johnston understood that curricular change was inevitable. Yet Wayland J. Chase of the University of Wisconsin, who wrote the history section of Johnston's textbook, had remarkably little criticism for the traditional history curriculum. He even credited the Committee of Five as presenting "fresh and pertinent suggestions as to the method of treatment" about the familiar four blocks from the Committee of Seven.[14] Thus, although the new "forces" of change were acknowledged, teachers were receiving mixed signals from academic education experts.

Three years after the education textbooks by Johnston, Monroe, and Thorndike, the shift from traditional educational concepts to social efficiency-responsibility, as found in the new education textbooks, was startling. Many education textbooks apparently broke all connections with past theories and stood firmly behind social education principles (of the generic sort; that is, that all course work be viewed from the societal perspective) and social efficiency theories.

Samuel Chester Parker, dean of the College of Education, University of Chicago, credited Dewey and Thorndike in his education textbook *Methods of Teaching in High Schools*, specifically for the pedagogical-psychological approaches used in the textbook. Parker added:

> Efficiency and economy in instruction are facilitated by (1) radically adapting all instruction to contemporary social needs, (2) basing methods of instruction on sound psychological principles which have been determined, as far as possible, experimentally, and (3) applying principles of scientific business management to the conduct of all teaching.[15]

Continuing with the shift in pedagogical direction, on the eve of the dissemination of the report of the Commission of the Reorganization of Secondary Education, Henry Eastman Bennett, of the Education Department of William and Mary, directed educators to check his list for making the schools more efficient by "eliminating waste in teaching and study." Bennett's list included the following as educational wastes:

1. Teaching subject matter which lacked practical value.
2. Teaching without clear aims and plans.
3. Teaching without systematic check upon deficiencies and attainments.
4. Continuing to teach a pupil what he already adequately knows.
5. Teaching without insuring the use and retention of that which is taught.

6. Teaching without training in the art of economical study.
7. Drudgery in either teaching or study.[16]

What were educators to make of these new demands on their schools? Were the programs in force at the time of the Committee of Five's dissemination (1911) as wrongheaded and as unsuccessful as the new educational experts made them appear? In all the confusion that surrounded the inevitable clash of competing theories, one wonders if all the rhetoric connecting the new socialization concept of education with the striking political, social, and economic changes, manifested in industrial, urban, and immigration problems, led educators to call for the reform of secondary education. Perhaps it could be more simply put by saying the social efficiency educators (of which the social studies insurgents were an integral part) merely believed that the traditional program of education was wrong and needed redirection no matter what social, economic, or political environment existed.

In spite of the new challenges of the social efficiency educators, the Commissioner of Education survey of education for 1911–1912 revealed that a substantial amount of progress was being made in many areas of education. Moreover, progress was being made largely under a traditional program of education. The traditional program continued to flourish throughout the decade particularly in rural districts that remained staunchly conservative. Furthermore, the traditional program showed little sign of weakening until well after the Commission on Reorganization of Secondary School Studies released their "Seven Cardinal Principles" in 1918.

The Survey of Education for 1911–1912 reported that "the year [had] been distinctly one of advance . . . it [had] been marked by substantial practical achievement, rather than by any signal [outstanding] development of educational theory."[17] The survey's "record of routine progress in education" included:

1. the gradual elimination of illiteracy where it has persisted most stubbornly;
2. pronounced improvement in the work of getting all children into the schools;
3. the extension of the amount of educational opportunities in terms of length of school year and period of compulsory schooling;
4. broadening the provisions of State education to include higher education;

5. the constant betterment of teaching standards;
6. the slow but certain transformation of the rural schools to make them adequate for rural life;
7. increased expenditures for suitable building and grounds;
8. the steady rise in college and professional standards, together with a greater uniformity in requirements.[18]

Notwithstanding these "fundamental lines of progress in routine efficiency," the Survey also noted that the nation's education system was "in a period of transformation" where "one of the most important results of recently developed theories has been to arouse lively discussion and criticism of existing school conditions as related to the new demands."[19] At "the present time," continued the Survey, "public education . . . [was being] subjected to searching criticism with respect to purpose, organization, administration, curriculum, teaching methods, and results."[20] The Survey outlined nineteen topics related to school criticism from the "changing purpose of education" to "democracy in the public school." The Survey indicated that the criticisms were a healthy sign for the school system. It noted:

> In the criticism that has come to a climax in the past year, there is much that is based on the best thought of our time; there is much that is the direct result of the discoveries of modern science; there is much that is backed by years of practical experience in the schoolroom and in the administrator's office; and there is naturally much that represents mere guesswork, misunderstanding, or even ignorance. Good or bad, significant and trivial, this mass of educational criticism is an indispensable guide to the progress of public education.[21]

Evidently educators were aware of the explosive nature of many issues in public education. Most if not all the criticisms articulated in the Survey were directly related to the swelling opposition to the traditional system of education, which favored a secondary school reorganization. Yet what sort of reorganization and how much the secondary curricula would change was not made clear. The Survey reported:

> Much is said and written nowadays of the school's inefficiency; one hears, too, a great deal of increasing its efficiency. Thus from both points of view the impression is given that some-

thing is wrong with the American school, that at least there is room for salutary changes. In the opinion of even the least critical, much remains to be done to perfect our school system. The chief count in the indictment against the school is that it is not meeting the needs of the community, and various panaceas for this ill have made their appearance. "Enrichment" of the curriculum, "socializing" the school, and industrial training are some of the "movements" of which one has often heard or read. . . . Some see in a complete reorganization of the school system the only effectual means of readjustment. But whatever may be the need or however great it may be, there is in some quarters a tendency to make radical changes in the organization and work of the city school.[22]

Although the Survey discussed the principal educational problems of the day, its report reflected a decidedly conservative school system. The report did, however, acknowledge that educational change was a major concern to educators. The Survey noted that while progress was being made, schools needed to improve even more. In addition, it was clear that older courses of study, methods, and organization be studied to reveal their viability. Nothing was of more profound consequence for American schools than an official document of the United States government, issued by a cabinet-level organization suggesting that the Federal government make the education system an agency of the State. "It is simply that the State," noted the Survey, "in its eagerness to allow the maximum of local self-government, has been reluctant to insist upon education as a State function. The first step in educational progress is recognition by the State of its direct school obligations."[23] From 1912 to 1918, in regard to secondary education, government "sponsorship" of the Commission on Reorganization of Secondary Education meant that the U.S. government supplied many of its key leaders and paid for the publication and distribution of all its committee reports. The Federal government had taken a decided step toward exercising a large measure of involvement with public school policy.

Although school policy was traditionally the domain of local and state authority, another prime example of the new Federal intrusion into local school concerns was the Smith-Hughes Act. This law, enacted in 1917, was designed to promote vocational education in "agriculture and the trades and industries, to provide cooperation with the States in the preparation of teachers of vocational subjects, and to appropriate money and regulate its expenditure."

To effect increased government involvement (leaning toward conformity and society in the twin paradoxes) what was needed was to organize the criticisms into a viable argument, not necessarily *against* the traditional system, but certainly *for* social education. The Commission on the Reorganization of Secondary Education was in essence that argument. Three individuals worked to undermine the influence of the traditional history curriculum: John Dewey, the chief protagonist and philosopher of social education who exerted a passive, though important, influence; David Samuel Snedden, the chief antagonist of traditional history and an active agitator for social education; and Clarence Darwin Kingsley, the chief "moderator," who, as chairman of the Commission on Reorganization of Secondary Education worked to institute the new socialized education curriculum in the nation's secondary schools. Dewey and Snedden are the subjects of the next two sections; Kingsley will be treated in the context of the social studies.

DEWEY ON HISTORY AND THE SOCIAL STUDIES ARGUMENT

Historian Richard Hofstadter has stated:

> The new education rested on two intellectual pillars: its use, or misuse, of science, and its appeal to the philosophy of John Dewey. Of the two, Dewey's philosophy was much more important. . . . Dewey's contribution was to take certain views of the child which were gaining force around the end of the nineteenth century, and to link them to pragmatic philosophy and the growing demand for social reform. He thus established a satisfying connection between new views of the child and new views of the world.[24]

The main lines of "progressive pedagogy," however, often erroneously attributed to Dewey alone, were expressed by a number of educational thinkers, many antedating Dewey. William Torrey Harris and Francis Wayland Parker, called by Dewey the father of the progressive movement,[25] as well as many others contributed ideas to the progressive concept of education. Among them was the notion of "forging the relations between the school and a changing society."[26] In addition, poet and social commentator Ralph Waldo Emerson caught the "essence" of the "theoretical base" of progressive educational thought when he exclaimed, "efficient universal education, that makes men producers as well as consumers, is the surest guarantee of progress in the arts of peace—is the mother of national prosperity."[27]

By the turn of the century three important variables were added to education to make the school curricula more dynamic. Taken together, these variables were crucial to the success of the new education proposals, especially social studies. Curricular reform was energized by developmental psychology, as represented by G. Stanley Hall, William James, and Edward Lee Thorndike; scientific methodology, as espoused by Herbert Spencer, Charles Peirce, Thorndike, Dewey, and others; and sociological objectivity, reflected in the writings of Lester Frank Ward, Albion Small, and Franklin Giddings. The total influence of these men on education as a whole is impossible to estimate.[28] But it is clear that these variables, as found in these thinkers' work, were represented in progressive education rhetoric. Collectively, these three variables were used to argue against the traditional curricula and to demonstrate for the new social studies program.

As Hofstadter surmised, perhaps Dewey's greatest contribution to progressive thought and social studies was the bringing together of these ideas, formulating them from so much educational palaver into palatable specifics, and allowing the strength of his dialectic to carry the reform of education.[29] This was not to say that Dewey did not augment progressive educational thought with original contributions, for he clearly did so; it is merely to emphasize the success of his unique ability to synthesize the various and often disparate progressive concepts of education from such influential thinkers as Peirce, James, Thorndike, Sumner, Spencer, Ward, Small, Hall, Jacob A. Riss, Jane Addams, and a host of others. It was this exceptional quality together with his own philosophy that made Dewey "the symbol and prophet for an incipient educational revolution."[30]

By 1912 the progressive education proposal for the reorganization of public education was well known to educators. The following is an inventory of progressive educational goals, summarized into seven broad elements:

1. concern for the child in all his or her complexity—interests, needs, desires, feelings, and attitudes;
2. recommendation of an advisory rather than authoritarian or directive role for the teacher;

3. advocacy of problem-solving techniques of instruction in preference to those stressing student passivity, rote memorization, and
   deductive learning;
4. rejection of the doctrine that education is more a preparation for
   living than a part of the process of living;
5. emphasis on a supportive, humane environment where cruel
   punishments have no place;
6. support for patterns of educational organization encouraging cooperative, communal experiences through which pupils would
   actually practice democratic modes of behavior;
7. curricula geared to the maturational level of each student, with
   learning proceeding out of pupils' spontaneous interests.[31]

Most, if not all, of these issues were discussed by Dewey in
some form in one of his most important and influential educational
works, *Democracy and Education*. In regard to the traditional history curriculum as presented by the Madison Conference and the
Committees of Seven and Five, Dewey launched no specific attacks,
nor articulated any particulars against it. Throughout the period
Dewey, was, however, fond of using such euphemisms as "our present instruction" or the "existing school system," in his assault on
the traditional application of such educational issues as the place of
subject matter in schools and student interest. There is little doubt
that Dewey rejected the underlying principles of traditional history
upon which the Committees of Seven and Five rested their views.
Dewey's offensive against traditional and formal education models
ran deeper and was far more profound than even the most bitter
objector among historians. There were, however, some areas where
both historians and Dewey could agree. For instance, traditional and
socially oriented educators both made provisions for experience in
the education process. Dewey wrote:

> The educator's part in the enterprise [was] to furnish the en-
> vironment which stimulates responses and directs the learn-
> er's course. In the last analysis, all the educator can do [is]
> modify stimuli so that response will as surely as is possible
> result in the formation of desirable intellectual and emotional
> dispositions.[32]

Both Dewey's teacher and the traditionalist's teacher were
engaged in "furnishing the environment" for learning. But what
should this environment look like? What would be the purpose of

providing the teaching situation? What materials should be studied? And in what context and at what level should the materials be presented?

It is at this point that any firm relationship between Dewey and the traditionalists breaks down. Dewey's concern was with the subject matter approach that he felt was not so much out of place in a modern school as it was simply a defective system. Dewey believed the first questions a teacher needed to address concerning the subject matter were:

> What is that study, considered as a form of living, immediate, personal experience? What is the interest in that experience? What is the motive or stimulus to it? How does it react with reference to other forms of experience? How does it gradually differentiate itself from others? And how does it function so as to give them additional definiteness and richness of meaning? We ask these questions not only with reference to the child in general, but with reference to the specific child—the child of a certain age, of a certain degree of attainment, and of specific home and neighborhood contacts.[33]

Here traces of Dewey's attacks on "subject matter first, student approaches second" were evident. Traditional historians held that the subject matter of history had intrinsic educative values that were the same for all students regardless of their age, sex, or capacity for learning: history was a one-size-fits-all curriculum. Dewey, by contrast, held that this dogmatic, provincial methodology was harmful and dangerous. To him, the foundation of student growth should be focused on the student's own interests and needs, and placed at the center of the curriculum, not on the subject matter. Hence, the traditional history curriculum, because it placed its subject matter at the center, violated students and prevented their development.

Leo J. Alilunas helped clarify Dewey's argument that interest had to be based within the child and that any subject that had "to be made interesting" or "an appeal to will power had to be made" created poor teaching situations and led to "bad . . . learner outcomes."[34] Genuine student interest was a necessary condition for real learning. Force-feeding students subject matter, determined outside their interests, would result in only short-lived, unconnected thoughts that passed very quickly through the student. Dewey wrote:

Genuine interest is the accompaniment of the identification, through action, of the self with some object or idea, because of the necessity of that object or idea for the maintenance of a self-initiated activity. . . . There are certain powers within the child urgent for development, needing to be acted out in order to secure their own efficiency and discipline, we have a firm basis upon which to build. . . . But this effort never degenerates into drudgery, or mere strain of dead life, because interest abides—the self is concerned throughout. Our first conclusion is that interest means self activity.[35]

Dewey's editor wrote in the preface to *Interest and Effort In Education* that the child needed to be "wholeheartedly active in acquiring the ideas and skill needed with problems of his expanding life."[36] Thus to Dewey to remove the child from "self-activity" was to remove the child from any possible meaningful learning. That the teacher generate subject matter from and with the interest and needs of the learner in view was fundamental to Dewey's attack on traditional methods of instruction. In this context, Dewey's principal arguments against history were cut and dried. He wrote in 1897:

History [was] vital or dead to the child according as it is or is not presented from the sociological standpoint. When treated simply as a record of what has passed and gone, it must be mechanical because the past, as the past, is remote. It no longer has existence and simply as past there is no motive for attending to it. The ethical value of history teaching will be measured by the extent to which it is treated as a matter of analysis of existing social relations—that is to say as affording insight into what makes up the structure and working of society. This relation of history to comprehension of existing social forces is apparent whether we take it from the standpoint of social order or from that of social progress. Existing social structure is exceedingly complex. It is practically impossible for the child to attack en masse and get any definite mental image of it. But type phases of historical development may be selected which will exhibit, as through a telescope, the essential constituents of the existing order.[37]

Dewey allowed that those "historical developments" that "may be selected" included data from the full range of history, from the beginnings of civilization to ancient Greece and Rome to the present. Dewey was *not* advocating or even remotely implying that history should not be offered in schools. Instead he believed that history as a discipline, to be consistent with the principles of education as conceived by him, needed to follow the tenets of social progress and individual growth. History as any subject in the school curricula had to be functional and presented with a specific social purpose. The "only way of securing the necessary perspective [necessary to make history functional]," wrote Dewey, "[was] by relating the past to the present, as if the past were a projected present in which all the elements [were] enlarged."[38]

Dewey noted that "one reason historical teaching [was] usually not more effective" was that students were called to "acquire information . . . reduced to the same dead level."[39] If the teacher made the study of history a social study in cooperation with the student, where the purposes and aims of the study were directly related to social progress and were not subject matter specific, then history study would be as vital as any other school subject. It is significant that Dewey reported that "historical teaching," as it was then taught under the dictates of the Committee of Seven, was not completely ineffective. The implication was that to be more effective history teaching needed to be socially based rather than subject specific. Dewey did credit history teaching with at least some measure of success, however, one has the distinct impression from him, in this piece as in others, that if the "existing system" of history did not subscribe to the "sociological standpoint," and the traditional history curriculum clearly did not, one may deduce that Dewey held it to be a "dead" study. This raises an important question: If history was dead, why did Dewey suggest that it could be more effective if taught from the "sociological standpoint"? He finalized his argument:

> Everything depend[ed] then upon history being treated from a social standpoint, as manifesting the agencies which have influenced social development, and the typical institutions in which social life has expressed itself.[40]

History as described by Dewey was something quite unlike the scientifically ordered discipline as espoused by traditional historians. Dewey in arguing *for* history, while very cleverly disputing traditional history, was not provoking a revision or reconsideration of history as it was then studied, but a complete reformation of history teaching. On the eve of the dissemination of the social efficiency prototype as formulated by the committee on social studies, Dewey wrote:

> The past just as past is no longer our affair. If it were wholly gone and done with, there would be only one reasonable attitude toward it. Let the dead bury their dead.[41]

In seeming contradiction, Dewey continued:

> But knowledge of the past is the key to understanding the present. History deals with the past, but this past is the history of the present. An intelligent study of the discovery, explorations, colonization of America, of the pioneer movement westward, of immigration, etc., should be a study of the United States as it is today: of the country we now live in. . . . Past events cannot be separated from the living present and retain meaning. The true starting point of history is always some present situation with its problems.[42]

Here, on the one hand, Dewey emphasized that the past was "no longer our affair"; while on the other hand, he maintained that "knowledge of the past" was the "key to understanding the future." In the rush to make schools efficient, to make schools socially progressive, Dewey had provided traditional historians with a philosophical escape hatch. Using Dewey's portal, without risk of stunting the intellectual or social growth of students, historians could conceivably maintain their trade and produce works of history, and educators could teach students about the past as long as they cast or reconceptualized history in light of sociological principles. "Whatever history may be for the scientific historian," reasoned Dewey, "for the educator it must be an indirect sociology—a study of society which lays bare its process of becoming and its modes of organization."[43]

Thus Dewey viewed history as having two levels: one of research and one of pedagogy. Historians could move between the two without restriction if they maintained a "sociological standpoint." They could not, however, cross the line into pedagogy unless they altered both their content and methodology. Given Dewey's distinction, many critics of history, however, would not have allowed any escape hatch. To such critics, history was a dead study and as such had no proper place in the reconstructed secondary school.

DAVID SNEDDEN ON HISTORY AND SOCIAL EDUCATION

As important as John Dewey was to the overall concept of progressive educational reform, it was David Snedden, introduced in chapter 1, who defined in practical terms the issue of what place history should hold in the public schools relative to social interests. Snedden was the most vociferous critic of the traditional history curriculum, agitating indefatigably for the ouster of history from the public school curriculum and for the placement of strictly socially functional studies.

Snedden's penetrating questions sharpened the distinction between the traditional historians on the right and the "new" historians on the left. More importantly, his arguments measured the way educators should appraise the two, a distinction that prompted J. Madison Gathany to divide the two emerging conceptualizations regarding history teaching between the "insurgent, progressive, radical school" and the "conservative, reactionary, stand-pat older school."[44] In this context, Snedden was the embodiment of a "gadfly" for social education.[45]

For Snedden the primary goal of social education was to effect "social control" and to induce proper "social conduct." Snedden believed that educators and other experts would identify the needs of society, then fit the child and the curriculum to those needs. Snedden's view of social control sought to capitalize on citizenship education by indoctrinating students in acceptable and appropriate social behaviors. He wrote:

> Under the head of citizenship we include all qualities making for the more effective group life, including submission to established political order, cooperative maintenance of the same, and a great variety of social qualities which we sometimes designate as the social virtues, or moral worths.[46]

That public schools allowed for and approved of indoctrinating students into "submission to established political order" was not anything new. But placing citizenship education at the "head" of social education and social education at the head of all public schooling was a radical departure from traditional curricula. Yet what prompted this radical shift? Borrowing from sociologist Edward A. Ross, Snedden set down:

> As a society comes to include more members, as its activities specialize, and its dependence upon friendliness and coopera-

tion among its members increases, the field for social education will increase rather than diminish. This explains contemporary solicitude for better training for citizenship, for [moral]
character formation, for study of nations towards ends of mutual understanding, and for greater social insight in general.[47]

The "demands of contemporary civilization," Snedden claimed,
were "forcing readjustments in education."[48] He carefully delineated
that it was societal demands, not philosophical agitators, that acti-
vated change. The distinction was important. Snedden was not proposing a "readjustment" of education, following a personal deep-
seated faith or intuition; he was reaching to a social, political, and
economic landscape that was changing very rapidly. As a progressive-
ideological thinker, he saw the opportunity to offer some guidance.
He duly noted, as others had, "the breakdown of faith in older customs and doctrines." He commented that this event was "always
accompanied by a boundless disposition to launch new experiments
and to form new parties or cults."[49] Although "boundless energy"
need not be a vice, undirected "boundless energy" certainly was.
Hence, with his thoughts well grounded in sociology and convinced
of the progressive nature of contemporary society, Snedden felt more
than qualified to provide not merely supporting rhetoric but functional, practical advice during the readjustment period of American
education.

With societal change at the forefront of educational reform,
Snedden raised several important issues. In dealing with the twin
paradoxes, if society through its institutions including education
inevitably changes, what place do individuals have in the process?
That is, can individuals enter into the picture of educational change
and perhaps influence outcomes? And if individuals can enter in the
process of change and find ways to influence the schools, and Snedden believed they could, what justification can be offered to assure
the integrity of the individual's intrusion into matters concerning the social whole? Given these important questions, Snedden
focused upon the justification of social education. He declared
confidently:

> Here then, do we find the chief justification of all forms of
> education in social science—our functioning objectives must
> be directed towards social conduct. This is particularly true of
> all education supported by public funds. The study of history
> or any other social science for purely cultural reasons or as a

high-grade diversion may be permitted to, or encouraged on behalf of, a few; but the study of social science in the interests of democratic citizenship in a highly complex civilization must be directed chiefly towards pragmatic ends—not, of course, in the narrowly utilitarian, but rather in the higher social sense.[50]

Unlike "the unscientific aims of contemporary education," Snedden believed that the social sciences could provide educators with all the data necessary for a modern school to not only function well but to make social progress. Statistics of all sorts could be generated from field observations to measure the worth and ultimately the efficiency of the schools. Snedden was certain that with carefully interpreted social science data, educators would be better able to "formulate valid aims" for schools.

Snedden called upon educators to "recognize" that:

All traditional subjects of secondary education [were] subject to more or less scrutiny, especially from the standpoint of their educational values. It is the spirit of the social economy of our time that, as far as possible, all forms of social activity should be purposeful and efficient. It was inevitable that we should become more and more critical of any form of education based largely upon tradition. Most of the subjects of the secondary school curriculum have never been consciously evaluated in terms of the actual needs of the society of the twentieth century.[51]

The most important question of the day to Snedden and other social education insurgents was, How shall education be made efficient?[52] Snedden's answer envisioned a two-tiered system of separate high schools under the concepts of specialization and differentiation that both featured flexibility. Snedden projected that the last years of general, social heterogeneous education would be given in the seventh or eighth grades, followed by attendance in either the cultural or general high school, or the vocational high school. Here students selected the school depending upon their interests: the general high school for those more intellectually inclined or the vocational high school for those more practically minded. Apparently, efficiency in either high school would be measured by how closely the administrators followed the dictates of social education. Those educators who failed to reconceptualize their studies in the light of the new social demands became the target of Snedden's attack.

Concerning his criticism of traditional history, Snedden concentrated his efforts on dismantling the history program of the Committee of Seven. Ironically, however, Snedden, like many other social education insurgents, believed that the traditional history classroom and the traditional history teacher, both reshaped of course, would make social education programs work. Because of what Snedden perceived to be the unsettled nature of educational aims for the curricula of vocational schools, Snedden offered no full description of a history program for vocational high schools. Instead, he centered all his attention to formulating a plan for social education in the general high school.

The reason why Snedden was so keenly interested in "revising" the history program was not so much that he was vitally concerned with history—Snedden confessed a lack of personal interest in the subject—[53] but that in the crowded, overburdened school curriculum the history program was the most likely candidate to provide a spot for a new social education agenda of citizenship education. With this is view, it was necessary, therefore, for Snedden (following the doctrine of social efficiency) to expose traditional history as an inefficient discipline, unsuitable for secondary schools.

Snedden noted the "high expectations" that historians, educators, and the public alike held for history in high schools. Yet despite the earnest work of history experts as well as educators, history as a school subject had generated "a great deal of disappointment." The reason for this "disappointment," declared Snedden, was that the subject had "no satisfactory pedagogy."[54] He wrote:

> The popular faith in the efficacy of history study has borne fruit in the recent enormous development of that subject in American colleges. It has also assumed prominence in the programs of secondary schools; and with it are not infrequently linked short courses in civil government and economics. The interest is primarily due to the conviction that the citizen— voter or not—needs a purposeful civic education, if he is to be prepared to meet the responsibilities of the modern social organization.[55]

But Snedden asked:

> Can an effective program of civic education be composed, in any considerable part, of courses in history as that general sub-

ject is now organized and taught in secondary schools? Or is any extensive study of that subject a necessary prerequisite to other studies which may be more purposefully directed toward education for citizenship?[56]

It was Snedden's "conviction" that traditional history did not express functional "civic attitudes, ideals, or knowledge," nor did "such study contribute essential or valuable elements to other studies" in the "interests of civic or social education."[57] To Snedden, citizenship education should "involve" history but the traditional history curriculum was simply "shaped along the wrong lines." Moreover, history was "pedagogically unadapted to the ends sought."

Like Dewey, Snedden distinguished between academic history and school history, acknowledging that history may indeed "hold a place" in higher education as one of the "pure sciences . . . with the pursuit of art 'for its own sake,'" but it served no real social purpose in the secondary school. Snedden believed that the history offered in the secondary school was, by its nature, a narrow, provincial study that affected a "relatively small number of individuals who [happened to] have special tastes and interests in the study of history."[58] This interest, however, if placed in the correct circumstances, should not be denied to students. Yet, according to Snedden, to center the narrow goals of the existing history program in the secondary school curriculum at the public's expense was simply wrong; democratic institutions were formulated to serve the many, not the few.

Dismantling traditional history was no easy task, especially "because of the growing popularity of the subject" that conflicted with the "obvious need of a more adequate social education."[59] In spite of any accomplishments of traditional history, Snedden argued that such achievements, if any, often came at the expense of citizenship education. Moreover, he held that the difficulties of teaching history arose specifically from the inherent nature of the discipline that ignored or discounted social educational values. "If measured in terms of better citizenship," continued Snedden, "the amount of time and of conscientious labor" given to history was "in large measure" like throwing "seed . . . upon a rock":[60]

We are now confronted by the most fundamental problem of all, [declared Snedden, bringing his argument to a climax,] namely as to whether in realizing the ends of sound social education, we shall not be obliged in large measure to substitute social sciences, exclusive of history, for history as it has been taught heretofore.[61]

Given his background in sociology and his attitude on history, it was no surprise that Snedden favored the social sciences. In place of what he called the "cold storage theory of education," which he claimed traditional history subscribed to, Snedden suggested basing citizenship education on the "assimilation or participation theory." Snedden's definition of the "cold storage theory" suggested that "the mind of the learner can be stored with certain knowledge," which consisted of "detailed facts and sometimes of generalizations" that "at some future time," if conditions were ideal, could be recalled from memory storage and utilized.[62] In contrast, Snedden described the "assimilation or participation theory" as furnishing the "keynote to the reorganization of the teaching of social science and history as we shall find it, I believe, in the future."[63] "Fundamentally," declared Snedden:

> The pupil will start with the present, becoming familiar with it and on the basis of this knowledge going into the past. The teacher of history under these conditions will, first of all, have to be a teacher of contemporary social science. She will not feel qualified to take her pupils into any period of the past until they have become thoroughly acquainted with what their own environment has to teach them as a basis for the remoter knowledge.[64]

Snedden's attitude toward social education was no less than a declaration of war against the traditional history curriculum. Unlike Dewey's radical compromise that allowed for a modified traditional history to still function, Snedden's attack was beyond radical; it was revolutionary, for it struck at the core of traditional history. By shifting the foundation of history to social education, Snedden rejected the very essence of traditional history teaching composed of chronology (forward or reverse) and historical unity. By turning the teaching of history over to the present-minded social scientists, in effect, Snedden was calling for the burning of any bridges back to the traditional history curriculum.

Although not actually reflected in the 1916 Social Studies report, Snedden asserted that the rationale for social education and citizenship education in particular was founded on scientifically derived data, not faith or intuition. Such data revealed that society was rapidly changing and becoming increasingly complex. Therefore, reasoned Snedden, social education (the new education) and citizenship education (its agent) became necessary. Snedden's social education was directed to secure "social control," to "make and shape" the "social instinct," provide for "effective cooperation," instil the "right attitudes and right conduct customary . . . the right social conduct," and to "discover how to utilize [and enlarge] the social environment."[65] In Snedden's attempt to reconciliation of the twin paradoxes, citizenship education became the agent to inculcate students with "functional," cardinal knowledge that included the values, attitudes, and feelings essential for life in a modern urban industrialized society.

In deemphasizing his conviction that the social sciences must be the backbone of social education, Snedden conceded:

> We can not use any of the social sciences as logically organized for the purposes of the most effective social education. . . . But [we] shall be obliged to develop new methods of pedagogical organization, dependent in large part upon the formation of large units permitting concentration of attack, and adapted to the maturity and capacities of those being taught. In every case, it would probably be desirable that the learners first familiarize themselves with observed facts and practical interpretations of social phenomena as accessible in the neighborhood and contemporaneously, after which on the basis of secondary materials they could proceed to study similar phenomena at a distance in both time and space.[66]

Snedden was suggesting that educators may wish to divide the newly formed contemporary based studies into two levels: the elementary for younger students, and the secondary for more mature students. At the elementary level the curriculum would emphasize "stories," "fables," and "biographies" concerning "social life" and "economic activity." From these, students would learn socially functional "knowledge," "interpretations," "insights," and "ideals" associated with group living.[67] As students matured they would be ready for accelerated "mental and spiritual growth."

If students showed a predisposition for "more abstract thinking and for more comprehensive generalization" and sought the "understanding" of "cause and consequence," under Snedden's program of social education they could receive it with the proviso that such study would be "regarded as means only to a useful knowledge of contemporary social life."[68] Moreover, should a student have the desire to study history "for its own sake," Snedden argued that "certainly nothing in the program here set forth will prevent such a consummation."[69] At any rate, Snedden was careful to emphasize that the end result of education must be functional knowledge that is "useful knowledge of contemporary social life." A program thus conceived would almost certainly exclude any semblance of the traditional history curriculum.

The following was Snedden's tentatively proposed program for social education:

> *Seventh Grade*—community civics (major study), socialized history (minor study)
> *Eighth Grade*—study of contemporary nations (major study), socialized history (minor study)
> *Ninth Grade*—economics of production and transportation
> *Tenth Grade*—economics of finance and consumption
> *Eleventh Grade*—evolution of cultural agencies
> *Twelfth Grade*—intensive study of democratic government.[70]

A cursory overview of this program in comparison to the established traditional history curriculum revealed to traditional educators and historians the revolutionary nature of Snedden's attack. For Snedden the break was sharp and clean. History as promulgated by the Madison conferees and the Committees of Seven and Five was judged as possessing no value in the new formulation of contemporary, progressive public schools, and would not be accorded any position therein. Snedden, as noted earlier, carefully delineated that the social sciences as were presently formulated were not suitable as secondary subjects. To adjust to the needs of the new education, a completely reformed program would have to be designed, organized, and implemented.

Nonetheless, Snedden's social education argument appeared much closer to the tradition of Herbert Spencer than John Dewey. Spencer's question, "What knowledge is of most worth?," was sounded by critics during the transition from one educational system to another; but its actual meaning was often lost in the translation.[71] Spencer believed educators should seek the knowledge of most worth in *relative* terms—that is, to study what was most valuable at a certain place and time. Spencer wrote:

> There is not a subject that has not some value . . . [and] before there can be a rational curriculum, we must settle which things it most concerns us to know. . . . We must determine

the relative value of knowledge. To this end, a measure of value is the first requisite. . . . Of what use is [the subject]?[72]

In regard to history, Spencer claimed:

The only history that [was] of practical value, [was] what may be called Descriptive Sociology. And the highest office which the historian can discharge, is that of so narrating the lives of nations, as to furnish materials for a Comparative Sociology; and for the subsequent determination of the ultimate laws to which social phenomena conform. . . . All social phenomena are phenomena of life . . . and can be understood only when the laws of life are understood.[73]

For Spencer the "laws of life" were generated through the study of the "organic sciences," sociology and the other social sciences. Borrowing heavily from Spencer, Snedden's argument for social education was centered on utilizing the data from the social sciences to generate and maintain the social education curriculum. Social education insurgents like Snedden resurrected Spencer, among others, and modified and shaped their arguments for teaching the relative worth of knowledge into the "new education" that sought the teaching of knowledge based on social efficiency and social responsibility.

Two years before the formation of the epoch-making Commission on the Reorganization of Secondary Education, Snedden demanded that educators teach "something that has not been named, but which [Snedden] call[ed] sociology."[74] Later Kingsley's Commission formed a subcommittee to address the need for a sound citizenship education that would include a new organization of education. Here Snedden's unnamed entity was given an official title: social studies.

HISTORIANS' REACTION TO THE NEW EDUCATION

The attack that Snedden launched on traditional history did not go unnoticed by historians. Following Snedden's address before the New England History Teachers' Association in May 1914, George L. Burr of Cornell University, and Frederick Jackson Turner, then of Harvard, both took exception to Snedden's remarks.[75] Burr, whose paper was later published next to Snedden's in *The History*

Teachers' Magazine, agreed that the "cold storage theory" should never be the goal of any academic subject. But he strongly disagreed that history should be made the servant of the present by basing all inquiries into the past on contemporary problems or the present needs and interests of students. Such a concept of history, according to Burr, was nothing short of "history with the history left out."[76] Moreover, Burr argued that giving the history curriculum over to the sociologists and other social scientists was to reduce the value of humankind to mere statistics.[77] "Heartily do I acclaim his earnest words," exclaimed Burr, "that our teaching of history must put our students in touch with the present."[78] Yet Burr stopped short of handing curriculum construction over to the interests and needs of students or to social scientists.

Snedden's effect on historians was that of a "gadfly," in that his questions (and answers) stirred up a lot of controversy. Because many of his assertions appeared to build paper tiger arguments, it is doubtful whether he led historians to become defensive of their discipline and methodology. By contrast, he did make a deep and lasting impression on educators. Clarence D. Kingsley, who had gained a national reputation as chairman of the Committee on the Articulation of High School and College, was persuaded by many—but not all—of Snedden's social education arguments. Kingsley learned much about Snedden's social education while working under Snedden in Massachusetts as his agent to high schools.

The circumvention and recasting of history's aims toward more direct social control appealed to many urban educators who faced the daily problem of assimilating the "foreign element" in their schools. The response of Charles H. Fisher, of the West Chester Normal School, Pennsylvania, to teaching "history for its own sake" arguments was typical of those that echoed Snedden. "I care not what defense you make of history as a subject. My main interest is in the needs of the pupil and the demands of society." Moreover, "At the present there seems to be a strong tendency to look at history from the standpoint of social science. From this standpoint only such history is useful as will make the present intelligible."[79]

Perhaps Snedden's greatest impact was his contribution to the argument for citizenship education.[80] The topic had been given serious consideration by the Committee of Seven, and more recently by the Committee of Five, yet historians continued to downplay its place in the curriculum. The traditional historian's concept of citizenship education, which they labeled civil government, emphasized the machinery of government, for example, the workings of the

Constitution or the Bill of Rights. With the curriculum outlined by Snedden, based on the present needs and interests of society, citizenship education took on a radical new look as the school and its community became the focus of the "new education."

In 1913, at the fall meeting of the Association of History Teachers' of the Middle States and Maryland, the chief topic of discussion was citizenship education. The principal speakers were James Lynn Barnard, representing the National Education Association's Committee of Social Studies; James Sullivan, a former member of the American Historical Association's Committee of Five; and Charles Beard, Columbia University and advocate of the "new history." Among the panelists asked to respond to Barnard, Sullivan, and Beard were two members of the Committee on Social Studies: Jessie C. Evans and Arthur William Dunn. That such a topic generated the interest of historians and was placed at the center of attention at a history teachers meeting illustrated the impact of the social studies advocates on traditional historians.

In spite of the tone of reform implicit in presenting a new idea, Barnard and Sullivan were not antagonistic to traditional history. Barnard did not seek to topple traditional history, but he did want to see a more secure place *in* the history curriculum for civics based upon "this all-important point: [that] the order followed [was] invariably that of the child's own interest and application."[81] Sullivan declared that he was not there to make a "plea" for civics or to outline a "program" in citizenship education. He did, however, offer two rather tame criticisms of the traditional history curriculum: (a) that, as "Dr. Barnard has stated so clearly here and elsewhere," civics [community civics] should replace civil government; (b) that civics should be taught apart from history.[82]

Despite the modest arguments of the nonhistorians, the third speaker of the evening, historian Charles Beard, delivered an extremely harsh criticism of the traditional history curriculum. In reference to finding a spot for teaching about the "rights and duties of citizenship," Beard surmised that the only way "to find room [was] to evaluate the work now given in the light of the needs of this age."[83] Rather bluntly, Beard asserted that "my method of solving the problem of overcrowding is a drastic one, deliberate eviction. Wherever the old four-year history schedule is in force, it should be cut."[84] Beard claimed that the traditional program was "worse than a crime," it was an "educational outrage" and clearly evident "to anyone who stops to think for a moment." Continuing, Beard argued that students left high school knowing more of the "constitution of [ancient] Athens than the charter of their home city."[85] Beard went so far as to say that if teachers were "responsible for any of the evils of American politics, the committee of the American Historical Association which devised the four-year historical course must assume the full burden."[86]

Beard, unrelenting in his criticism of the traditional history, questioned:

> How great was the wrong done to American democracy through this usurpation of dominion by history is apparent now, even to some historians, and a few are willing to concede a reduction of their overgrown domain.[87]

According to the Commissioner of Education's statistics for 1912, however, nearly 99 percent of school-age children avoided the "wrong done to American democracy" by dropping out of high school or not attending long before having received any civil government instruction. The measurement of the damage done to that 0.016 percent of the school-age population for having had civil government for a semester during their senior year instead of civics, only Beard could explain. Following the presentations, none of the respondents publicly addressed or even questioned Beard's claims. Instead they concentrated exclusively on Barnard and Sullivan's presentations. The meeting did conclude by adopting eight resolutions regarding secondary civics. Two of the more controversial resolutions were that the "work should be based on the pupil's experience and immediate surroundings" and that the "keynote of the course should be the obligation of the citizen to serve the community."[88]

On the eve of the release of the report of the Committee on Social Studies, Rolla Tryon reported, "the chief question among those in charge of history in the secondary schools was, 'Shall we join the revolters or stand pat on the four-block system of the Committee of Seven?'"[89] Given the actual situation of history in schools, this was a curious question. Until 1916 at least, according to data from the field (as noted in chapters 2, 3, and 4) the traditional history program of the Committee of Seven was in particularly good shape and solidly entrenched in the secondary curriculum.

For instance, while addressing the membership of the Association of History Teachers' of the Middle States and Maryland in 1915, William E. Lingelbach declared that despite "men like Mr. Kingsley, of the N.E.A., [who] would apply the knife ruthlessly to all subjects that do not show a distinct influence in increasing efficiency in the affairs of daily life," there was "very little evidence" or "real danger" that "history was losing ground."[90] Continuing, Lingelbach admitted that although history faced "vigorous competition" from other studies including vocational subjects and "social studies," he claimed that "despite this, the results of recent investigations all indicate that history is not only holding its own, but gaining ground."[91]

If traditional history was solidly entrenched in 1916, and the data seemed to indicate that it was,[92] what prompted Tryon to mark that a great division was taking place, a division that required educators and historians alike to either declare their loyalties to traditional history or to social education? The answer appears to lie in the force and inertia of the progressive movement and the determination of social studies advocates to reorganize public education. Some traditional historians, and obviously a majority of school administrators, were not eager to upset the established history curriculum. The result of the Committee of Seven, noted John R. Sutton at the Berkeley American Historical Association meeting (July 1915) was the "fair degree of uniformity in the history work of the secondary schools." Sutton asked:

> Now, why should a new committee be appointed to send out the history teachers of the nation a new recommendation relative to the content of history courses? Such a recommendation would not make for greater uniformity. On the other hand, it would tend to destroy such uniformity as now exists; for some schools would follow the new recommendation, while others would abide by the old plan.[93]

In arguing that another history committee on schools was not needed, Sutton tacitly acknowledged that the insurgents' movement was gaining attention. That a rival organization (rival in the sense that it accepted a competing view of history) was preparing a social efficiency prototype program specifically aimed to dislodge traditional history (Committee on Social Studies) most likely disturbed Sutton. Similarly, other historians, seemingly discounting the idea that the National Education Association's Committee of Social Studies could wrestle the forum of curricula responsibility away from academic experts, collectively put their heads in the sand.

Remarkably, the debate between traditional historians and the advocates of social studies was played out with great drama in the pages of *The History Teachers' Magazine*, then under financial sponsorship of the American Historical Association. Beginning in 1910 and continuing up through the beginning of America's entrance into the Great War, articles of controversy and conservatism appeared side by side, as in the case of Snedden and Burr. Historians Henry Johnson, Rolla M. Tryon, Edgar Dawson, James Harvey Robinson, and William C. Bagley, and social studies insurgents, such as Kingsley, Barnard, Arthur William Dunn, and Thomas Jesse Jones, all authored articles for the magazine. Notwithstanding the free exchange of ideas in the magazine, what impact did this debate have on mainline historians? That is, how did social studies affect those who were then considered to be the voices of the American Historical Association?

At a joint session of the Association of History Teachers' of the Middle States and Maryland and the American Historical Association, held after the publication of what was the final report of the Committee on Social Studies, the AHA Committee on History in Schools gave a conference on the teaching of history in schools. Among the principal speakers were Henry Johnson, Teachers College, Columbia University; Rolla M. Tryon, University of Chicago; Herbert D. Foster, Dartmouth College; and Henry E. Bourne, Western Reserve University. Johnson in delivering the main address remarked with great stoicism that "since the report of the committee of five [1910] we [traditional historians] seemed to have suffered a relapse."[94] With a sense of irony, secured by his faith and knowledge of history's place in schools, Johnson discussed the social education program:

> What is important to us in the present, we are being told, must determine what is important to us in the past, and what is important to us in the present is our own community. The history program must, therefore, be determined by the special interests and special programs of the community. There must be as many kinds of programs as there are kinds of community interests and problems, and a uniform program in history is neither possible nor desirable. Furthermore, these programs must change with the changing interests and problems of the community. What is important this year, or even this month, or this week, may not be important at all next year, or next month, or next week. The coming of the war [World War I] has, it is true, directed the principle into broader channels. The need of international friendships and national patriotism, and incidentally the need of a reasonable and proper hatred of our

enemies, tend in these tremendous and tragic days to over-shadow the narrower interests and problems of the community. But the principle of confining history to issues directly suggested by present issues remains the same.[95]

In Johnson's dissection of the issues, as stated above, he discounted the insurgents' proposals as misplaced and reactionary. Johnson argued that to design the curriculum according to "current events" was a reduction to absurdity. "If the content of history," reasoned Johnson, "is to be determined by present interests and problems, and if such interests and problems are constantly changing, only a prophet could plan a connected, organic course in history."[96] Johnson held that history textbooks were often written with the impression that "history had something to do with the past as the past; that the past itself can be explained only in terms of what is important in and to the past," and "that the past itself must be explained if the past is to be of any service in explaining the present."[97] Johnson, turning the tables on the insurgents, noted that the "real innovators, the real radicals, the real revolutionaries" were the textbook authors who wrote of the "past as the past," because they were attempting to make their work, unlike the social studies insurgents who were interested only in citizenship, "not only educational but also historical."[98]

Finally, Johnson declared that "to that supreme purpose [winning the war] every other consideration must be subordinated. . . . What can be blended must for the moment be ended."[99] Johnson was willing to concede the great temptation of teaching "national patriotism," but warned, given the example of imperial Germany, of its potential disastrous results. Johnson continued that given the "mood for generalization," teachers were "ready to grant . . . that the better we can understand other peoples, and the more other peoples we can understand, the better we shall be able to understand and to appreciate that part of ourselves which is distinctly American."[100] The type of "patriotism" Johnson advocated was not one resting unsteadily on "self-satisfied isolation," but rather one that comes from "an understanding of other peoples" by which develops "a sense of duty to our neighbors as well as ourselves."[101] For Johnson, any other consideration or application of the history curriculum would have to wait for the war's end.

Until a return to normalcy, Johnson reiterated the value of the traditional history program and emphasized the need to maintain it, despite the attacks of the social education insurgents (see chapter 6).

Johnson outlined the three vital elements of the program that must remain unaltered: (a) that "our facts must be historical and must be recognized as historical," (b) these "facts must be selected and arranged from the standpoint of development . . . look[ing] primarily for interests and problems that shaped the past, and not primarily interests and problems now shaping the present," and (c) "we must strive for continuity, for history one and indivisible, one continuous, continuing process."[102] Other speakers present at this meeting agreed unanimously with Johnson. At the conclusion of the conference, Marshall S. Brown, New York University, chairman of the conference, appeared somewhat surprised that no one questioned or "dissented" from Johnson's view of patriotism, or that "the past should be interpreted by the motive that induced the action of the past," and not "by the motive of the present." Exclaimed Brown, "the fact that [Johnson's points] have not [met with opposition] seems to imply that we have reached a consensus of opinion on that proposition [the place of history in schools]."[103]

Thus, the traditional historians made their stand at the same time the social studies insurgents made theirs. The ultimate decision, however, as to what direction the curriculum should take was left to legislatures, school administrators, and the field's practitioners.

During the political transition from conservative programs to the progressive agenda, educators came under the influence of the phenomena of social efficiency. Nationwide, educators adopted social efficiency as the slogan for the "new education" movement. Social studies, too, embraced the slogan and philosophy of social efficiency. The major problem for the new socially based programs was finding a place in the crowded secondary curricula. Concurrently, the traditional history program that had appeared so firmly entrenched in school curricula, fell under the close scrutiny of social studies insurgents.

In summary, shortly following the release of the report of the Committee of Seven, that was for all intents and purposes the traditional history program, historians began to reconsider their proposal. Complaints and criticisms of traditional history curriculum were aired during meetings of the various history teachers associations and eventually culminated in the American Historical Association's appointment of the Committee of Five to review the earlier report and suggest improvements or revisions to the general membership of the association.

The primary criticisms and complaints that led to the reconsideration of the traditional history program by the Committee of Five including the following:

1. No general history program was proposed or even advised, despite widespread popularity of such.
2. The program was not practical for those schools that lack funds, facilities, staff, and time necessary to complete the recommended four years of history.
3. No provision was made for diverting the aims of history to accommodate the needs of the nation in regard to the "Americanization" of newly arrived immigrants. In this view, history was described as a processing agent for social control.
4. No allowance was made for assimilating newly arrived immigrants into the mainstream of American thought and values.
5. "An immoderate amount of work" was required in ancient history.
6. The curriculum required far too much material than was possible to learn or teach.
7. Too much emphasis was placed on college teaching methods, and very little on practical pedagogical methods for secondary schools.
8. Insufficient time was provided for topics in modern history.
9. Too much emphasis was accorded the relationship between high schools and universities.
10. Civil government was not given sufficient emphasis or time in the curriculum.
11. No provision for history study was made for the new industrial high school.
12. Unwittingly, the program encouraged the study of generalized over specific knowledge.
13. Given the nature of the program, in that it was not practical for most schools to offer the full four years or to staff specially trained history teachers in those history courses offered, educators preferred the use of a "good" history textbook. This phenomena resulted in a host of complaints against the traditional history program from being too bookish and too boring to stressing far too much memory work.
14. Not enough attention was given history teacher education programs.

Given the number and nature of the criticisms against the traditional history program, the American Historical Association appointed the Committee of Five to reconsider the program of the Committee of Seven. The primary recommendations of the Committee of Five were:

1. The maintenance of the basic principles of history was to be retained: chronology and historical unity.
2. The intellectual nature of traditional history was restated and reaffirmed.
3. It was suggested that English history be moved from the eleventh to the tenth grade.
4. Medieval history could be dropped as a separate course, by selecting the most important personages, events, ideas, and issues to be presented as part of either ancient or modern history.
5. If possible, modern history should be given a greater emphasis.
6. Better prepared teachers were an absolute necessity for the success of the program.

Despite the earnest efforts of many traditional historians to revamp their own program, social studies insurgents took the initiative to bring the history curriculum in line with the push for more socially efficient and socially responsible schools. The social studies agenda had four basic objectives: (a) debunk traditional history; (b) argue for the ouster of traditional history from school curricula; (c) develop and disseminate a social studies proposal; and (d) argue for the placement of social studies in the school curricula at the expense of traditional history programs.

The insurgents' argument against traditional history differed from the historians' arguments. The primary criticisms against the traditional history curriculum, as voiced by the social studies insurgents, claimed that traditional history:

1. was not socially functional and lacked in social objectivity.
2. failed the test of social efficiency in both the managerial and Deweyan sense.
3. was not based on the present needs and interests of students or centered on the contemporary problems of the community, therefore it was not related to social progress.
4. actually was undemocratic because its program catered to the needs of the few about to attend college and ignored the needs of the many who had no hope of attending college.
5. did not reflect functional "civic attitudes, ideals, or knowl-

edge," and did not contribute "essential or valuable elements to other studies" in the school curricula.

6. was "shaped along the wrong lines" and was, therefore, unadapted to its own ends.
7. lacked a satisfying pedagogy.
8. rested upon the faulty principles of chronology and historical unity.
9. failed to recognize the value of citizenship education.
10. was founded on the intuition and faith of its practitioners, not on sound scientific principles.

During the often vicious attacks on the traditional history curriculum, launched primarily by David Snedden, many historians committed themselves to the decision to stand firm on the history curriculum as promulgated by the Committee of Seven and reconfirmed by the Committee of Five. The voices of dissent among historians, as represented by Charles Beard, Carl Becker, and James Harvey Robinson, who will be treated in the following chapter, argued that history should be modernized and transformed along more socially responsible lines. Despite the efforts of the insurgents and the transformed "new" historians, mainline-traditional historians such as Henry Johnson argued for the maintenance of the three basic principles of pedagogical history: (a) the concept of historicism (chronologically based study); (b) the reliance of fact selection and arrangement interpretations from the standpoint of their value and importance in their historical context, not their relative value for contemporary society; and (c) the concept of continuity of history. Furthermore, Johnson insisted that the search for and teaching of historical truths was not to be violated by circumventing the purposes of history to match what he believed were selfish special interests.

The decade had begun with historians firmly in control of both school history theory and practice. Slowly, through the persistent efforts of such men as David Snedden and Clarence Kingsley, traditional history's hold at the theoretical level in school curricula began to erode. Between 1912 and 1916, the struggle between the traditionalists and insurgents sharpened. In its clearest sense, the turf fight between these groups centered upon philosophical differences in attempting to reconcile the twin paradoxes of liberal democracy through education. The following chapter outlines and describes the social studies prototype designed to harmonize the twin paradoxes. Additionally, the chapter introduces those individuals responsible for the formulation of this new prototype.

6. THE SOCIAL STUDIES-EFFICIENCY PROTOTYPE

IN THE MIDST OF THE Great War, while all of Europe and most of the world were caught in a turmoil of death and destruction, the Committee on Social Studies of the Commission on the Reorganization of Secondary Schools argued for a reformation of history and civic instruction within American secondary schools. Despite Edgar Bruce Wesley's prediction to the contrary, as well as the recent efforts of the Bradley Commission, in the more than seventy years since 1916, there has been no national committee reform effort in history or social studies education with the impact and acclaim of the 1916 Committee or the 1899 Committee of Seven.[1]

Inasmuch as the 1916 committee was the last truly significant agency of reform for history and social studies education for public schools, it merits the careful attention of persons presently engaged in the field. This chapter will seek to describe and outline the social studies program as formulated by the legendary NEA Committee on Social Studies. This chapter also presents the leading figures of the Committee and discussed their contribution to the creation of the first social education prototype entitled social studies.

THE COMMITTEE ON SOCIAL STUDIES

The beginnings of our present social studies programs can be traced back to the work of the Committee on Social Studies, which published what was its last official report in 1916. This committee, originally formed in 1912 as the Committee on Social Science, was part of the larger Commission on the Reorganization of Secondary Schools sponsored by the National Education Association. The Commission was an outgrowth of Clarence Kingsley's earlier report to the Committee on Articulation between Colleges and Secondary Schools.[2]

Shortly after the Commission was reorganized under the chairmanship of Clarence Kingsley, Thomas Jesse Jones was named chairman of the Committee on Social Science. Kingsley had been actively involved in the development of a new civics course for New York schools and felt a deep commitment for the improvement of secondary education. Although Kingsley had been employed by David Snedden as the Massachusetts state agent for high schools and shared many common notions on education with the noted education reformer, they disagreed fundamentally on the issue of tracking students in different high schools for different educational purposes. Kingsley, more influenced than Snedden by the factor of social efficiency, supported the concept of the "cosmopolitan high school" composed of all the variations necessary in one setting for a modern education. Snedden also supported "social efficiency," but his version was more directed at social control.[3] Both views were reflected in the Committee's report, represented in the recommendation for community civics and the Problems in American Democracy course.

In Kingsley's view, social efficiency could be realized only in a high school where young people of all walks of life intermingled. In this heterogeneous setting, he placed a heavy emphasis on the development of a new civics program for socializing young people into the new "cosmopolitan society." Kingsley's selection of Jones aimed to realize that goal. After Jones's appointment in 1912, the committee's title was changed to the Committee on Social Studies. As noted in chapter 5, this subtle conceptual shift marks the beginnings of social studies in American school curricula.

The Committee on Social Studies was composed of twenty-one members from various educational backgrounds.[4] Unlike the Committee of Ten subcommittee on History, Political Economy, and Civil Government (Madison Conference) and the Committee of Seven, the 1916 Committee membership heavily favored professional secondary school educators over professional college and university historians. Of the twenty-one members of the committee only James Harvey Robinson of Columbia University, who was also a member of the original Committee of Ten history subcommittee as well as the

Committee of Five, and William Mace of Syracuse could be counted as professional university historians. In contrast, the earlier committees were dominated by college and university historians, who, ostensibly, favored their discipline over the newly emerging social sciences. It appeared, however, that despite the educationally diverse composition of the committee, committee policy was dominated by a few government bureaucrats (Kingsley, Jones, and Arthur William Dunn) and a few historians (mainly Robinson and James Lynn Barnard).

At the time of the committee's formation, an increasingly antagonistic attitude toward traditional history instruction in secondary schools was being voiced by the emerging progressive minded critics, as noted in chapter 5. Since the turn of the century, critics, such as John Dewey, David Snedden, and G. Stanley Hall, among others, while not completely condemning history instruction, advocated a more modern approach in which only that history which followed the dictates of "present needs and interests" was thought appropriate. The progressive educators argued that history should serve the present needs of students, and that any history not of direct value, particularly ancient and medieval, should be eliminated from the secondary curriculum to make room for other more vital studies based in the social sciences. In the committee's preliminary statement of 1913, Jones wrote that history as king-of-the-curriculum was to be dethroned and replaced with the social studies:

> Good citizenship should be the aim of social studies in the high school. While administration and instruction throughout the school should contribute to the social welfare of the community, it is maintained that social studies have a direct responsibility in this field. Facts, conditions, theories, and activities that do not contribute rather directly to the appreciation of methods of human betterment have no claim. . . . History, too, must answer the test of good citizenship. The old chronicler who recorded the deeds of kings and warriors and neglected the labors of common man is dead. . . . In this spirit recent history is more important than that of ancient times; the history of our own country than that of foreign lands; the record of our own institutions and activities than that of strangers; the labors and plans of the multitudes than the pleasures and dreams of the few.[5]

Jones's statement set the tone for the committee's work: to attack and dismiss traditional history instruction and to introduce a secondary curriculum that specialized in attending to the present growth needs and interests of the learner. The committee set about to introduce the notion that instruction in social studies began with the research of a "real" community problem that made use of content from social science to help identify and solve that problem. The emphasis was no longer on strengthening the individual character of students, but on developing the good citizen who was cognizant of and responded to the concepts of social service, welfare, utility, efficiency, and responsibility.

The committee, including its two "new" historians, largely supported the notion of practical or functional history. It may be more accurate to say, however, that the committee adopted a decidedly ahistorical approach. The academic background of committee members Jones, Kingsley, William Arey, Arthur William Dunn, and Samuel Howe can be traced to sociologists Franklin H. Giddings, George Vincent, and Albion Small. All these committee members had studied with Giddings at Columbia University, except Dunn, who studied with Small and Vincent at the University of Chicago. It was no coincidence, therefore, that the committee, particularly with the influential Jones, Kingsley, and Dunn present, took on a sociological outlook. Only historian James Harvey Robinson appeared to bridge the gap between those who would reject outright and those who sought an accommodation with the popular recommendations of the Committee of Seven.

In accepting Robinson's view of the "New History," the committee reported that "history instruction should be organized, not on the traditional basis of chronology and politics, but on that of [the students] own immediate interests."[6] Rather than "modify the existing course of study" as defined by the Committee of Seven, the committee, with Robinson's urging, encouraged its readers to "take up the whole matter afresh," to "experiment" and use "initiative" in designing the social studies curriculum in secondary schools.[7] In effect, the committee rejected the familiar "four block" system of the Committee of Seven and adopted a "sociological point of view" as the basis of the new social studies curriculum.

Significantly, the American Historical Association did not sponsor any the activities of the committee. For the previous two decades, as noted earlier, the American Historical Association along with other local and regional historical associations such as the History Teachers' Association of the Middle States and Maryland, Mississippi Valley Historical Association, and the New England History Teachers' Association had controlled the primary forum of debate and policy generation for history and civic instruction in public school curricula. The Social Studies Committee, as well as the sponsoring Commission on the Reorganization of Secondary Education, were interested in diverting the passage of influence from the AHA historians, traditional history advocates, to professional educators of the National Education Association, labeled here as progressive education, new education, and social education insurgents. That traditional history advocates showed a strong reluctance to merge their agenda with the insurgents implied to the insurgents that historians were unwilling or unable to reconceptualize their values and attitudes with respect to secondary history instruction. The insurgents took this cautious attitude as a refusal to cooperate, thus mandating their call to action.

THE REPORT OF THE 1916 SOCIAL STUDIES COMMITTEE

Much like the earlier Madison Conference report, and unlike the report of the Committee of Seven that concentrated on the secondary curriculum, the Committee on Social Studies sought to outline a program that would span grades seven through twelve. Although mentioned briefly, the elementary grades were not given much attention. Ironically, the insurgents accepted the history-centered approach generally accepted in the elementary grades; no suggestion of social studies content was made in the report.[8] The 1916 Committee's notion of a connected curriculum of interrelated subjects appealed to many educators. Although the focus of the report was on the senior high school, attention was also given to the newly emerging junior high school curricula. The report of the Committee on Social Studies began appropriately with a definition of the field of social studies relative to secondary education:

> The social studies are understood to be those whose subject matter relates directly to the organization and development of human society, and to man as a member of social groups.[9]

The committee assigned "content course[s]" centered in geography, history (nonspecific), and civics to the new junior high school arrangement (seventh, eight, and ninth grades). European history, including ancient and oriental civilizations, medieval, and English histories; American history; and Problems of American Democracy were directed to the new senior high school arrangement (tenth through twelfth grades). Despite this brief description, the committee's definition of social studies was essentially open-ended. The definition specifically allowed for the inclusion of any of the social sciences such as economics, sociology, anthropology, archeology, or political science if the particular school system viewed such study appropriate and practical.

Dramatizing that the social studies differed from the other studies as found in junior and senior high schools curricula, the committee distinguished that the report followed the dictates of "social efficiency," which they reasoned was "the keynote of modern education." Because the social studies were expressly devoted to "social content," they "afford[ed] peculiar opportunities for the training of the individual as a member of society."[10] Here, the social studies aim or purpose was revealed to be directly related to attending to the twin paradoxes of freedom versus conformity and the individual versus society. The necessary "training" to address these issues was recognized by the conferees to be citizenship education:

> The social studies of the American high school should have for their conscious and constant purpose the cultivation of good citizenship. We may identify the "good citizen" of a neighborhood with the "thoroughly efficient member" of that neighborhood; but he will be characterized, among other things, by a loyalty and sense of obligation to his city, State, and Nation as political units.[11]

On the one hand, "loyalty" and "obligation" associated with education in a social context reflect a philosophy of social control, leaning toward the conformity side of the first paradox. Here, teachers were to "teach" the child that a good citizen was one who was loyal to the state and possessed a sense of obligation to the government and its elected officials. On the other hand, the concept of "neighborhood" and being neighborly implied a sense of duty or social service to the child's fellow neighbors and citizens, leaning toward the society of the second paradox. The conferees sought to combine the two—that is, to recommend that educators adopt social control measures as well as social service concepts. The educational goal of furthering the development of the student's intellectual capacities apart from social concerns or issues was not an expressed aim of the social studies program. In sum, citizenship and group socialization were to stand paramount to any other consideration.

In the explanation of their "point of view," the committee

noted that they were not appointed to "obtain justice for a group of social studies . . . or for one social study" against another, "but to consider wherein such studies might be made to contribute most effectively to the purposes of secondary education."[12] The conferees were resolved to introduce new civics into the schools "to train for citizenship."[13] Thus, if any social study was to be placed in the schools, that social study was to be community civics. Interestingly, as a disclaimer, the committee underlined that the "superficial" and "more or less mechanical" alterations of the existing curriculum, which they admittedly were proposing, would amount to little "unless the subject matter and methods of instruction [were] adapted to the pupil's immediate needs of social growth."[14] Nonetheless, the committee addressed the demand for more civics to be taught by requiring civics for all students, transferring it from the last year of high school to the first, so that more students would be exposed to it, and by introducing civics in the elementary school, and shifting the emphasis from the national government to the local municipal government.

No matter what course the school offered, however, if the principal and teachers did not adjust the course to the "immediate needs of social growth," the class would be of little value to the child, the community, the state, or the nation. The dilemma presented to educators by this line of reasoning seemingly precluded the outlining of a curriculum prior to instruction, as Henry Johnson predicted. Following this idea, the committee stressed that it was their purpose to "establish certain principles, to illustrate . . . and to stimulate initiative on the part of the teachers and school administrators in testing proposed methods or in judicious experiments of their own."[15] The conferees unequivocally "refrained from offering detailed outlines of courses, on the ground that they tend to fix instruction in stereo-typed forms inconsistent with a real socializing purpose." They insisted that "the selection of topics and the organization of subject matter should be determined in each case by immediate needs."[16]

If "immediate needs" was to be the guiding principle of social studies, and we have every reason to believe it was for the committee, then any explanation or suggestion that followed ran the risk of contradicting this stated basic principle. Nevertheless, apparently fully aware of any possible inconsistencies, the committee proposed a program. Following a Deweyan line of thought, the committee stated:

The high-school course has heretofore been determined too largely by supposed future needs and too little by present needs and past experience. The important fact is not that the pupil is getting ready to live, but that he is living, and in immediate need of such mental and social nourishment and training as will enable him to adjust himself to his present social environment and conditions. By the very processes of present growth he will make the best possible provision for the future. . . . [That] means merely that such instruction should be given at the psychological and social moment when the boy's [or girl's] interest are such as to make the instruction function effectively in his processes of growth.[17]

Several important questions were raised here, but unfortunately none were adequately addressed in the text of the report. For example, if the present needs and interests were to determine the social studies curriculum, then it appears that the sort of program "developed" would be a spontaneous, dynamic curriculum, everchanging according to the dictates of present interests and needs. Who, however, would determine what the present interests and needs were? Who spoke as the final authority: the child, the teacher, the principal, parents, the business community, the local government, the state, the federal government? Also, who decided the proper "psychological and social moment" for the presentation of information or the inquiry into a problem or issue? Was it possible for teachers to prepare any sort of lessons in geography, history, civics, or the social sciences prior to class and apart from the mental consent of the individual students or without consideration of other interested parties?

In the committee report the answers to these questions were not made entirely clear. Certainly socialization, citizenship education, and social efficiency were at the core of the social studies curriculum. The concept of beginning instruction with the individual child in the tradition of Parker and Hall, however, appeared glossed over. Instead, it appeared that the committee in their explanation of the social studies expected the teacher and principal to follow their lead in deciding the needs and interests of their students, despite whatever their students' literal needs and interests may have been. This stance has its origins in Dewey, who held that although the child's needs and interests are a vital part of any school program, students were not to dictate curricula.

The conferees referred to the needs of pupils, native-born Americans, immigrants, local communities, local conditions and requirements, and industrial concerns, yet the various needs and interests necessary for outlining a social studies program were largely identified and established by the committee. Unlike the history committees that offered statistical data to support their assertions and recommendations, the committee appeared to be dictating a course of action without benefit of empirical support, using instead Deweyan philosophy as a base.

Nonetheless, the committee was interested in the development of the individual, where the socialization of the group far outweighed specific attention to the individual. To the conferees, the individual student *did* have to make a choice, with the teacher's careful guidance, between selfish interests and the "common general interests." The difference between the traditional program and the new education was divided by this significant point. The traditional program was essentially an intellectual one centered on the individual; whereas, the new education was based on the social development of the group. "The best question that can be asked in class," wrote the conferees, "[was] the question that the pupil himself asks because he wants to know, and not the question the teacher asks because he thinks the pupil some time in the future ought to know."[18] It appeared that the committee was concerned with individuals and their thoughts when this statement is taken out of context. But in the context of the full social studies program, individual interests and needs were clearly a secondary concern. For example, the statement assumed that children would ask pertinent questions, questions that the teacher could answer or assist the child to find an answer to. The statement, like the entire social studies program, assumed that the questions asked would be social questions of common interest to the group or at least pertinent to their particular neighborhood.

The committee's attempt to make a "distinction" between "the needs of present growth" and "immediate, objective utility" only worked to obscure the philosophical foundation of the social studies program. Although the committee described the concept of "present needs and interest," they failed to adequately define or illustrate it, the concept of "immediate, objective utility" was not described, defined, or illustrated. The picture that educators may have been left with had the social studies program preparing students as citizens first, learners second. This notion implied a preplanned curriculum based upon what the conferees defined as the "good citizen," not what the student or parents considered the "good citizen" to be.

The problem of outlining a program on a national level, prepared without consulting present interests and needs of groups or individuals created a curious contradiction. Nevertheless, the committee produced a "general outline of the social studies" with the single provision that the school attend to the "social aspect of education" by addressing present needs and interests, which were left largely undefined. Apparently, the conferees reasoned it would be more productive to offer educators something tangible, something that could be utilized as a guideline, and run the risk of schools violating the guiding principle, than to confine the report to a revolving philosophical argument.

Essentially, the Social Studies Committee's program employed a two-cycle system. Students were to be introduced to geography, European history, American history, and civics in the junior high school (grades 7 through 9), then repeat the cycle in the senior high school (grades 10 through 12). The primary rationale for the two-cycle system was that the program provided a "comprehensive, and in a sense complete, course of study for each period."[19]

The first cycle was viewed as elementary, where the basic or essential skills and knowledge were offered by the social studies. The second cycle was designed with a "broader horizon," to include "new relations and more intensive study" for the advancing student. The secondary rationale for the cycles was far more pragmatic; large numbers of pupils left school after the eighth or ninth grade rather than attending high school. This condition resulted in a dropout rate as high as 90 to 95 percent. With fewer than 10 percent of the high school–aged students actually graduating from secondary schools, the two-cycle program served to give all students at least some exposure to social studies before they departed.

THE JUNIOR HIGH SCHOOL SOCIAL STUDIES PROGRAM

The main emphasis of the social studies program, as previously described, was community civics. The Committee referred the reader of the 1916 Social Studies report to the earlier, more detailed, special committee report on civic education. Despite the referral to the 1915 Community Civics document, the 1916 Social Studies report did include an outline of civic education. Community civics, their preferred term, was not only to be included in each year of the first cycle, but was to be the focus of the social studies program. Again stressing the importance of local curriculum development, the conferees suggested be "adapted to local conditions." The committee suggested the following "alternative" programs for the junior high school:

Seventh year:
(1) Geography—one-half year
European History—one-half year
Civics—taught as a phase of the above and of other subjects, or segregated in one or two periods a week, or both
(2) European History—one year
Geography—taught incidentally to, and as a factor in, history
Civics—taught as a phase of the above and of other subjects, or segregated in one or two periods a week, or both

Eighth year:
American History—one-half year
Civics—one-half year
Geography—taught incidentally to, and as a factor in, the above subjects

Ninth year:
(1) Civics: continuing the civics of the previous year, but with more emphasis upon state, national, and world aspects—one-half year
Civics: economic and vocational aspects
History: much use made of history in relation to the topics of the above courses
(2) Civics—economic and vocational
Economic History.[20]

The committee suggested that any of the above courses could be presented in sequence or parallel to one another, and emphasized both the flexibility and interrelatedness of the social studies proposal.

Specifically, the history program in the seventh and eighth grades was primarily to utilize the "problem" or "topic" methods. With the "problem" method, the teacher was to present a particular problem for the students to consider. For example, the students may be asked to investigate, "Why was the development of Brazil so retarded?" The answer would involve studying the geography of Brazil, its culture, its economic and political situation, and its history as well. Students who wished to study history in a different manner were directed to the "topic" method as an alternative to the "problem" method. Here students were suggested to select a topic from a list prepared by the teacher, such as how the British Empire was organized. Again, geography, history, and the social sciences would be called upon to aid in investigating the question or formulating an answer.

Topics and problems from American history, however, were viewed as the best companion for community civics. For instance, the committee noted that students would find that "the motives that lead to colonization were the same as those which have led to the development of their own community and State."[21] Notwithstanding the attention to history, in the selective sense of meeting the test of social efficiency, no matter what the topic or problem under study, everything in the social studies curriculum at the junior high level was to be related to community civics. The committee described community civics as civics with the "emphasis upon the local community":[22]

It [was] the community with which every citizen, especially the child, comes into most intimate relations, and which [was] always in the foreground of experience; it [was] easier for the child, as for any citizen, to realize his membership in the local community, to feel a sense of personal responsibility for it, and to enter into actual cooperation with it, than is the case with the national community.[23]

"Membership in the local community" was an important concept for social studies and all instruction was to be centered on the community first. This membership was to be determined, of course, by local conditions and specifically geared to benefit the community directly. Accordingly, the general aim of community civics was simply "to help the child to know his community." The realization of this goal, explained the conferees, involved leading students "to see the importance and significance of the elements of community welfare" of which they were a part, "to know the social agencies" that operated in and among the community, and "to recognize [their] civic obligations" to the community at large.[24] It was from these three "elements" that teachers were to direct their attentions to in relating civics to the other subjects of the social studies as well as other subjects in the secondary school curriculum. The committee suggested that teachers present the following eleven topics as the "elements of welfare" and basic to the community civics program:

(1) Health; (2) Protection of life and property; (3) Recreation; (4) Education; (5) Civic beauty; (6) Wealth; (7) Communication; (8) Transportation; (9) Migration; (10) Charities; and (11) Correction.[25]

Since the 1916 Social Studies Committee released their proposal two years before the overall Reorganization Commission report, it is probable that the "elements of welfare," as manifested in the report of the Social Studies Committee, may have directly influenced the preparation of the Commission's famous "Seven Cardinal Principles."[26]

Matched to the "elements of welfare" were the committee's "social facts," which the conferees suggested should be utilized in determining the method of teaching community civics. Among the "social facts" related to community civics were:

1. The pupil is a young citizen with real interests at stake. . . . It is the first task of the teacher, therefore, not to create an interest for future use, but to demonstrate existing interests and present citizenship.
2. The pupil as a young citizen is a real factor in community affairs. . . . Therefore, it is a task of the teacher to cultivate in the pupil a sense of his responsibility, present as well as future.
3. If a citizen has an interest in civic matters and a sense of his personal responsibility, he will want to act. Therefore the teacher must help the pupil to express his conviction in word and deed. He must be given an opportunity . . . to live his civics, both in the school and in the community outside.
4. Right action depends not only upon information, interest, and will but also upon judgment. Hence the young citizen must be trained to weigh facts and to judge relative values, both in regard to what constitute the essential elements in a situation and in regard to the best means of meeting it.
5. Every citizen possesses a large amount of unorganized information regarding community affairs. . . . It is, therefore, important to teach the pupils how to test and organize their knowledge.
6. People are . . . most ready to act upon those convictions that they helped to form by their own mental processes and that are based upon their own experiences and observation. Hence the teacher should . . . lead the class: (1) To contribute facts from their own experience; (2) To contribute other facts gathered by

themselves; (3) To use their own reasoning powers in forming conclusions; and (4) To submit these conclusions to criticism.
7. The class has the essential characteristics of a community. Therefore, the method by which the class exercises are conducted is of the utmost importance in the cultivation of civic qualities and habits.27

With these "social facts," joined with the concepts of "social feeling, social thought, and social action," the committee laid out the essential important components of community civics for the eighth grade. Teachers were to begin in the community itself, treat the student as a vital element in the present life of the community, and process the "unorganized information" from the student by means of the scientific method: begin with a real problem, gather and observe data, test the data, form conclusions, and "submit" the conclusions to review.

As students developed their ability to observe local community problems and to better observe and monitor the way social agencies dealt with these problems, or failed to, students would be prepared to begin study of ninth-grade civics. No recommendation of the Social Studies Committee was as radical to traditional history advocates as the suggestion to place civics in the ninth grade in place of Ancient History, the cornerstone of traditional history. Despite the risk of challenging the status quo, the committee was convinced that placing civics in the ninth grade, following the eighth-grade program in community civics, would by its "very nature . . . tend to keep in school . . . many of those whom the traditional history courses [Ancient History] usually given in the ninth year would offer no inducement to remain."28 Community civics was not only good for the community, state, and nation, but it also provided "the pupil with a motive for the continuation of his education." Thus, to the conferees, community civics was a practical course that would persuade more children to stay in school at least to the ninth grade.

Ninth-grade civics enlarged the scope of community study to include the study of the state, the nation, and the world. Here, the committee outlined the notions of "amplification of national concepts" and "world interests." The conferees identified health, education, and industrial or urban problems as universal to state, national, or worldwide interests. "As our population grows," wrote the committee, "means of communication perfected and the interests of the individual more closely interwoven with the interests of oth-

ers, the opportunities for friction and conflict increase." This potential condition created the "necessity for training the pupil to recognize the common interest in the midst of conflicting group interests." Given the choice between provincial or individual interest
and the common interest, the committee declared that teachers
needed to "cultivat[e] the will [of their students] to subordinate"
individual interest to create a feeling of "national solidarity."[29]

To identify the "common interest," the committee stated the
importance of teaching students to conceptualize the world as one
"community." The goal was to extend the notion of "common interest" or "national solidarity" beyond the local community, the city,
the state, and the nation. These various elements were all "dependent upon one another and [were] bound together into the larger
community life by their common interests and cooperative action."[30] As the peoples of the earth were "becoming more and more
closely dependent upon each other," teachers needed to foster the
attitude or feeling of "internationalism" and one "world community," together with the concept of national solidarity.[31]

Another important topic of the ninth-grade civics was "civic
relations and vocational life." The committee felt it was vital to the
overall social studies program to have teachers guide students in the
selection of socially useful work. Teachers were to present a survey of
vocations, and with their teachers' careful "vocational guidance,"
students would be better able to make a "wise choice of vocation"
and an "intelligent preparation for it."[32] The underlining rationale of
civic education was that "one of the essential qualities of the good
citizen" was the ability "to be self-supporting." Returning again to
the concept of "social efficiency," the conferees stressed that it was
"through the activities necessary to [the students'] self-support" that
they "contribute[d] efficiently" to "the world's progress."[33]

The Social Studies Committee summarized that the "chief
purpose" of ninth-grade civics:

> Should be the development of an appreciation of the social
> significance of all work; of the social value and interdepen-
> dence of all occupations; of the social responsibility of the
> worker, not only for the character of his work but for the use of
> its fruits; of the opportunities and necessity for good citizen-
> ship in vocational life; of the duty of the community to the
> worker; of the necessity for social control, governmental and
> otherwise, of the economic activities of the community; and of

the part that government actually plays in regulating the economic life of the community and the individual.[34]

These "purposes" made history a viable subject for the junior high school. "Community civics," noted the conferees, "afford[ed] the opportunity to use history to illuminate topics of immediate interest."[35] Here, "local history" together with "community civics" laid the groundwork for further study in history by "developing an appreciation of what history means and for giving historical perspective to the present." As community civics began with the individual in the community and expanded to encompass the world, history instruction, too, began in the community and was amplified to include a study of all nations.

Specifically, the committee suggested that under the topic of health, one of the eleven "elements of welfare," in a general history course the student may study, for example, "the development of sanitation, sanitary conditions in medieval cities," or the "Greek ideal of physical development."[36] Under the topics of transportation and trade the student could study "early trade routes and road building" or "early methods of trading and transportation." Although the topics in history would vary, chronological approaches were clearly not advocated. No matter what the topic, everything had to relate directly to the present, and all topics had to deal specifically with "real situations and relations in the pupil's own life" to be considered sociallly efficient.[37]

THE SENIOR HIGH SCHOOL SOCIAL STUDIES PROGRAM

After a successful junior high school experience in community civics with relevant attention to history and geography, the student was prepared to begin the senior high social studies course. The committee recommended that students take social studies in each of the three years of the senior high school to complete the full six-year social education program. The four courses suggested were to be dependent upon local conditions. The program for grades ten through twelve was as follows [only the last course (Problems of American Democracy) was specifically slotted for a particular year in school]:

1. European history to approximately the end of the seventeenth century (one year). This would include ancient and oriental civil-

ization, English history to the end of the period mentioned, and the period of American exploration.

2. European history including English history since approximately the end of the seventeenth century (one year or one-half year).

3. American history since the seventeenth century (one year or one-half year).

4. Problems of American democracy (one year or one-half year).[38]

These courses were designed specifically to "repeat the cycle of social study provided" in the junior high school, and were not intended to be an introduction to just another set of disconnected courses. The same "principle of organization" that applied to the junior high cycle was to apply to the senior high courses. Instruction and course development were to begin with the interests and needs of the student who was acting and thinking in terms of the common good of the community. To the committee the notion that the "social aspect" determined course development allowed social studies to be "extremely flexible and easily adaptable to the special needs of different groups of pupils" and "different high-school curriculums" such as the traditional, commercial, scientific, technical, or agricultural high school.[39]

Consequently, no matter what the high school curriculum, social studies could be adjusted to fit the school's purpose. Only the guiding principle of "needs and interests" needed to remain constant. By contrast, the traditional history curriculum had a relatively fixed course program that was to be given to all students regardless of the type of high school they attended. The pedagogy of social studies, however, was less flexible; primarily students were to utilize the scientific method when dealing with social problems and special topics. The pedagogy of the traditional history curriculum varied widely; sometimes the scientific method was used, sometimes the source method, at other times a chronological approach (straight narrative), and so forth. These differences manifested themselves especially in the history program of the two curricula.

In the social studies program, history was to be organized either as a "topic-centered" or "problem-centered" study according to two basic principles: "the selection of topics or problems for study" were to be used "with reference to the pupil's own immediate interest" and to the "general social significance" of the study.[40] As noted earlier, the committee equivocated on the issue of who exactly determined needs and interests, or in this case the "pupil's own immediate interest." In the final analysis, however, as presented in the study of community civics, students were to bend their individual will to conform to the interests and needs of the community for the "common general interest." With this in mind, the first principle would not apply unless the student's "own immediate interest" corresponded to what was thought to be in the "common interest" of the community, city, state, or nation. For the student to disregard the "common good," acting apart from the interest of the community, was the same as acting socially irresponsible. For the teacher to allow this sort of nonsocial behavior was to run against the fundamental principles of social studies, social service, and social control. Consequently, the teacher was to avoid this sort of individualized behavior at all costs.

In the junior high school, community civics was seen as the best means to promote proper social behavior. In the senior high school, history best served that function. The "primary aim in American history," declared the conferees, "should be to develop a vivid conception of American nationality."[41] This was not intended to be a promotion of the "narrow and partisan" type of patriotic study that the committee erroneously attributed to the traditional history curriculum. Instead, the committee explained that a "strong and intelligent patriotism, and a keen sense of the responsibility of every citizen for national efficiency" was to be instilled in every student. It was "only on the basis of national solidarity, national efficiency (economic, social, political), and national patriotism that this or any nation could expect to perform its proper function in the family of nations":[42]

> [For] one of the conscious purposes of instruction in history . . . should be the cultivation of a sympathetic understanding of [other] nations and their peoples, of an intelligent appreciation of their contributions to civilization, and of a just attitude toward them. So important has this proposal seemed that a proposal has recently been made that one year of the history course be supplanted by a course to be known as "A Study of Nations."[43]

The study of the world's nations, a logical extension of community civics, was not given attention and was not outlined in the proposed list of social courses, as were courses in the traditional subjects in history. Nonetheless, the committee gave the impression of being interested in promoting such a course. Clarence Kingsley designed a world studies program for the committee. Wrote one reviewer:

> Instead of focusing attention upon the past [the teacher] would start frankly with the present or typical modern nations— European, South American, oriental—and would use history in explanation of these nations and of clearly defined problems of supreme social importance at the present time. Not only would the use of history organized in this way, according to Mr. Kingsley, "tend to reduce friction in international relations [relating to the World War], as such friction often results from popular clamor, born of a lack of understanding of foreign nations," but "it would help to a truer understanding and appreciation of the foreigners who come to our shores," and "it would lead us to be more helpful in our relations with backward peoples, because it would help us to value them on the basis of their latent possibilities, rather than on the basis of their present small achievements."[44]

Kingsley's course, with strong undertones of Snedden's view of history, emphasized the present. In spite of the philosophical closeness to community civics, the Social Studies Committee pragmatically faced the reality that the vast majority of the secondary schools offered the familiar four-block program of the committee of Seven and that they were not likely to derail that program in toto for a specialized, untested course in history.

In view of the prevailing situation concerning the traditional history subjects, the committee sought to work within the traditional framework by reshaping the existing courses to a form more in line with the social studies concept of history. The committee asked three basic questions in regard to those secondary schools that offered the "customary four units":

1. To what extent and in what ways are the college requirements and life requirements mutually exclusive?
2. To what extent does an increase in the amount of history offered insure more universal or better social education?
3. What "tests" must the history course meet if it is "to hold its own in our schools?"[45]

The committee provided answers to each of the three with direct quotes from Dewey (question one), and statements from

James Harvey Robinson and William Mace (question three), and paraphrased arguments from Snedden without citation (question two). Essentially these supporting answers attacked the traditional history program as being "ill adapted to the requirements of secondary education" and recommended in its place a socialized approach to history that was better suited to modern educational needs. Because the "traditional type of history" failed to "meet the tests" of "efficiency," socialized history that placed the problems of the present at the forefront of the discipline was the only logical choice for secondary study. From this position the committee offered a solution.

The committee declared in a statement that would, of course, be contested by traditional historians, that there was "general agreement that history to be of value in the education of the boy or girl, must 'function in the present.'" There was, however, "disagreement over two questions: (1) What [was] meant by 'functioning in the present'?" and "(2) How shall the material of history be organized to this end?"[46] The conferees presented "two interpretations of the phrase":

(a) The sociological interpretation, according to which it is enough if history be made to explain present conditions and institutions; [and] (b) the pedagogical interpretation, according to which history, to be of value educationally, must relate to the present interests of the pupil.[47]

Although the committee spoke of "two interpretations of the phrase," they also suggested a third interpretation borrowed from Robinson, which was a mixture of both:

The selection of a topic in history [or a problem], and the amount of attention given to it should depend, not merely upon its relative proximity in time, nor yet upon its relative present importance from the adult or sociological point of view, but also chiefly upon the degree to which such topic can be related to the present life interests of the pupil, or can be used by him in his present processes of growth.[48]

"Acceptance of the principle," argued the committee, "raised the new questions. What history does meet the needs of the child's growth? and, How may a given topic be related to the child's interest?"[49] In spite of the importance of these "new questions," the conferees explained that they could "not be disposed of once and for all by a jury of historians or sociologists," but that the classroom teacher must provide the answers specific to one's "own particular pupils." Thus for the teacher a dual problem was created. On the one hand, what topics should be studied? And on the other hand, how should these topics be approached once they were developed? Without illustration, the committee offered a guideline to follow. Again borrowing from Robinson, the conferees suggested that teachers should:

> Organize all history instruction on the basis of these interests [those of the "common men and women"], selecting from any part of the past those facts that "meet the needs of present growth"; and [they] would utilize these facts at a time when the pupil has a need for them in connection with any subject under discussion or any activity in progress.[50]

Surprisingly, given its rhetoric, in presenting this guiding principle, the committee was working carefully not to blatantly upset the status quo traditional history courses; schools could continue with their present history curriculum. The important difference, of course, was that the organization of the program as well as its content was being recast. Rather than presenting their lessons in the traditional narrative, chronological fashion, teachers were to select from the whole of the traditional history course those facts that met the qualifications of "functioning in the present"; everything else was to be discarded. Cognizant of the difficulties that such a "radical reorganization" of history would create, the committee emphasized the importance of teachers being trained enough in pedagogical skills, which they labeled "the art of teaching," and content to make these important decisions. This was, of course, the old escape hatch clause used earlier by the traditional historians: if only we had trained teachers, the program would work.

Nonetheless, the committee urged educators, both principals and teachers, to work against the "impression of history" and "to work boldly and without timid reservation," to "take up the whole matter afresh, freed . . . from the impression of history."[51] Apart from this bit of advice and encouragement, the conferees left the matter there and offered no specifics on how teachers should go about reorganizing their history programs. Instead the report moved on to the next topic, the "culminating course" in the social studies program, Problems of American Democracy. This course was the vital link in the effort to harmonize the twin paradoxes.

The purpose of the Problems of American Democracy course was to provide students with a "more definite, comprehensive, and deeper knowledge of the vital problems of social life, and thus of securing a more intelligent and active citizenship."[52] The course appeared very similar in form to that of the Madison Conference recommendation made twenty-five years earlier for a full year of intensive study of some special topic in history. However, sidestepping the controversy of which social science should be highlighted, the committee stressed that no one social study was to take precedence over another. Instead, the course should ideally involve all social studies, including history, by centering the class on a study of "actual problems, or issues, or conditions, as they occur in life, and in their several aspects, political, economic, and sociological,"[53] not in subject matter. According to the committee:

> These problems or issues [would] vary from year to year, and from class to class, but they should be selected on the ground (1) of their immediate interest to the class and (2) of their vital importance to society.[54]

As with community civics and history, the committee suggested that the Problems course be organized with the same guiding principle. Beyond this, however, "the committee believ[ed] . . . that it should go no farther than to define principles, with such meager illustration as it [had] available, and to urge experiment."[55] The conferees discussed the whole course, which was a radical departure from the norm, in less than five pages.

In all probability, as will be discussed in the following section, the political climate cast by World War I served to tone down or eliminate the more liberal aspects of the Problems of Democracy course.[56] Even after the dissemination of the report, teachers rarely experimented with the notion of questioning status quo positions. In fact, Dawson called the new social studies offerings (which included the problems course) in 1924, "the confusion of tongues."[57] Despite these conditions, although stated in the context of community civics, the conferees emphasized four central points of methodology that were applicable to the problems course:

> People are . . . most ready to act upon those convictions that they have helped to form by their own mental processes and that are based upon their own experience and observation. Hence the teacher should . . . lead the class: (1) To contribute

facts from their own experience; (2) To contribute other facts gathered by themselves; (3) To use their own reasoning powers in forming conclusions; and (4) To submit these conclusions to criticism.[58]

All the essentials of a sound scientific method were presented: start from what you know; seek and generate new data; form your own conclusions; and be prepared to authenticate and validate your data, as well as to support, defend, and justify your conclusions. At least in rhetoric, the conferees had stimulated teachers and their students to chart their own territory of ideas. Training the collective will, as was found in the earlier mental discipline theory, was not the purpose of the 1916 social studies.

Clearly, the Problems course was hardly standardized in title, form, method, or content. It became, exactly as the conferees might have suspected, an experimental course. Either this condition indicated the acceptance of the experimental-elastic ability of social studies, or, more unfortunately and probable, the diversity of course work in social studies exhibited a serious lack of understanding, misconception, or agreement as to what social studies was to be. The examination of this important issue, however, falls beyond the scope of this work.[59] Nonetheless, the notion or seed of experimentation was planted for others to nurture.[60] Despite the unsettled nature of what the course was suppose to do or be, it turned out to be an enduring legacy of the Social Studies Committee and eventually became a fixture in many secondary curricula over the next fifty years.[61]

THE LEADING CONTRIBUTORS OF THE 1916 SOCIAL STUDIES

Which of the original twenty-one members of the 1916 Social Studies Committee made the most significant contribution to the cause of social education? If the pen is any indicator, those on the committee who exerted the greatest influence on the shaping of social studies would have to include James Lynn Barnard, Arthur William Dunn, James Harvey Robinson, Thomas Jesse Jones, and Clarence Kingsley, who served as chairman for the Commission on the Reorganization of Secondary Education to which the Social Studies Committee was to report, as well as a conferee with the social studies group. Collectively, these five wrote more articles, books, curricula projects, government reports, and gave more speeches related to the beginnings of social studies than did the other original seventeen members combined.

Given the committee's composition—that is, its heavy focus on secondary school personnel—control over policy and philosophical positions appeared to rest squarely upon these five individuals. Evidence for this assertion lies with their collective and individual thoughts largely expressed *prior* to their appointment to the Committee: Kingsley, Dunn, and Barnard had been early advocates of community civics; Jones championed the use of social sciences at Hampton Institute; Robinson was the leading spokesman of the "new history"—all well before the Social Studies Committee came into existence. By comparison, their fellow conferees offered little in terms of new formulations or conceptions other than those that were already in print and credited to these men. In effect this left the seventeen other members more like political dressing than actual contributors—political dressing in the sense that the seventeen supporting players were needed to fill out the impression that the committee was not top-heavy with college professors and government bureaucrats, which, of course, it was, but more representative of secondary practitioners.

The first report of the Committee, entitled "The Preliminary Report of the Committee on Social Studies," issued in 1913, was written primarily by Jones. It included a brief section on history prepared by Robinson, a slightly longer section on community civics prepared by Barnard, and a short section on economics by Henry R. Burch. The second report, *The Teaching of Community Civics*, released in 1915, was actually a separate work prepared by a special subcommittee of the committee co-authored by Barnard, Dunn, Kingsley, and F. W. Carrier. This subcommittee credited David Snedden, Jones, and fellow Social Studies Committee member Jessie C. Evans with providing "valuable suggestions" in the preparation of the paper. Much of this work was reproduced in the major report of 1916. It supports the notion that policy formulation was actually in the hands of a few individuals and closed to other influences or perspectives.

The rationale for the community civics report was similar to that offered for a course in community civics outlined by Jones at the Hampton Institute in 1905, Snedden in his many addresses and writings on citizenship education, and Dunn in the preface of his 1907 text, *The Community and the Citizen*.[62] This report is vital to understanding the outlook of the overall committee. The basic idea was that in "community civics" young citizens would learn to become part of the political system. They would work within the system rather than merely memorize such trivia as the number of senators and the qualifications of the president, which was commonplace in the standard civic offerings of the time.

The preliminary statement of 1913 and the civics report of 1915 provided several clues as to who exerted the most influence within the committee. It is in these reports that Jones, Barnard, Dunn, Kingsley, and Robinson instilled the working spirit, and defined and organized the content of the committee's work. Moreover, the preliminary report outlined the method or "tests" that educators needed to give their current curriculum to ascertain if it did or did not contribute to "human betterment."[63] The notion that schooling was tied or linked to "social betterment" or "social efficiency" was underlined in these early works.

By inference, three other individuals merit mention because of their significant contributions to the 1916 Social Studies program. The notion of using principles to guide a particular study, as used by the committee, was earlier outlined by William Mace in his *Study in History*.[64] Although he believed knowledge was not a fixed entity, to Mace, a less prolific writer of the Social Studies Committee when compared to Robinson, when a subject or topic was studied carefully, certain principles began to appear. These principles, once discovered, could be used to guide a student's investigation into a topic more efficiently than beginning on page one of a history text and working through to the end. Utilization of the guiding principle concept was consistently applied throughout the Social Studies report by the conferees. The primary principle used, of course, was Dewey's "needs and interests," thus making Dewey another important, though somewhat passive contributor, as discussed in chapter 5.

Dewey's influence on the committee was strong. Most, if not all, the selected philosophical points that appeared in the report were specifically drawn from his writings. Although he may not have personally agreed with all that the committee wrote or with the direction the conferees took with social studies, most of Dewey's ideas on social education blended nicely with the committee's avowed interest in promoting social education.

Unlike Dewey, however, David Snedden, who led the fight against unseating traditional secondary history, received little credit (with just a brief mention in the committee's second report) for his views on community civics, modern history study, presentism, and social studies in general. Snedden was vitally interested in education for social control. Although pledged to social service, the committee appeared to accept in full Snedden's view of community civics as the best educational means available to secure social control. That is, the committee established that public education and in particular social education (social studies) needed to be centered on working toward the goal of social efficiency. Social control, as formulated in the social studies prototype, appealed to urban educators overburdened by the massive influx of immigrants from Europe as well as from the southern states. Here Snedden's concept of a two-tiered school system, students attending either a vocational high school or general high school complete with a program for tracking students by ability, found a receptive audience with educators.

As mentioned earlier, Snedden's attack on traditional history was no less than a declaration of war. He came to view traditional history as not expressing functional "civic attitudes, ideals, or knowledge," nor contributing "essential or valuable elements to other studies" in the "interests of civic or social education." Consequently, Snedden lobbied heavily to remove traditional history and its curricular baggage from the secondary curriculum to provide space for the social education program.

WAR AND SOCIAL STUDIES REFORM

During World War I, war became the enemy of freedom of thought and expression, as well as of truth. This is not to naively suggest freedom and truth were a given in a peaceful America, or that people, by nature, always sought out truth. The struggle and definition of freedom and truth are enduring themes. Even in countries that declared themselves a democracy, it made little difference if the nation was preparing for war or was presently engaged. The ability to openly question the actions or reactions of government was sharply curtailed, if not banned outright. In the name of victory, overt censorship was given full reign.

When the United States became indirectly and later directly involved in World War I, strict laws and other "unofficial" sanctions were made to repress certain opinions and actions regarding belligerents, in particular Germany.[65] One of the victims of this repression[66] policy was the 1916 Social Studies report and, in particular, the Problems of Democracy course. The report, produced in the spirit of progressive humanitarianism, inevitably clashed with the martial spirit necessary for war. Even sympathetic progressives who came to embrace the war effort understood the toll that war would extract from American institutions and the people.

In selling the notion of war to the American people, Wilson himself attempted to "preserve. . . humanitarian feelings by couching the entry into the war, and the later peace negotiations, in the language and rhetoric of the progressive movement."[67] Yet, as Richard Hofstadter noted, by associating the war with progressive rhetoric and progressive values, Wilson "unintentionally insur[ed] that the reaction against Progressivism would be intense."[68] By uniting the reality of war and the necessary martial spirit for warring with progressivism, "the American people [came to] repudiate progressivism."[69] Thus, for social studies, rather than being celebrated as a balanced approach to confronting the twin paradoxes, initially the 1916 report became a casualty, because of its association with progressive ideology.

The point, however, is not to debate American government policy during wartime, but to note that the type of academic freedom necessary to nourish an open forum–style course was leveled by 1917. Simply put, the war created a "war hysteria" in the United States that made objective and impartial analysis and discussion of war issues inside or outside the classroom impossible.[70] Clearly, the freedom to hold certain opinions or to speak out on issues was literally absent in public schools. On fear of dismissal or worse, a jail sentence, teachers either avoided war issues altogether or, more likely, strictly followed accepted policy and accepted official war information.[71]

Remarkably, among the first to enlist in the war effort were academic historians.[72] Historian James Shotwell of Columbia University, at the request of the Carnegie Endowment for International Peace, that saw the war against Germany as "an opportunity to reconstruct the international organization of the world,"[73] organized the National Board for Historical Service by resolution of the American Historical Association on April 29, 1917. In addition to the connection to the Carnegie group[74] and the AHA, the Board also worked in close cooperation with the Committee on Public Information and the Bureau of Education. The Board, acting in a "semiofficial" advisory position, came to represent some three thousand historians by 1918. Board membership included Shotwell, who was named chair, and several leading historian-educators such as Henry Johnson, Frederick Jackson Turner, James Schafer, and William Lingelbach, among others.[75]

The mission of the board was to "prepare," for public schools, "literature" that supported and justified American war efforts. Clearly, one "truth" had been decided upon at the outset: German leadership and its militaristic philosophy were responsible for the Great War.[76] The task of the historians was to confirm this assertion, which they did with conviction.

Henry Johnson summed up the historians' position on history in schools:

> The traditional and conventional attitude toward history as a school study has been accentuated and illustrated anew under the pressure of war. We must, as all of us know, win the war. To that supreme purpose every other consideration must be subordinated. Personal convictions, personal emotions, even the love for truth, must blend in one harmonious, overpowering, stern will to victory. What can not be blended must for the moment be ended. Inevitable, therefore, the question uppermost in the minds of thousands of history teachers to-day, and in the other thousands who are not history teachers, is, "What can I do for victory?"[77]

Statements such as "we must win the war," "other considerations must be subordinated," and "even the love for truth, must blend in one harmonious, overpowering, stern will to victory," worked to cast doubt upon impartial and open debate. In the classroom their could be no truth with the German side of the story. For example, historians were quick to document that the root of German brutality could be found in the past, such as Clausewitz's "War is an act of violence pushed to its utmost bounds,"[78] while ignoring Sherman's famous remark that was used to justify his soldiers' brutality, "War is war."[79] In like manner, paradoxically, Wilson, together with many Americans, proudly proclaimed America's strongly willed impartial neutrality, but openly displayed pro-Allied sentiments and actions.[80]

Johnson and the Board's principal "avenue of expression" to school teachers was no less than Albert McKinley's *The History Teacher's Magazine* and his publishing firm. The same publication had been the open forum of debate between the traditional historians and the social studies insurgents since 1909. Incidently, as war neared, responses to the 1916 Social Studies report (published in the magazine three months *before* the American declaration of war on April 6, 1917), as well as the continuing debate between historians and insurgents, promised by the editors of *The History Teachers' Magazine*, never materialized. Instead, the war led the magazine's editors, together with the historians, to close ranks and shut out the insurgents.[81]

One explanation for this action could have been the antihistory tenor of the 1916 report and that history study was then needed to support the war effort. Speculation aside, the fact remains that none of the principal authors of the 1916 social studies, except James Lynn Barnard,[82] were able to publish any articles for the magazine relating to the social studies between 1917 and 1919. At any rate, by design or circumstance, the war effectively silenced the insurgents. Even in the report itself, despite being prepared and disseminated during the war, only one vague reference was made regarding the world war through an exercise on the question of neutrality in the War of 1812.[83] Although current problems were an important aspect of the report, the 1916 document virtually remained silent on one of the most critical issues of the day: the Great War and related war concerns and issues.

While the intent of this book was to conclude with the 1916 report, some explanation is warranted as to why the suggestions of 1916 report, in particular, the Problems of Democracy course, never realized the potential inherent in their design. As the late Lawrence Metcalf's response to the question "Whatever happened to the Social Studies?" explains, "social studies did not fail, it was never tried."[84] The context of Metcalf's statement, that reflected the intention of the 1916 insurgents, referred to the failure of "social studies" teachers to use experimentation, honest reflection, and persistent and unvarnished examination of social, cultural, economic, religious, or political issues with students.[85] With the steady outpour of anti-German articles, written by or through the National Board for Historical Service, and with the backing of popular opinion for the Allied cause, open dialogue on such issues as neutrality, imperialism, propaganda, war atrocities, and war guilt was impossible to treat in schools.[86]

Moreover, by 1918, the National Education Association, too, seemingly turned its back on the 1916 Committee report by asking the National Board, then under the sponsorship of the American Historical Association, to reexamine the public school curriculum. The Board then organized the Committee on History and Education for Citizenship, naming one of its own members as chair (James Schafer). Henry Johnson also served on this committee. None of the leaders of the 1916 Social Studies Committee took an active leadership role in the National Board for Historical Service, nor any of its related agencies. Henry Johnson, by contrast, was an original member of the Board and prepared the "general scheme," according to Harold Rugg, of the Committee on History and Education for Citizenship report.[87]

In addition to the action of historians, universities, too, were enlisted or drafted into the war effort. For example, Columbia University faculty, which had spawned many of the social studies leaders and was a principal forum of progressive educational ideas only a few years before, was forced to turn against open debate when President Nicholas Butler called for all professors to support the war without question, or face dismissal.[88] Butler warned the Columbia faculty:

> I say with all possible emphasis, that there is and will be no place in Columbia University for any person who opposes or counsels opposition to the effective enforcements of the laws of the United States, or who acts, speaks, or writes treason. The separation of any such person from Columbia University will be speedy as the discovery of his offense. This is the last warning to any among us who are not with whole heart and mind and strength committed to fight with us to make the world safe for democracy.[89]

War hysteria and such tactics as Butler's warning ended by 1920. The damage done to social studies, however, was not so easily overcome.[90] In fact, the argument could be made that the war helped historians maintain some degree of curricular control through the potent appeal of patriotism; history could explain why America had to assist the Allies to defeat Germany. Without question the war emphasized and increased the study of history in schools, and this condition helped the traditional historians' case. On the other hand, the war worked to dismantle traditional history's key concept, "historical continuity," by highlighting the need for the study of modern history. This rendered ancient and medieval history, the foundational rock of the Committee of Seven's four-block system, expendable. This condition served to confirm one of the key concepts of social studies, "the present should be the focus of social studies." Although the war both helped and hurt the case for traditional history, the effect on the emerging social studies was more pronounced. Ultimately, schools vacillated between these positions and curricular chaos was the end result.

For example, following the war, the Committee on History and Education for Citizenship struggled to have its report accepted. AHA historians opposed it, most likely because it strayed too far from the earlier Committee of Seven historical philosophy. On the other hand, NEA advocates rejected the recommendations for grades seven, eight, and nine. In the end, the sponsoring AHA failed to adopt the committee resolutions. Harold and Earle Rugg argued that the "ineffective work" of the committee was another example of a group of individuals dictating curriculum. What was needed to bring order to the curricular chaos, claimed the Ruggs, was a new scientifically based organization composed of subject-field and curriculum specialists.[91] This union of specialists would then prepare a "scientific program [in social studies]." The organization that developed from the Ruggs' suggestion was the National Council for the Social Studies.[92]

Epilogue

In summary, it is important to highlight that new interests were being served by the 1916 Committee's adoption of a fresh line of philosophy. Ostensibly, through its rhetoric, the major concern of the committee was to prepare and present a program to expedite social efficiency in an era where educators were taken in and consumed with the "cult of efficiency."[93] In this regard, the 1916 Social Studies Committee membership was no exception. They envisioned their curriculum as an integral part and major step toward the development of a viable progressive education program for secondary schools. However, in Deweyan terms, the social studies prototype was an experiment, especially the Problems of Democracy course. In fact, this course, and the philosophy behind it, provided educators with the foundation of experimentation amid conservatism.

In attending to the twin paradoxes, the committee advanced a conservative-acceptance type of curriculum, as reflected in the standard history-civics offerings, as well as a thought and action experimental type of curriculum, as revealed in the Problems of Democracy course. In effect, the necessary elements to treat the paradoxes through education were presented in the 1916 report. Perhaps the most important component of the report was the Problems of Democracy suggestion. This course could be portrayed as analogous to the "elastic cause" of the Constitution, because it outfitted future social studies with a platform from which to adapt to conditions as they arose; a fact that few social studies practitioners have since recognized.

Although the formulators of the 1916 Social Studies saw the need to develop a specialized program for public schools apart from a university approach to subject matter, the intention was not to create a discrete field of study called social studies. Nonetheless, the program of the 1916 Committee led many later educators to the conclusion that social studies should indeed be fashioned into a discrete field of research, inquiry, and teaching.

The Social Studies Committee grounded its own argument for reform in a unique combination, or formulation, of three key variables wherein developmental psychology was represented by the committee's interest in the developing individual, scientific methodology was reflected in their demand for truth and objectivity, and sociology served the needs of a dynamic social structure. As cited in the text of the committee report, as well as the preface of Arthur William Dunn's influential civics text, the major acknowledged source for the assertion that the individual and society are inextricably bound together was Dewey's essay, "Ethical Principles Underlying Education."[94] The committee attempted to address both individual and social concerns. But its members were very clear that the "common interest" or "social aspect" of the social studies program was to take precedence over any individual concern. In attending to the twin paradoxes of education, the committee's socio-psychological-scientific fusion underlined the aim and spirit of the progressive school movement that claimed the good citizen and social efficiency as its ultimate educational goal.

The notions of experimentation and free discussion of social problems were represented in the proposal for community civics and the Problems of American Democracy course, to be guided by reflective thinking. The teaching of traditional values was incorporated in the recommendations for history instruction that emphasized great institutions, great men, and great ideas *selected* from our near and distant past. In addition, the committee encouraged teachers to help their students study the problems of their society (in school, community, state, and nation). However, all instruction was to stem from an interpretation of what the immediate needs and interests as well as social problems suitable for classroom study. Again, teachers were to apply the guiding principle that all needs, interests, and social problems were to be viewed in terms of the collective or common good.

Notwithstanding the acknowledged popularity of traditional history and its familiar four-block program, the committee favored the 6–3–3 system and designed the connected six-year social studies program to match the new formulation of junior and senior high school. In both the junior and senior high schools the study of modern-day life (presentism) and community civics was to occupy the center of the curriculum. History, if it was taught at all, was to be organized not by chronological or narrative methods, but by how well the facts selected met the test of social efficiency.

The committee argued for the introduction of "community civics" and social studies into the secondary curriculum as the best means to promote good citizenship and to effect social efficiency. To accomplish these goals, the committee found it necessary to displace one or more of the more established subjects in the curriculum. Believing that traditional history had become obsolete and had failed to meet the present needs and interests of students, the committee launched its attack. The basis of this attack centered on the belief that although facts from the past may indeed serve the present, only those facts that directly serve the present needs and interests of students were required in secondary school curricula. Facts from the distant past were to be discarded if they failed to meet this test. Ancient, Medieval, and English Histories, as well as the intellectually oriented psychology that supported them, did not fair well by this criterion; it was "their slots" in the curriculum that were usurped by social studies.

———————

As this chapter on the history of social studies closes, the question of origins remains somewhat inconclusive and tentative. Did social studies come into existence as a curricular subject through the efforts of the 1916 Committee alone, much like a "big bang"? Or did the social studies begin merely as a natural evolutionary reaction to social, political, and economic conditions of the turn of the century? Or, as a third position, was the development of social studies a result of serious philosophical differences between historians and the new social advocates? The answer revealed in this book does not maintain any single one of these positions; rather, this work supports all three assertions.

Clearly many educators, both from history and social studies backgrounds, recognized the curricular chaos that existed in the period. That social studies insurgents attempted to activate a new model, given the prevailing conditions, should not be surprising. In the 1890s historians, too, acted to standardize what amounted to curricular chaos with school history. The chaos of the early 1910s was created by increasing numbers of diverse students as well as a host of other political, social, cultural, and economic issues; some left unattended, some newly created. The need to bring management to the chaos was apparent to these new insurgents. As professionalization of education grew, so did the new education of which social studies was a part. In the end, the battle for social studies during the 1910s embodied this new professional spirit.

Although rhetoric was used to persuade educators to turn from traditional history to social studies symbolically, many schools remained solidly behind history while others vacillated between both. Though briefly, historians during the Great War had succeeded in standardizing-maintaining the history curriculum. Following the war, the old, submerged curricular chaos returned. Again, educators sought to reform education. As social studies, through the efforts of the NCSS and later the AHA, became established in theoretical circles during the 1920s and 30s, the battle continued between traditionalists and insurgents.

As a footnote, although still a "working committee" of the Commission of the Reorganization of Secondary Schools, the committee met formally only once after 1916 (Cleveland, February 24, 1920) to "consider the desirability of supplementing or revising its original report [1916]," and consequently did not produce any further reports.[95] Nonetheless, a subcommittee "to undertake such revision of the details of the 1916 report as suggested by the trend of events since it was published, and to submit a revision or a supplement to the original report" was appointed at the Cleveland meeting.[96]

In the period between the release of the 1916 report and this meeting, seven of the original twenty-one members of the committee resigned or simply left, and eleven new members were appointed, six being appointed to the special ten-member revision subcommittee. Among the notable new faces appointed to the NEA Social Studies Committee were J. Montgomery Gambrill (Columbia University and chair of the revision subcommittee), Edgar Dawson (Hunter College), Ross L. Finney (University of Minnesota), Daniel C. Knowlton (Columbia University), Albert E. McKinley (University of Pennsylvania and editor and publisher of *The Historical Outlook*, formerly *The History Teacher's Magazine*), and Harold Rugg (Columbia University).

Despite the formation of the subcommittee, Gambrill apparently took on the revision investigation by himself and reported his findings through the pages of *The Historical Outlook* with a grant from the Commonwealth Fund under the auspices of the newly formed National Council for the Social Studies.[97] Although not on the revision subcommittee, Edgar Dawson, too, completed an examination of the social studies for the American Historical Association (*The History Inquiry*).[98] These investigations worked to put social studies in perspective for educators by measuring and documenting the growth of the field's infancy.

The individuals who developed social studies conceptions as found in the 1916 Social Studies Committee report deserve the attention of those currently interested in studying the foundations of the field. It was, however, the men who worked at the "revision" of the social studies and led the social studies movement into the 1930s and beyond, Rugg in particular of the above group, that our latter-day historians of the field have identified as the "old masters" and "founders" of social studies.[99] Indeed the "Old Masters" contributed much to social studies, yet their noteworthy accomplishments would not have been what they were had they not stood on the proverbial shoulders of those who forged the first social efficiency prototype.

Thomas Jesse Jones, Arthur William Dunn, James Lynn Barnard, James Harvey Robinson, and Clarence Kingsley, whose greatest accomplishment, in terms of social education, was the prudent selection of these men, were the most influential members of the social efficiency prototype team that produced the inaugural social studies program. These men, together with the contributions of such other notable individuals as William Mace, John Dewey, and David Snedden, were responsible for the preparation and presentation of the argument that led to the introduction of social studies in America's secondary schools.

Ironically these educators sought to enact their social studies program within the traditional history classroom, which they were attempting to supplant, using traditional history instructors. In another sense, it was also ironic that the teachers called upon to instil democratic values and principles, that included voting rights, were themselves deprived of universal suffrage. Despite the serious nature of these ironies and their implications for education, the social studies prototype survived its first challenge from the status quo traditional historians and managed to gain a foothold in the public schools.

The developers of the 1916 social studies prototype gave expression and emphasis to many issues raised by social reformers since the mid-1850s. After 1916 the prospects and progress of the social studies program, outlined by the conferees without full specifics, was handed over to a different, more committed group of educators in the late 1910s and 20s. These later social studies theorists, such as Harold and Earle Rugg, Bessie Louise Pierce, Rolla Tryon, Paul Hanna, Hilda Taba, Howard Wilson, and others, took the 1916 Committee's rough conceptualization of social studies and began to focus and fashion a more specialized social studies.

Although a history of these and later social studies theorists, as well as social studies curricula in general to the present, does not exist in a single volume,[100] a record of their individual and collective effort and achievement is available. When interest in the historical foundations of social studies grows, and indeed it has grown enormously over the past decade, additional chapters of the history of social studies will be prepared. As each of these future histories account for and clarify social studies, the social studies enterprise will move closer to full status as a profession. This account and analysis of the beginnings of social studies will, I hope, be merely one of many historical works that shed light upon the work of social studies practitioners, as well as highlight the importance of the attempt to reconcile the twin paradoxes of liberal democratic education.

APPENDIX

Throughout the twentieth century, on those rare occasions when the beginnings of social studies are discussed, the 1916 report of the Committee on Social Studies is mentioned as the originator of the concept of social studies. This book has labored to shed light upon the work of that committee, as well to account for much of the trail that led to this report. The 1916 report, however, has not been available to the general reader of social studies for more than seventy-five years. As discussed in the Preface of this book, knowing the history of social studies is an important part of the professional equipment for social studies practitioners and researchers. Given this qualification, that is, because they are central to the field's early history, selected contents of the three published works of the Committee on Social Studies are reproduced here ("Statement of the Chairman of the Committee on Social Studies," 1913; *The Teaching of Community Civics*, 1915; and *The Social Studies in Secondary Education*, 1916). Hopefully, the text of this book together with these original documents, will spark (or renew) new interest in social studies and lead to a better understanding of teaching social studies in schools.

STATEMENT OF CHAIRMAN OF THE COMMITTEE ON SOCIAL STUDIES.[1]

THE POINT OF VIEW.

It is probable that the high-school teachers of social studies have the best opportunity ever offered to any social group to improve the

---

[1] The term "social studies" is used to include history, civics, and economics.

citizenship of the land. This sweeping claim is based upon the fact that the million and a third high-school pupils is probably the largest group of persons in the world who can be directed to a serious and systematic effort, both through study and practice, to acquire the social spirit.

Good citizenship should be the aim of social studies in the high school. While the administration and instruction throughout the school should contribute to the social welfare of the community, it is maintained that social studies have direct responsibility in this field. Facts, conditions, theories, and activities that do not contribute rather directly to the appreciation of methods of human betterment have no claim. Under this test the old civics, almost exclusively a study of Government machinery, must give way to the new civics, a study of all manner of social efforts to improve mankind. It is not so important that the pupil know how the President is elected as that he shall understand the duties of the health officer in his community. The time formerly spent in the effort to understand the process of passing a law over the President's veto is now to be more profitably used in the observation of the vocational resources of the community. In line with this emphasis the committee recommends that social studies in the high school shall include such topics as the following: Community health, housing and homes, public recreation, good roads, community education, poverty and the care of the poor, crime and reform, family income, savings banks and life insurance, human rights versus property rights, impulsive action of mobs, the selfish conservatism of tradition, and public utilities.

Long as the foregoing list is, it is quite apparent that many more vital topics could be added. It is therefore important to understand that it is not the purpose to give the pupil an exhaustive knowledge of any one of these subjects, but rather to give him a clue to the significance of these matters to him and to his community, and to arouse in him a desire to know more about his environment. It is to help him to think "civically" and, if possible, to live "civically." Teacher and pupil must realize that they are studying living things. They must not be content with the printed page. Everything and everybody in the community must be drafted into the service of the boy and girl striving to become an effective part of the "body politic" and a constructive member of the social group. Companions in the schoolroom and on the playgrounds, workers in philanthropy and reform, Government officials and business leaders, voters and laborers of every class are all material for the classroom and laboratory in social studies.

History, too, must answer the test of good citizenship. The old chronicler who recorded the deeds of kings and warriors and neglected the labors of the common man is dead. The great palaces and cathedrals and pyramids are often but the empty shells of a parasitic growth on the working group. The elaborate descriptions of these old tombs are but sounding brass and tinkling cymbals compared to the record of the joy and sorrows, the hopes and disappointments of the masses, who are infinitely more important than any arrangement of wood and stone and iron. In this spirit recent history is more important than that of ancient times; the history of our own country than that of foreign lands; the record of our own institutions and activities than that of strangers; the labors and plans of the multitudes than the pleasures and dreams of the few.

In order that the aim described above shall be realized, the committee proposes to outline the five following units of social studies:

(1) Community civics and survey of vocations.

(2) European history to 1600 or 1700 (including English and colonial American history).

(3) European history since 1600 or 1700 (including contemporary civilization).

(4) United States history since 1760 (including current events).

(5) Economics and civic theory and practice.

COMMUNITY CIVICS.

The term "civics" is used here to include all the possible activities of the good citizen, whether as an individual or with private organizations or with government. Community civics is intended to acquaint pupils with the civic condition of their own community. Pupils visit in person and study at close range the vital elements of their city, village, or rural area. Personal visitation and first-hand information is a distinctive feature of the course. It insures the reality and simplicity necessary to a vital knowledge of social forces. It tends to dignify those forces and those places which the pupil usually despises because they are familiar. Finally, knowledge of the neighborhood will show the pupil how an effective education will make him a productive citizen.

It is the belief of the committee that such a course should be offered to the pupil as early as his powers of appreciation allow. The advantages of early acquaintance with the civic conditions are: First, that the larger number of pupils in the lower grades would be reached; and, second, that many pupils realizing the value of education would remain longer in school.

The subject matter of community civics will vary with the community in which the school is located. Communities differ almost as much as individuals. There are the large cities, the villages, and the open country. They differ also as to the characteristics and occupations of the people. It is the hope of the committee to prepare outlines for each of the main types of communities, certainly for rural and urban. The topics given below are merely suggestive.

An explanation of the value of "community health" as one of the topics for this introductory course will make clear the various elements to be considered in selecting topics. The value of a topic for this course depends upon its intrinsic importance to the pupil as a citizen or potential citizen; upon the possibility of presenting it to the boy or girl mind; upon the attitude of the community toward the subject, such as sensitiveness to the discussion of unfavorable conditions; and upon its relation to other studies. There is probably no subject which so well meets all of these requirements as community health. Certainly there is no other topic of more immediate interest to everyone. Health can be made so concrete that even a child can understand much about it. While the community may be sensitive about certain conditions, it is possible to present the facts so definitely as not to injure the teacher's influence. Community health and civic biology when taught in the same school seem to overlap, and yet with the cooperation of the teachers one course should help the other. Civic biology goes to the health department and observes the microscopic analysis of sputum and the multiplication of bacteria in milk. Community health considers the economic loss caused by deaths from impure milk. Civic biology explains what is meant by "death from preventable causes"; community health shows the scandalous carelessness of a social system that permits 650,000 deaths from preventable causes every year in the United States, and then points out civic remedies.

HISTORY.

The committee is now prepared to submit only two provisional suggestions on history, namely, first, the conception of history according to which pupils should be instructed; and second, the division of the field of history into three unit courses. This conception of history is so well stated by Prof. James Harvey Robinson, a member of this committee, that we quote from his article in the Proceedings of the American Philosophical Society, May–June, 1911.

The older traditional type of historical writing was narrative in character. Its chief aim was to tell a tale or story by setting forth a succession of events and introducing the prominent actors who participated in them. It was a branch of polite literature, competing with the drama and fiction, from which, indeed, it differed often only in the limitations which the writer was supposed to place upon his fancy.

In order to appreciate the arbitrary nature of the selection of historic facts offered in these standard textbooks and treatises, let us suppose that a half dozen alert and well-trained minds had never happened to be biased by the study of any outline of history and had, by some happy and incredible fortune, never perused a "standard" historical work. Let us suppose that they had nevertheless learned a good deal about the past of mankind directly from the vast range of sources that we now possess, both literary and archae-ological. Lastly, let us assume that they were all called upon to prepare independently a so-called general history, suitable for use in the higher schools. They would speedily discover that there was no single obvious rule for determining what should be included in their review of the past. Having no tradition to guide them, each would select what he deemed most impor-tant for the young to know of the past. Writing in the twentieth century, they would all be deeply influenced by the interests and problems of the day. Battles and sieges and the courts of kings would scarcely appeal to them. Probably it would occur to none of them to mention the battle of Issus, the Samnite wars, the siege of Numantia by the Romans, the advent of Hadrian, the Italian enterprises of Otto I, the six wives of Henry VIII, or the invasion of Holland by Louis XIV. It is tolerably safe to assume that none of these events, which are recorded in practically all of our manuals to-day, would be considered by any one of our writers as he thought over all that men had done, and thought, and suffered, and dreamed through thousands of years. All of them would agree that what men had known of the world in which they lived, or had thought to be their duty, or what they made with their hands, or the nature and style of their buildings, public and private, would any of them be far more valuable to rehearse than the names of their rulers and the conflicts in which they engaged. Each writer would accordingly go his own way. He would look back on the past for explanations of what he found most interesting in the present and would endeavor to place his readers in a position to participate intelligently in the life of their own time. The six manuals, when completed, would not only differ greatly from one another, but would have little resemblance to the *fable convenue* which is currently accepted as embodying the elements of history.

Obviously history must be rewritten, or, rather, innumerable current is-sues must be given their neglected historic background. Our present so-called histories do not ordinarily answer the questions we would naturally and insistently to them. When we contemplate the strong demand that women are making the right to vote we ask ourselves, "How did the men win the vote?" The historians we consult have scarcely asked themselves that question, and so do answer it. We ask, "How did our courts come to control legislation in the exceptional and extraordinary manner they do?" We look in vain in most histories for a reply. No one questions the inalien-able right of the historian to interest himself in any phase of the past that he chooses. It is only to be wished that a greater number of historians had greater skill in hitting upon those phases of the past which serve us best in understanding the most vital problems of the present.

The three unit courses in history that the committee intends to outline are as follows:

(1) European history to 1600 or 1700 (including English history and colonial American history).

(2) European history since 1600 or 1700 (including contemporary civilizations).

(3) United States history since 1760 (including current events).

The best method of abbreviating the work in history to two units, when such abbreviation is necessary, is still an open question.

The plan of the committee is to refer each period to some historian who has given evidence of "skill in hitting upon those phases of the past which serve us best in understanding the most vital problems of the present," with the request that he give us a statement of such phases as are useful to the high-school boy and girl. This material will then be assembled, reviewed, and referred to high-school teachers of history for trial.

In comparison with community civics, this course stresses the formal elements of civic thought. One of the main purposes here is to help the pupil determine the mutual relation of the forces and events which he has been observing and studying throughout his school days.

Frequent use will be made of well-written reports published by public and private organizations on such topics as sanitation, housing, pure food, child labor, recreation, and social education. Emphasis on the formal study must not be permitted to crowd out the observation of actual conditions nor such experience in social service as the time will permit.

The following tentative outline is offered only as indicating the points of emphasis. It is given also in response to demands for immediate aid by teachers who desire to reorganize their work in civics.

I. Government and public welfare.

Fully two-thirds of the time should be devoted to this topic. Here the pupil studies those activities of the Government which influence his life more frequently than those ordinarily classified under the next topic—Government machinery. Here he learns how broad is the work of the Government and how intimately it influences the life of the individual. The real meaning of government dawns upon the pupil when he learns of the roads, of the weather, of mineral resources, of labor and commercial conditions, and of many other things too numerous to mention. Nongovernmental organizations engaged in work for social improvement should be discussed in connection with the governmental functions to which their efforts are most closely related.

The following topics are suggested: (1) Health and sanitation: Housing, pure food and milk, sewerage, waste disposal, contagious diseases, statistics, medical inspection of school children, health crusades. (2) Education. (3) Recreation. (4) Charities. (5) Correction, juvenile courts, reform schools, etc. (6) Public utilities: Transportation, light, telephone, telegraph, postal system, water, etc. (7) City planning: Sanitation and beauty.

II. Government machinery.

Local, State, National; legislative, executive, judicial; courts and legal processes; election and political activities, including such topics as initiative and referendum.

III. The development of government.

Social psychology, democracy, the family, and other social organizations.

THOMAS JESSE JONES,
Chairman.

UNITED STATES BUREAU OF EDUCATION,
Washington, D.C.

THE TEACHING OF COMMUNITY CIVICS.

PART I.
AIMS AND METHODS IN TEACHING COMMUNITY CIVICS.

I. WHO IS THE GOOD CITIZEN?

The good citizen may be defined as a person who habitually conducts himself with proper regard for the welfare of the communities of which he is a member, and who is active and intelligent in his cooperation with his fellow members to that end.

The welfare both of the individual and of the community depends upon various factors, such as health, education, recreation, civic beauty, wealth, communication, transportation. In order to secure these *elements of welfare* the individual and the community are dependent upon many *social agencies,* such as pure-food laws, schools, playgrounds, parks, factories, post offices, railroads. The usefulness of such social agencies depends upon the intelligence and readiness with which the members of the community establish, direct, and cooperate with them. They may be classified as governmental or voluntary according to the nature of their support.

It is evident, therefore, that the good citizen will possess an abiding interest in the welfare of the community, a working knowledge of social agencies, and good judgment as to those means and methods that will promote one social end without at the same time defeating other social ends. Furthermore, he must have the point of view that progress is essential in order that he may do as well by civilization as did his fathers before him. Every community also needs citizens who possess a large measure of social initiative and the power of leadership.

II. STAGES IN DEVELOPING GOOD CITIZENSHIP.

Training for good citizenship must begin even before the child enters school and must continue through school, and indeed through life. Four stages in the process are well marked.

1. Before the child enters school he receives from the family life itself his first impressions of cooperation and responsibility. Whether these impressions and the social habits inculcated shall be for good or for ill depends upon the atmosphere and efforts of the home. Home education is thus the first factor in the development of good citizenship.

2. Between the ages of 6 and 12 the child enters the larger community, the school. The establishment of right social relations by and within the school is now of prime importance. Moreover, the school should consciously interpret to the child the community nature of the home, for the teacher can speak as an interested outsider regarding the relation of the child to the parent. The school should also lead him to see how the grocer, the iceman, the policeman, the postman, and many others in the larger community outside of the home and the school enter into his life and contribute to his welfare and the welfare of others. Civic education at this stage need not consider the organized agencies through which men cooperate, but the pupils must become more and more conscious of the interdependence of individuals in the community. Through the study of appropriate literature and through acquaintances with noble characters of history he should form ideals of loyalty and of personal honor and integrity.

3. Between the ages of 12 and 15, the early adolescent period, the outside community enters more largely into the pupil's experience, and it should be interpreted to him in terms of wider human relationship. Accordingly, the civic education of the youth should include elementary history, community civics, and some study or survey of typical vocations.

Community civics should be taught during this period in the child's life, so that when the psychological changes of adolescence occur there shall have been laid a basis for turning the social instinct displayed in the gang spirit of boys and in the groping sentimentality of girls into useful channels of *social feeling, social thought,* and *social action.* In this course the civic grasp of the pupil should be strengthened by helping him to compare the conditions in his own community with those in other communities, and the conditions in his own time with those of other times. Moreover, this habit of comparing social conditions will be almost indispensable to the pupil when he comes to the history that should follow, because the new type of history is placing its emphasis on such comparisons.

The study of vocations here suggested should be taught during this period not merely to help the pupil choose his vocation intelligently, when the time comes to make such choice; but it should be so taught as to make it perfectly clear to the pupil that each citizen in his choice of vocation, in his preparation for it, and especially in the way in which he conducts himself after he has entered upon it, shows the quality of his citizenship. This study should also give the pupil a respect and an appreciation for many vocations and should thus develop a better understanding between citizens of diverse callings, including a better understanding between capital and labor.

4. Between the ages of 15 and 18, the civic education of the third period should be continued by means of courses in history and elementary economics, culminating in an advanced course in civics.

Not civics alone, but the entire group of social studies—civics, history, and economics—should have for its immediate aim the training of the good citizen. It should still further be recognized that the work of the public school in training for citizenship is not limited even to the social studies, but involves a socialized point of view for all instruction and for all school management and discipline. With this recognition of the problem of civic education in all its breadth, this bulletin is designed to give help in one phase of the subject only, namely, community civics.

III. WHAT IS COMMUNITY CIVICS?

The social study to which the name "community civics" has been applied is well defined or described in Civic Education Circular No. 1, issued by the United States Bureau of Education:

The aim of community civics is to help the child to know his community—not merely a lot of facts about it, but the meaning of his community life, what it does for him and how it does it, what the community has a right to expect from him, and how he may fulfill his obligation, meanwhile cultivating in him the essential qualities and habits of good citizenship.

Community civics lays emphasis upon the local community because (1) it is the community with which every citizen, especially the child, comes into most intimate relations, and which is always in the foreground of experience; (2) it is easier for the child, as for any citizen, to realize his membership in the local community, to feel a sense of personal responsibility for it, and to enter into actual cooperation with it, than is the case with the national community.

But our Nation and our State are communities, as well as our city or village, and a child is a citizen of the larger as of the smaller community. The significance of the term "community civics" does not lie in its geographical implications, but in its implication of community relations, of a community of interests. * * * It is a question of point of view; and community civics applies this point of view to the study of the national community as well as to the study of the local community.

IV. PLACE OF COMMUNITY CIVICS IN THE SCHOOL PROGRAM.

Community civics should be taught in the elementary grades, and should be continued in a more comprehensive course in the first year of the high school. Many pupils do not enter high school at all; and those who do should already have begun to acquire habits of civic thought and action. Experience proves that pupils who have had such training in the elementary schools are the better prepared for their high-school work, especially in the field of social studies. They are also the better prepared for the transition to the larger freedom and responsibility of the high school. But civic training must be a continuous process, and the greater maturity of the high-school pupil makes possible the development of phases of the subject that are impracticable in the elementary school.

It is suggested that five periods per week be devoted to community civics through the entire freshman year, although a part of the year may well be used for a survey of vocations whenever the teachers are prepared. (See p. 10.)

The methods and subject matter suggested in this bulletin are adapted both to the seventh and eighth grades of the elementary school and to the freshman year of the high school; but the scope of the elementary and high-school courses, when both are given, should be agreed upon by teachers and local school authorities to avoid duplication. It may be found desirable, however, for the high-school class to study from a new angle some of the topics considered in the elementary school.

V. SPECIFIC AIMS OF COMMUNITY CIVICS.

To accomplish its part in the training for citizenship, community civics should aim primarily to lead the pupil:

1. *To see the importance and significance of the elements of com-*

munity welfare (see below and p. 1) in their relations to himself and to the communities of which he is a member;

2. *To know the social agencies*, governmental and voluntary, that exist to secure these elements of community welfare;

3. *To recognize his civic obligation, present and future*, and to respond to them by appropriate action.

These three aims are given in the above order because it is essential to the success of this course that at the outset the interest of the pupil be attached to the elements of common welfare, and that he be taught to think of each agency as a means to an end and not as an end in itself. Each part of the study should culminate in a recognition of personal responsibility as a good citizen, and, as far as possible, in appropriate action.

Many courses in civics fail because they fix attention upon the machinery of government rather than upon the elements of community welfare for which government exists; that is, they familiarize the pupil with the manipulation of the social machinery without showing him the importance of the social ends for which this machinery should be used. Consequently, the pupil, upon leaving school, uses his knowledge for ends which are most evident to him, namely, his own selfish interests.

VI. ELEMENTS OF WELFARE SUGGESTED AS TOPICS.

For the purpose of this course in community civics it is suggested that the following elements of welfare be studied as topics: (1) Health; (2) Protection of life and property; (3) Recreation; (4) Education; (5) Civic beauty; (6) Wealth; (7) Communication; (8) Transportation; (9) Migration; (10) Charities; (11) Correction.

The attempt has been made to arrange these elements of welfare in an order that seems suitable for teaching rather than in the order in which the sociologist would think of them. But each teacher should exercise judgment in adapting the order to the needs and current interests of the class.

In addition, the course may well include the following topics dealing with the mechanism of community agencies:

(12) How governmental agencies are conducted.

(13) How governmental agencies are financed.

(14) How voluntary agencies are conducted and financed.

VII. METHOD OF TEACHING COMMUNITY CIVICS.

(A) SOCIAL FACTS UPON WHICH THE METHOD SHOULD BE BASED.

1. The pupil is a young citizen with real present interests at stake. He is dependent upon the community for his education, which will

largely determine his ability to earn a livelihood and to enjoy both his work and his leisure. He is dependent upon the community for recreation; for the protection of health, life, and property; for the beauty of his surroundings; for the ease with which he may communicate with his friends.

It is the first task of the teacher, therefore, not to *create* an interest for future use, but to demonstrate *existing* interests and present citizenship.

2. The pupil as a young citizen is a real factor in community affairs. His cooperation in many phases of community life is quite as important as that of the adult. He may help in forming public opinion, not only among his mates, but in the home and in the community at large.

Therefore it is a task of the teacher to cultivate in the pupil a sense of his responsibility, present as well as future.

3. If a citizen has an interest in civic matters and a sense of his personal responsibility, he will want to act.

Therefore the teacher must help the pupil to express his convictions in word and deed. He must be given an opportunity, as far as possible, to *live* his civics both in the school and in the community outside.

4. Right action depends not only upon information, interest, and will, but also upon good judgment.

Hence the young citizen must be trained to weigh facts and to judge relative values, both in regard to what constitute the essential elements in a situation and in regard to the best means of meeting it.

5. Every citizen possesses a large amount of unorganized information regarding community affairs. The amount of such information possessed collectively by an ordinary class of wide-awake young citizens 12 to 15 years of age is surprisingly large. But it is fragmentary, often erroneous, and usually unorganized.

It is, therefore, important to teach the pupils how to test and organize their knowledge regarding community affairs.

6. People are, as a rule, most ready to act upon those convictions that they have helped to form by their own mental processes and that are based upon their own experience and observation.

Hence the teacher should act as a guide and should lead the class:

(1) To contribute facts from their own experience,

(2) To contribute other facts gathered by themselves,

(3) To use their own reasoning powers in forming conclusions, and

(4) To submit these conclusions to criticism.

7. The class has the essential characteristics of a community.

Therefore the method by which the class exercises are conducted is of the utmost importance in the cultivation of civic qualities and habits. Cooperation in contributing information; the give-and-take of class discussion; regard for the contributions and opinions of others; personal responsibility for the class welfare; the attitude of the teacher as a fellow citizen with the pupils, and a learner along with them; all of these help to cultivate interest, judgment, initiative, cooperation, power to organize knowledge, and other qualities of good citizenship. In short, the class should exemplify the right community spirit.

(B) THREE STEPS IN TEACHING AN ELEMENT OF WELFARE WHEN TAKEN AS A TOPIC.

The study of each topic of this kind should consist of the following steps:

1. Approach to the topic.

2. Investigation of agencies by which the element of welfare is secured.

3. Recognition of responsibility, present and future, with respect to the topic under consideration.

(1) *Approach to the topic.*—In beginning the study of an element of welfare the teacher should lead the pupils to realize its importance to themselves, to their neighbors, and to the community, and to see the dependence of the individual upon social agencies.

Much depends upon the method of approach. The planning of an approach appropriate to a given topic and applicable to a given class calls for ingenuity and resourcefulness. In this bulletin the approaches to various topics are suggested by way of illustration, but the teacher should try to find another approach whenever he thinks the one suggested is not the best one for his class.

In the approach it is especially important to draw upon the experience and observation of the class. As facts are contributed, the teacher may summarize them upon the blackboard or use some other device to have the class consciously pool their experiences.

(2) *Investigation of agencies.*—The knowledge of the class should now be extended by a concrete and more or less detailed investigation of agencies such as those suggested in this bulletin. These investigations should consist largely of first-hand observation and study of local conditions.

It is advised that the first agency considered in the course be investigated by the entire class under the direction of the teacher, so as to get a method of work. After that, agencies may be studied sometimes by the class as a whole and sometimes by groups of pupils, the choice of procedure depending on the difficulty of the agency, its importance, and the degree to which the class has secured a social point of view.

The agencies suggested under each topic in the outline are so many that no attempt should be made to have the class as a whole study them all intensively. Such an attempt would result in superficiality, kill interest, and defeat the purpose of the course. In general, the more skillful the teacher, the more will he find that the class can do profitably under any agency. It will often be found advisable to study in detail one or more agencies under a given topic, and then to make a rapid survey of others.

The following considerations will be helpful in selecting the agencies for intensive study.

(a) Agencies of current interest to the community.—A proposed State road, new health regulations in view of a recent epidemic, or a new system of fire protection, may be so prominently in the thought of the community that the class can secure a large amount of material from the newspapers and from the opinions of their parents. This of course would add to the interest and effectiveness of the study.

(b) Agencies of immediate interest to the class.—An athletic field, a new school building, moving-picture shows, school lunches, rules of athletic associations, and boy scouts, may be of immediate interest to the pupils themselves.

(c) Agencies of special interest to the teacher.—The teacher may be so familiar with certain agencies that he can deal with them effectively, but his own knowledge is of importance only so far as it helps him to make the study more profitable to the pupils. In dealing with an agency with which he is not familiar, he should never hesitate to take the role of learner and join with his pupils in the work of investigation.

(d) Significance of the agency.—The agencies studied intensively should always be those that serve to bring out important facts, conditions, or obligations and should never be chosen merely because they are superficially interesting. They should be those that contribute directly and vitally to the element of welfare under which they are discussed.

(3) Recognition of responsibility.—A lesson in community civics is not complete unless it leaves with the pupil a sense of his personal responsibility and results in right action. To attain these ends is perhaps the most difficult and delicate task of the teacher. It is

discussed here as the third step in teaching an element of welfare; in practice, however, it is a process coincident with the first two steps and resulting from them. A proper sense of responsibility can only grow out of a correct perception of one's community relations; and a desire to act, from a realization of vital interest in a situation. If the work suggested in the foregoing paragraphs on "approach" and "investigation of agencies" has been well done, the pupil's sense of responsibility, his desire to act, and his knowledge of how to act will thereby have been developed. Indeed, the extent to which they have been developed is in a measure a test of the effectiveness of the "approach" and the study of agencies.

A distinction should be made between the present and future civic duties of high-school pupils. They have some civic responsibilities now; others await them in adult life. They must be prepared for both. The teacher should be careful to cultivate judgment as to the kinds of things for which pupils should assume responsibility now.

For example, pupils can hardly have any large responsibility for the water supply of their community; but they can help to conserve it by avoiding waste from water taps, and they can help to prevent the spread of disease by using individual drinking cups and by cultivating a sentiment at home against contaminating the sources of water supply (especially if wells or springs are used). It is hardly appropriate for a child to reprove the milkman for carelessness in handling milk; but he may exert influence in securing proper care of milk and milk bottles in the home.

A distinction should be made also between the duties of the *citizen* and the duties of the *official.* The citizen selects the official and should hold him to his task. The citizen must know the purpose to be achieved, the official must find out how to achieve it; the citizen needs a sense of values, the official technical knowledge; the citizen must be a competent employer, the official a competent executive. For example, in a town meeting, the citizen elects officials and votes on appropriations of money. To discharge this duty he must be a judge of the kind of men who will serve faithfully and efficiently and must understand the purposes for which appropriations are asked. But the duty of that citizen does not end with the town meeting. He should insist that these officials make reports that will show what they have accomplished and keep generally informed as to the way in which officials are discharging their duties.

It is important, in relation to either present or future duties, to develop intelligence regarding the proper channels through which to act, and how to go about it. There are cases in which a direct appeal from children to public officials may be entirely proper, as, for example, in regard to the establishment of a playground. But such appeals should be made under proper supervision. The good citizen should be able to write a courteous letter to the public official. Practice in writing such letters should be given to pupils, preferably relating to actual conditions observed by the pupils, or containing practical suggestions by them. Such letters should be discussed and revised by the class and teachers, but should be sent to the official only after approval by the principal or superintendent. Regard for the time of public officials should be cultivated, and no class should be permitted to send a number of letters where one would suffice.

It is sometimes desirable for the class to undertake a special piece of work of direct use to the community. In some places pupils have helped to exterminate insect pests. It is important that the teacher should be careful to set up right motives in work of this sort. Arthur W. Dunn, of the United States Bureau of Education, cites the following case in which wrong motives were set up. He says:

A group of boys who were studying their own community from the standpoint of cleanliness and beauty were "interested" by the offer of a prize to the boys who should bring in the largest number of discarded tin cans. The motive set up was wrong, and uncivic action resulted. Intense rivalry supplanted community cooperation, selfish personal interest took the place of community interest, and some of the boys actually hauled into the city wagonloads of cans from the city's dumps. Good citizenship can only grow out of right motives.

Participation in community affairs requires good judgment as well as right motives. The following lesson, also reported by Mr. Dunn, shows how such judgment was developed in one case:

One morning after a heavy fall of snow the question was raised in a number of civics classes, "What will be the effects of this snowfall upon the life of the community?" It was soon developed that it would interfere with traffic; that it would impede the work of the fire department; that if allowed to melt and freeze it would become dangerous to life and limb, and that if it lay in dirty heaps it would mar the beauty of the city. The snowfall was thus seen in various community relations previously discussed in other aspects. Who cleans the snow from the roadways? This is done for the citizens by the street-cleaning department of the city government. Who cleans the sidewalks? This is not done by the city but is left in the hands of the individual householders. The children observed on their way home how many of the sidewalks were cleaned and reported on the number not cleaned. Were the citizens left to their own discretion in this matter? No; a city ordinance commanded them to clean their sidewalks. Why was it not obeyed? Why was it not enforced? What is the effect of having a law that is not regarded?

The children took the matter to heart. They talked about it at home. They wanted to do something about it. The question arose as to what they could do. Here is where the training of judgment came in. Some wanted to complain to the authorities. It was decided after discussion that mere complaint seldom accomplishes much. Some thought that they could speak personally to offenders. This was decided to be slightly officious and perhaps offensive to older citizens. It was suggested that groups of boys organize to go about their neighborhoods cleaning walks. As a commercial venture this was approved, and in a few cases such groups also cleaned walks before vacant lots as a public service. It was concluded, however, that for boys to go about cleaning other people's walks as a public service when these people should do it themselves was shifting the burden of responsibility in a harmful way. What actually happened was that the boys pretty generally saw to it that their own walks were cleaned, learning the important lesson that in the regular course of one's daily tasks, such as caring for one's own premises, lies an ever-present opportunity for good citizenship; and further, a public sentiment on the subject was created starting in the classrooms, extending into the homes, and spreading through civic organizations and the newspapers, until the householders themselves saw to it after later storms that their walks were cleaned.

In this instance, besides the cultivation of interest and motive in a striking degree, we see a splendid lesson in cooperation; a whole community aroused, largely through the initiative of the children; the children participating, but not being led to assume too much responsibility in the matter; judgment exercised in regard to method of attacking the problem, and finally, "action, which is the end of all good citizenship and of all good teaching."

VIII. APPLICATION OF PRINCIPLES TO CONDUCT.

In the past much civic instruction has been ineffective because it has left the pupil to work out for himself the application of general principles to conduct. The translation of principles into conduct is more difficult than the comprehension of the principles themselves. It is largely a matter of motive, reinforced by judgment and initiative. To cultivate these is the teacher's greatest task. The natural human motive of self-interest should be recognized. It is not only legitimate but in every way desirable to demonstrate the relation of civic conduct to self-interest and to utilize the latter as a channel through which to develop a broad spirit of service. With this in view it may be helpful to analyze the conduct of the citizen:

1. Conduct that has self-interest as an evident end.

Under this head would come, first, care for one's own health, education, and character. But these things are not only necessary to individual success; they are also essential if one is to be useful to the community. They have direct civic bearing. If the citizen impedes the welfare of the community through physical incapacity or lack of education and good character, it follows that he, as a member of the community, will also suffer the consequences of the same defects in others. It is, therefore, to the interest of the citizen to care, not only for his own health, education, and character, but also for those of others. Thus a starting point is afforded for the development of a real sympathy and a real altruism.

Under this head may also be included the citizen's economic or vocational activities, and his care for his property. He works for a living primarily in his own interest; but he also owes it to the community to be self-supporting and to contribute to its economic welfare. Industry, efficiency, and thrift are civic, as well as individual, virtues. The citizen who is himself industrious, efficient, and thrifty can not get the full benefit of these qualities in himself if they are lacking in other members of the community upon whom he has to depend. Thus, again, self-interest may lead to an appreciation of the civic relations of conduct.

2. Conduct that is more evidently social in character and based primarily upon the *interest of others* or upon *a common interest.*

This includes the citizen's activities in cooperation with social agencies, voluntary and governmental. Thus he may become a member of such voluntary agencies as school organizations, boy scouts, consumers' leagues, child-labor committees, boards of trade, labor unions. He may cooperate, as an individual or in association with other individuals, with the health department by reporting contagious diseases; with the street-cleaning department by not littering the street; with teachers and school authorities in the work of the schools; with the charity organization society by not giving aid indiscriminately. Sometimes the citizen's cooperation may take the form of money contributions for the support of social agencies; and again, in proportion to intellectual endowment and force of character, it may take the form of leadership in organizing and directing such agencies.

The citizen also has a responsibility for the support and direction of government, which is the recognized agency of cooperation for the entire community. He not only pays taxes for the support of government, but he also has a voice, directly or indirectly, in determining the amount of money that shall be devoted to the support of each governmental agency. Through public opinion and the use of the franchise he decides what kind of public officers shall occupy governmental positions, and may exert an influence in holding them to the proper performance of their duties.

Finally, the citizen may, on occasion, be called upon to fill positions in government, and thus to direct and guide the affairs of the community as a whole.

The point of emphasis in all this, however, is that while we urge that the citizen should engage in these activities as far as opportunity offers, it is necessary to cultivate a motive sufficiently strong to lead him actually to do so. This motive is to be found in the *common interest*, which includes *his* interest, at least until such times as an ideal altruism may lead to the placing of the interest of others and the community above the interest of self.

THE SOCIAL STUDIES IN SECONDARY SCHOOLS

PREFACE.

The committee issues this report with the conviction that the secondary school teachers of social studies have a remarkable opportunity to improve the citizenship of the land. This conviction is based upon the fact that the million and a third secondary school pupils constitute probably the largest and most impressionable group in the country that can be directed to a serious and systematic effort, through both study and practice, to acquire the social spirit. If the two and a half million pupils of the seventh and eighth grades are included in the secondary group, according to the six-and-six plan, this opportunity will be very greatly increased.

The committee interprets this opportunity as a responsibility which can be realized only by the development in the pupil of a constructive attitude in the consideration of all social conditions. In facing the increasing complexity of society, it is most important that the youth of the land be steadied by an unwavering faith in humanity and by an appreciation of the institutions which have contributed to the advancement of civilization.

The following report is the result of three years of continuous inquiry by the committee whose membership is given on page 6. This committee as a whole has met at various times in each of these years for sessions of one or two days each, subcommittees have met on other occasions, and individual members designated by the committee have given prolonged service and made specific contributions to the general result. It has corresponded widely in search of suggestions and criticisms, and has conferred with many persons not members of the committee in various parts of the country. It has met in conference with representatives of the American Historical Association and the American Political Science Association. In short, the committee has sought for every available source of suggestion, criticism, and contribution of material that would aid it in formulating and explaining its conclusions.

In 1914 a preliminary report was prepared by the chairman of the committee and printed by the Bureau of Education in Bulletin, 1914, No. 41, together with other preliminary reports of the Commission on the Reorganization of Secondary Education. The report as presented herewith was compiled by Arthur William Dunn, who for the past year has been the secretary of the committee. Mr. Dunn's pioneer service and long experience in civic education enabled him to make a very valuable contribution to the deliberations of the committee. His connection with the United States Bureau of Education as Special Agent in Civic Education has also given the committee unusual opportunity to keep in touch with the experience and thought of the entire country. The committee owes much to the cordial cooperation of the Bureau both in the preparation and in the publication of the report.

In 1915 the United States Bureau of Education published a bulletin on "The Teaching of Community Civics" (Bulletin, 1915, No. 23). This bulletin was prepared by J. Lynn Barnard, F. W. Carrier, Arthur W. Dunn, and Clarence D. Kingsley, who were constituted a special committee of the Committee on Social Studies for the purpose. This bulletin, which is referred to in the body of the present report, should be considered, therefore, as an integral part of the Report of the Committee on Social Studies.

The committee is fully conscious that available data derived from actual experience are not adequate for final judgments. It has endeavored at all points to avoid any suggestion of finality. It believes, however, that its report is more than a mere expression of personal opinion, in that the principles that it endeavors to formulate and illustrate are derived from an apparently clear and definite trend in actual practice.

A summary of this report has been approved by the Reviewing Committee of the Commission on the Reorganization of Secondary Education. This approval does not commit every member of the Reviewing Committee individually to every statement and every implied educational doctrine. It does, however, mean essential agreement as a committee with the general recommendations. On the basis of this summary, the Reviewing Committee has authorized the publication of the report by the Bureau of Education as one of the reports of the commission.

THOMAS JESSE JONES,
Chairman Committee on Social Studies.
CLARENCE D. KINGSLEY,
Chairman Reviewing Committee.

THE SOCIAL STUDIES IN SECONDARY EDUCATION.

PART I.—INTRODUCTION.

1. *Definition of the social studies.*—The social studies are understood to be those whose subject matter relates directly to the organization and development of human society, and to man as a member of social groups.

2. *Aims of the social studies.*—The social studies differ from other studies by reason of their social content rather than in social aim; for the keynote of modern education is "social efficiency," and instruction in all subjects should contribute to this end. Yet, from the nature of their content, the social studies afford peculiar opportunities for the training of the individual as a member of society. Whatever their value from the point of view of personal culture, unless they contribute directly to the cultivation of social efficiency on the part of the pupil they fail in their most important function.

More specifically, the social studies of the American high school should have for their conscious and constant purpose the cultivation of good citizenship. We may identify the "good citizen" of a neighborhood with the "thoroughly efficient member" of that neighborhood; but he will be characterized, among other things, by a loyalty and a sense of obligation to his city, State, and Nation as political units. Again, "society" may be interpreted to include the human race. Humanity is bigger than any of its divisions. The social studies should cultivate a sense of membership in the "world community," with all the sympathies and sense of justice that this involves as among the different divisions of human society. The first step, however, toward a true "neighborliness" among nations must be a realization of national ideals, national efficiency, national loyalty, national self-respect, just as real neighborliness among different family groups depends upon the solidarity, the self-respect, and the loyalty to be found within each of the component families.

High national ideals and an intelligent and genuine loyalty to them should thus be a specific aim of the social studies in American high schools.

3. *The point of view of the committee.*—(1) The committee adheres to the view that it was appointed, not to "obtain justice" for a group of social studies as against other groups, or for one social study as against others, but to consider wherein such studies might be made to contribute most effectively to the purposes of secondary education. It believes that the social studies require "socialization" quite as much as other studies, and that this is of greater moment than the number of social studies offered or the number of hours assigned to each.

The subject of civics may be taken to illustrate this point. Its avowed purpose is to train for citizenship. The various attempts to secure a more perfect fulfillment of this purpose by increasing the quantity offered, by making the subject required instead of elective, by transferring it from last year to first year of the high school or vice versa, by introducing it in the elementary course of study, by shifting the emphasis from the National Government to municipal government—such attempts have been more or less mechanical and superficial. Unless the subject matter and the methods of instruction are adapted to the pupil's immediate needs of social growth, such attempts avail little. What is true of civics is also true of the other social studies, such as history and economics.

(2) The committee has refrained from offering detailed outlines of courses, on the ground that they tend to fix instruction in stereotyped forms inconsistent with a real socializing purpose. The selection of topics and the organization of subject matter should be determined in each case by immediate needs. The attempt has been, therefore, to establish certain principles, to illustrate these as far as possible by examples from actual practice, and to stimulate initiative on the part of teachers and school administrators in testing proposed methods or in judicious experiments of their own.

No sensible teacher of history asks how many facts he is to teach. No two teachers—if good ones—would teach the same number of facts or just the same facts to the same pupils or class, and much less to different classes. No sensible teacher asks what kind of facts he shall teach, expecting to receive in answer a tabulation of his material. He knows that general rules accompanied by suitable illustrations are the only useful answer to these questions. (Elementary course of study in geography, history, and civics, Indianapolis.)

(3) One principle the committee has endeavored to keep before it consistently throughout this report because of its fundamental character. It is contained in the following quotation from Prof. Dewey:

> We are continually uneasy about the things we adults know, and are afraid the child will never learn them unless they are drilled into him by instruction before he has any intellectual use for them. If we could really believe that attending to the needs of present growth would keep the child and teacher alike busy, and would also provide the best possible guarantee of the learning needed in the future, transformation of educational ideals might soon be accomplished, and other desirable changes would largely take care of themselves.

The high-school course has heretofore been determined too largely by supposed future needs and too little by present needs and past experience. The important fact is not that the pupil is getting ready to live, but that he is living, and in immediate need of such mental and social nourishment and training as will enable him to adjust himself to his present social environment and conditions. By the very processes of present growth he will make the best possible provision for the future. This does not mean that educational processes should have no reference to the future. It does not mean, to use a concrete illustration, that a boy should be taught nothing about voting until he is 21 and about to cast his first ballot. It means merely that such instruction should be given at the psychological and social moment when the boy's interests are such as to make the instruction function effectively in his processes of growth. A distinction should be made between the "needs of present growth" and immediate, objective utility. As a boy's mental and social horizon broadens with the processes of education, he will become inquisitive about facts and relations perhaps long before he has direct use for them in the affairs of life. The best question that can be asked in class is the question that the pupil himself asks because he wants to know, and not the question the teacher asks because he thinks the pupil some time in the future ought to know.

(4) For effective social training in the high school more consideration must be given to its organic continuity with the work of the
elementary school in the same field. Opinion differs as to the grades
when the social studies as such should be introduced, especially in
the case of civics. This question is beyond the scope of this committee's consideration, except in its relation to the seventh and eighth
years. These years are now in some places included with the ninth
year in the junior high school, and must, therefore, be considered in
any plan for the reorganization of secondary education. But even
where the junior high-school plan is not adopted, the foundations of
secondary education must be laid in the years preceding the present
high school.

4. *General outline of social studies for secondary schools.*—
Assuming that provision has been made for the social aspect of
education in Grades I–VI of the elementary school, the following
general plan of social studies is proposed for the years VII–XII:

Junior cycle (years VII–IX):
  Geography.
  European history.
  American history.
  Civics.
Senior cycle (years X–XII):
  European history.
  American history.
  Problems of democracy—social, economic, and political.

5. *The "cycle" plan of organization—two three-year cycles preceded by an earlier six-year cycle.*—From the foregoing general outline it will be seen that the course of social studies proposed for the
years VII–IX constitutes a cycle to be followed by a similar cycle in
the years X–XII, and presumably preceded by another similar cycle
in the six elementary grades. This grouping coincides roughly with
the physiological periods of adolescence, but is based chiefly upon
the practical consideration that large numbers of children complete
their schooling with the sixth grade and another large contingent
with the eighth and ninth grades. The course recommended in this
report aims to provide a comprehensive, and in a sense complete,
course of social study for each period. Those pupils who continue
through the third period cover the same cycle provided for in the
first and second periods, but with broader horizon, new relations,
and more intensive study.

The Philadelphia course of study now in preparation and soon to be published, and the Indianapolis course of study described in Bulletin, 1915, No. 17, United States Bureau of Education, illustrate with variations the cycle organization of the six elementary grades. Within this period the pupils get at least some picture of the development of civilization as typified in the customs, historic personages and dramatic events of ancient and modern nations. They also acquire the simpler elements of American history from the period of exploration to the present time. This historical study is made in close relation with geographical study. Civic and social relations, beginning with the simple relations of home life in the first grade and gradually including the elemental relations of the larger community life, form a continuous phase of the work. In the sixth year of the Philadelphia course emphasis is placed upon economic or vocational relations, largely through a concrete study of occupations. In the Indianapolis course a similar though perhaps less intensive study of occupations is made, chiefly in connection with geography (general and local) and with especial emphasis in the fourth, fifth, and sixth years; while in the sixth year a somewhat systematic though elementary study is made of the more important "elements of community welfare."

With such a course of study, the pupil who leaves school after completing the sixth grade will have acquired some experience with practically the whole range of social studies—history (both ancient and modern, European and American); government in its relations to community welfare; economics in its simpler occupational relations, and also on the side of saving, thrift, conservation; and even sociology in very elementary and concrete terms. Elementary as the course is, and inadequate as it may be from the point of view of the pupil's future social efficiency, it is doubtless all that he can well assimilate at his stage of mental and social growth.

It will now require only a glance at the outline of courses suggested for the years VII–IX and X–XII of this report to make apparent without further discussion the completeness with which the cycle organization is provided for.

6. *Differentiation of courses.*—The course of study outlined is flexible and permits of differentiation to any extent necessary to meet the needs of characteristic groups of pupils. It is an open question how far such differentiation is desirable, especially in the years VII–IX. It is a fallacy, for example, to imagine that the children of native-born Americans need civic education any less than the children of immigrants; or that the pupils of a school in a purely

residential suburb require instruction in industrial history or vocational civics any less than the pupils of a school in an industrial district. But the scope and emphasis of such courses may well vary in the different cases. It is conceivable that in a class of immigrant children more emphasis might be given to American history and less to European history than in a class of native children. In both European and American history the selection of topics for emphasis should, within certain limits at least, be made to meet industrial or other specific needs. As suggested, community civics needs special adaptation to rural conditions and requirements.

The committee can not emphasize too strongly its belief in the desirability of such careful adjustment of courses to local and current circumstances. It is believed that the flexibility of the course of social studies offered and the principles suggested for the organization of subject matter (see especially under the section on History), lend themselves readily to such adjustment.

7. *Adaptation to the 8–4 and 6–3–3 plans of organization.*—The validity of the committee's recommendations and suggestions is not dependent upon the adoption of the junior and senior high-school organization. There is only one point at which the adoption or non-adoption of this organization would seem to make any difference in the completeness with which the course of social studies herein proposed for the years VII–IX could be carried out. If it is true that under the 8–4 organization more pupils are likely to leave school at the end of the eighth year than would be the case under the 6–3–3 organization, it would mean simply that a larger percentage of pupils would fail to complete the cycle of social studies provided for the years VII–IX.

The committee believes, however, that the very nature of its proposed course in civics in the ninth year will tend to keep in school, even under the 8–4 organization, many of those to whom the traditional history courses usually given in the ninth year would offer no inducement to remain. However, it is partly to meet the needs of those who, under either organization, leave school at the end of the eighth year that the committee urgently recommends the inclusion of an elementary course in community civics in that year. This course, if planned with that end in view, will consummate a complete, though necessarily abbreviated, cycle in the years VII–VIII. Let it be repeated, however, that one of the chief purposes of both eighth and ninth year civics should be to provide the pupil with a motive for the continuation of his education.

PART II.—SOCIAL STUDIES FOR THE SEVENTH, EIGHTH, AND NINTH YEARS.

(A) ADMINISTRATIVE FEATURES.

Geography, history, and civics are the social studies that find a proper place in the seventh, eighth, and ninth years. The geography should be closely correlated with the history and civics, and should be thoroughly socialized. The history should include European as well as American history. The civics should be of the "community civics" type. In addition, it is desirable to emphasize the social aspects of other studies, such as hygiene or other science, and even arithmetic. (For a description of "community arithmetic" see "Civic Education in Elementary Schools as Illustrated in Indianapolis," Bulletin, 1915, No. 17, United States Bureau of Education.)

1. *Alternative programs for years VII–IX.*—Opinion and practice vary as to the organization of the social studies in these three years. It is the belief of the committee that the organization should be adapted to local circumstances, and that no one plan should be recommended as best for every case. The following alternative plans are suggested; it is not intended, however, to preclude the possibility of other adjustments that local conditions may require.

Seventh year:
   (1) Geography—½ year.   } These two courses may be taught in se-
      European history—½ year. } quence, or parallel through the year.
      Civics—taught as a phase of the above and of other subjects, or segregated in one or two periods a week, or both.

Or, (2) European history—1 year.
> Geography—taught incidentally to, and as a factor in, the history.
> Civics—taught as a phase of the above and of other subjects, or segregated in one or two periods a week, or both.

Eighth year:
> American history—½ year. ⎫ These two courses may be taught in se-
> Civics—½ year. ⎭ quence, or parallel through the year.
> Geography—taught incidentally to, and as a factor in, the above subjects.

Ninth year:
> (1) Civics: Continuing the civics of the preceding year, but with more emphasis upon State, national, and world aspects (see pp. 25, 26)—½ year
> Civics: Economic and vocational aspects (see pp. 26–29)—½ year.
> History: Much use made of history in relation to the topics of the above courses.

Or,
> (2) Civics—economic and vocational. ⎫
> Economic history. ⎭ 1 year, in sequence or parallel.

2. *Organization of social studies in the seventh and eighth years.*—The alternative programs given above suggest three methods of organizing the social studies in the seventh and eighth years.

(*a*) By the first method, the three social studies ran parallel to each other, with more or less direct dependence upon each other, and with a good deal of one subject taught as an aspect of the other two. This method is exemplified in the Indianapolis schools, according to their course of study in geography, history, and civics published in 1914, and explained in Bulletin, 1915, No. 17, United States Bureau of Education. In the seventh year geography occupies three periods a week throughout the year, alternating with European history on the other two days. Civics is taught only as a phase of the geography, history, and other subjects, with more or less attention to it in the opening exercises. In the eighth year United States history occupies three periods a week, alternating with civics on the other two days. Geography is taught in this year only as a factor in the other two subjects. It should be said in passing that while civics does not appear as a distinct subject in the Indianapolis schools until the eighth year, it is systematically taught as an aspect of other subjects throughout the elementary grades beginning with the first.

The aim in the Indianapolis elementary schools seems to be to make of education, not a process of instruction in a variety of subjects, but a process of living, of growth, during which the various relations of life are unfolded—civic, geographical, historical, ethical, vocational, etc. In the first grade, for example, the pupil does not even study "English" or "language"; he merely does things, and talks about things, and hears and tells stories about things, the teacher alone being conscious that she is giving the child his first organized lessons in civic life, as well as in the use of the English language. (Civic Education in Elementary Schools as Illustrated in Indianapolis, Bulletin, 1915, No. 17, United States Bureau of Education, p. 9.)

Even in the eighth year, where civics appears as a separate "subject," alternating throughout the year with American history, the coordination is so close (in the hands of a skillful teacher) that the pupils are hardly conscious that they are studying two "subjects." They are rather studying certain phenomena of life in two aspects— historical and civic.

It is this aim that gives to the Indianapolis plan its chief distinction. It is perhaps an ideal aim. Its accomplishment, however, requires skillful teaching. It is only fair to say that even in Indianapolis there are principals and teachers who prefer the plan which existed in that city prior to the adoption of the present plan a year or two ago, and ago, indeed, still follow it. This plan is next described.

(b) By this second plan the social studies are taken up in sequence. Civics occupies the entire attention (so far as the social studies are concerned) five days in the week, in the last half of the eighth year. It is preceded by the courses in history, and these in turn by geography. Of course geography also appears as an element in the history work, European and American. More or less civics instruction may be given prior to the last half of the eighth grade as a phase of history, geography, and other subjects.

The chief advantage claimed for this plan is the concentration and continuity of interest and attention. It is perhaps particularly important that attention be concentrated upon civics at the time just before the pupils enter high school or leave school altogether. This last argument may doubtless lose some of its force under the Junior High School plan of organization, if it be assumed that the latter would keep pupils in school at least a year longer and would provide further civic training in that year. At all events, of the two plans described, the second is perhaps more likely to be effective in the hands of the great majority of teachers, and especially of those who are inexperienced.

(c) A third general plan of organization, which admits of variations, is characterized by the introduction of civics as a distinct subject in the lower grades for one or more periods a week, and its continuation in increasing amount until the climax is reached in the seventh and eighth years. A plan of this kind is now being developed in Philadelphia. The advantages claimed for it are the cumulative effect of continuous civics instruction through the pupil's early years, and the definiteness secured by fixing attention upon the subject as such, even if for only one or two periods a week, instead of depending upon the interest and skill of the teacher to develop the subject incidentally to the teaching of other subjects.

Objections that have been raised to this plan are (1) the multiplication of "subjects" in the elementary curriculum; (2) the difficulty of maintaining interest and securing effective results from subjects taught one or two periods a week; (3) the belief that the very fact of designating a few periods a week for the study of "civics" would tend to the neglect of the civic aspects of instruction in other subjects. Data are not available to prove the validity of these objections.

3. *Time allotment for civics in years VII–IX.*—An objection has been raised to the amount of civics recommended for the years VII–IX on the ground that it is out of proportion to the time available for the social studies. This objection appears to be due in part to a misconception of the meaning of the term, and of the scope of the work intended to be included under it. The term "community civics" has arisen (it was not invented by this committee) to distinguish the new type of civics from the traditional "civil government," to which the name civics was also applied. Unfortunately, the term has been interpreted by many as applying to a purely local study. From what is said on pages 23 and 25, it should be clear that the committee is not recommending a course, even in the eighth year, that is restricted to a study of "the pupil's own town"; and much less that it is recommending two consecutive years of such study. The proposed ninth year course is "civics" in that it is a specific course of training for citizenship; it is "community civics" solely in the sense of maintaining the point of view, the spirit, the general method, though not the same content in detail, which characterize the earlier course to which the name has been applied.

Although the committee recommends a course in civics in both eighth and ninth years, it does not necessarily follow that there must be or should be two full years of the subject. The committee has only suggested a half-year course in the eighth year (a daily period for one-half year, or two or three periods a week for the entire year). And while it has suggested a course for the ninth year that, in the committee's opinion, might well occupy the entire year under certain circumstances, this course is capable of adjustment to half-year requirements when conditions make it desirable.

(B) GEOGRAPHY AND HISTORY IN SEVENTH AND EIGHTH YEARS.

There are here given, with some comment, extracts from the course of study in geography and history in the sixth, seventh, and eighth grades of the Indianapolis schools, as published in 1914. These illustrate, as well as anything available to the committee, the socialization of geography and the coordination between geography, history, and civics. It has seemed well to include the sixth year in order to show the continuity of method from the elementary to the secondary period and because of its relation to the cycle organization.

Sixth-grade geography.—The geography of this year includes a study of Africa and South America in the fist half and of the United States in the second half.

By the time children reach the sixth grade they are sufficiently mature to approach the study of a continent or country with some problem in mind. Facts are needed in the solution of this problem; they should not, however, be given as isolated scraps of knowledge, but should be made to contribute to the working out of the problem.

The most vital problems, however, grow out of current events that stimulate questions in the minds of the children. Therefore problems may change from year to year.

Sixth-grade history.—The prominence of the historical factor in the geography of this year will be suggested by the typical outline given above. In addition to this "incidental" historical study, the period of discovery and colonization is studied in story form parallel with the geography of the first half year, and that from the Revolution on in the second half year parallel with the geography of the United States. The stories of Livingstone, Cecil Rhodes, Stanley, and Kitchener are taken up along with the geography of Africa. A very elementary textbook in history is used for the first time in this grade.

It should be remarked that this sixth-year history work is the culmination of the elementary six-year cycle, which began with a study of the meaning of national holidays and of Hiawatha's childhood in the first two grades, was continued in the third and fourth grades with pioneer stories and biography from American history, and in the fifth grade with the elements of European and oriental history, based on "Ten Boys." In the fifth grade, also, the modern awakening of Japan is studied, with the story of "Perry and Japan" as a basis.

Seventh-grade geography.—The geography of the first half of the seventh grade is a study of "Some prominent nations of the world," including, for example, Holland, France, Italy, Austria, Hungary, Switzerland, China, Japan, Argentina, Brazil. In the second half of the year, "The world in general," "The conditions of commerce," and "Four great nations of the world—British Empire, German Empire, Russian Empire, the United States"—are the subjects of study. A general geography and a commercial geography are used as texts to supply the material for study. The method of study is the same as in the sixth year.

Seventh-grade history.—Again the strong historical element in the geography of this year is to be noted. History, however, is also given a separate place throughout the year. In the history study geography becomes an essential factor.

Owing to the use of different texts, no attempt is made to outline the work in history of the 7B grade in detail. The point of view used in teaching this work should, however, be the same throughout.

In his "Moral principles in education" Dewey says: "History is vital or dead to the child according as it is, or is not, presented from the sociological standpoint. When treated simply as a record of what has passed and gone, it must be mechanical, because the past, as past, is remote. Simply as the past there is no motive for attending to it. The ethical value of history teaching will be measured by the extent to which past events are made the means of understanding the present." No history, therefore, should be treated as though it had meaning or value in itself, but should constantly be made to show its relation or contribution to the present. . . .

In the work of this grade make the children feel that the history of our country is a part of the history of the world and that it had its beginnings many centuries before its discovery. . . .

Accordingly, the elements of European history, which are studied throughout this grade, are organized under the general title, "European beginnings in American history," and are treated as such.

Eighth-grade history. Geography has no place in this grade as a separate subject, though it is always an important factor in the study of history. The history of this year is American history, taken up systematically in connection with a text. A somewhat full suggestive outline is given in the course of study, but need not be repeated here. The spirit controlling the history instruction in this grade is the same as that which controls in the preceding grade.

The characteristic feature of this year is the introduction of "community civics" as a separate subject throughout the year, and its close coordination with the history. This means primarily that the history of the Nation is treated as the story of the growth of a national "community," involving all the "elements of welfare," with which the pupils are made familiar in their civics work, the same development of means of cooperation, especially through government, and so on. More particularly, it means that special aspects of civic life and organization are emphasized in connection with those periods of American history in which they are most significant. The pupils find, for example, that the motives that led to exploration and colonization (whether on the Atlantic coast or in the far West) were the same as those which have led to the development of their own local community and State, and that the process of development is the same in the one case as in the other. Advantage is taken of the period of development of transportation and communication to emphasize the importance of these factors from the point of view of the study of the same topics in civics.

Before leaving the subject of geography and history in the seventh and eighth years, attention should be called to the emphasis that is given in the Indianapolis course of study to economic facts and relations, not only in the subjects of geography and history, but also in civics. This has an important relation to the development of the same field of social study in the later cycle of the years X–XII.

(C) CIVICS FOR YEARS VII–IX.

1. *Special report on community civics.*—A special committee of the Committee on Social Studies has prepared a detailed report on the aims, methods, and content of community civics adapted particularly to the eighth and ninth grades.[1] This special report has been approved by the Committee on Social Studies, adopted as a part of its present general report, and issues as a manual on "The Teaching of Community Civics" in Bulletin, 1915, No. 23, United States Bureau of Education. Its availability in that bulletin makes unnecessary, in the present report, a detailed description of the course and its methods. Some of the essential features, however, are here summarized.

(a) *Significance of the term "community."*—Community civics lays emphasis upon the local community because (1) it is the com-

---

[1] This committee consisted of J. Lynn Barnard, School of Pedagogy, Philadelphia; F. W. Carrier, Somerville (Mass.) High School; Arthur W. Dunn, specialist in civic education, United States Bureau of Education; and Clarence D. Kingsley, high-school inspector, Massachusetts Board of Education.

munity with which every citizen, especially the child, comes into most intimate relations, and which is always in the foreground of experience; (2) it is easier for the child, as for any citizen, to realize his membership in the local community, to feel a sense of personal responsibility for it, and to enter into actual cooperation with it, than is the case with the national community.

But our Nation and our State are communities, as well as our city or village, and a child is a citizen of the larger as of the smaller community. The significance of the term "community civics" does not lie in its geographical implications, but in its implication of community relations, of a community of interests. . . . It is a question of point of view, and community civics applies this point of view to the study of the national community as well as to the study of the local community.

(b) *Aims of community civics.*—The aim of community civics is to help the child to know his community—not merely a lot of facts about it, but the meaning of his community life, what it does for him, and how it does it, what the community has a right to expect from him, and how he may fulfill his obligation, meanwhile cultivating in him the essential qualities and habits of good citizenship.

More specifically this aim is analyzed as follows:

To accomplish its part in training for citizenship, community civics should aim primarily to lead the pupil (1) to see the importance and significance of the elements of community welfare in their relations to himself and to the communities of which he is a member; (2) to know the social agencies, governmental and voluntary, that exist to secure these elements of community welfare; (3) to recognize his civic obligations, present and future, and to respond to them by appropriate action.

A unique feature of the method of community civics described in this report lies in the fact that there is the closest relation between these three essential aims and the three steps by means of which each of the main topics is to be taught.

(c) *Content of community civics.*—A characteristic feature of community civics is that it focusses attention upon the "elements of community welfare" rather than upon the machinery of government. The latter is discussed only in the light of a prior study of the "elements of welfare," and in relation to them. The "elements of welfare" afford the organizing principle for this new type of civics.

It is suggested that the following elements of welfare be studied as topics: (1) Health; (2) Protection of life and property; (3) Recreation; (4) Education; (5) Civic beauty; (6) Wealth; (7) Communication; (8) Transportation; (9) Migration; (10) Charities; (11) Correction.

In addition, the course may well include the following topics dealing with the mechanism of community agencies: (12) How governmental agencies are conducted; (13) How governmental agencies are financed; (14) How voluntary agencies are conducted and financed.

(d) *Methods of community civics.*—I. Social facts upon which the method should be based:

(1) The pupil is a young citizen with real present interests at stake. . . . It is the first task of the teacher, therefore, not to create an interest for future use, but to demonstrate existing interests and present citizenship.

(2) The pupil as a young citizen is a real factor in community affairs. . . . Therefore it is a task of the teacher to cultivate in the pupil a sense of his responsibility, present as well as future.

(3) If a citizen has an interest in civic matters and a sense of his personal responsibility, he will want to act. Therefore the teacher must help the pupil to express his conviction in word and deed. He must be given an opportunity . . . to live his civics, both in the school and in the community outside.

(4) Right action depends not only upon information, interest, and will, but also upon good judgment. Hence the young citizen must be trained to weigh facts and to judge relative values, both in regard to what constitute the essential elements in a situation and in regard to the best means of meeting it.

(5) Every citizen possesses a large amount of unorganized information regarding community affairs. . . . It is, therefore, important to teach the pupils how to test and organize their knowledge.

(6) People are . . . most ready to act upon those convictions that they have helped to form by their own mental processes and that are based upon their own experience and observation. Hence the teacher should . . . lead the class: (1) To contribute facts from their own experience; (2) To contribute other facts gathered by themselves; (3) To use their own reasoning powers in forming conclusions; and (4) To submit these conclusions to criticism.

(7) The class has the essential characteristics of a community. Therefore the method by which the class exercises are conducted is of the utmost importance in the cultivation of civic qualities and habits. . . .

II. Three steps in teaching an element of welfare:

(1) *Approach to the topic.*—In beginning the study of an element of welfare the teacher should lead the pupils to realize its importance to themselves, to their neighborhood, and to the community, and to see the dependence of the individual upon social agencies. Much depends upon the method of approach. The planning of an approach appropriate to a given topic and applicable to a given class calls for ingenuity and resourcefulness. In this bulletin approaches to various topics are suggested by way of illustra-

tion, but the teacher should try to find another approach whenever he thinks the one suggested is not the best one for the class.

(2) *Investigation of agencies.*—The knowledge of the class should now be extended by a concrete and more or less detailed investigation of agencies such as those suggested in the bulletin. These investigations should consist largely of first-hand observation and study of local conditions. The agencies suggested under each topic are so many that no attempt should be made to have the class as a whole study them all intensively. Such an attempt would result in superficiality, kill interest, and defeat the purpose of the course. . . .

(3) *Recognition of responsibility.*—A lesson in community civics is not complete unless it leaves with the pupil a sense of his personal responsibility and results in right action. To attain these ends is perhaps the most difficult and delicate task of the teacher. It is discussed here as the third step in teaching an element of welfare; in practice, however, it is a process coincident with the first two steps and resulting from them. If the work suggested in the foregoing paragraphs on "Approach" and "Investigation of agencies" has been well done, the pupil's sense of responsibility, his desire to act, and his knowledge of how to act will thereby have been developed. Indeed, the extent to which they have been developed is in a measure a test of the effectiveness of the approach and the study of agencies.

2. *Ninth-year-civics.*—When provision is made for community civics in the eighth year the way is prepared for work in the ninth year that would not otherwise be possible. The work of the ninth year should build upon, or grow out of, the eighth-year course; but it should have a broader horizon, develop new points of view and new relations, and emphasize aspects of social and civic life that were only lightly touched upon or wholly omitted in the earlier course. Incidentally, also, this ninth-year course should lay substantial foundations for the social studies of succeeding years.

(a) *Amplification of national concepts.*—The reaction against the exclusive and formal study of national government and the increasing attention given to the study of local community relations have resulted in a noticeable tendency to minimize the study of civics in a national sense. It would be inexpressibly unfortunate if the study of local community life and local civic relations should supplant a study of national community life and national civic relations. The two aspects of civic life should clearly supplement each other. While we are impressing the pupil with the importance of his local civic relations and utilizing them as a means of cultivating fundamental civic concepts and habits, we should not allow this to divert attention from the increasingly intimate relations between local and national interests, and the increasing importance of a recognition by the individual of his responsibility for the national welfare.

It is extremely difficult for the average citizen in a democracy to think in terms of national interest, especially when there is any apparent conflict between it and the local or group interest. An illustration of this is seen in the local influences brought to bear upon the members of the National Congress which often prevent them from voting on public questions in the interest of the Nation as a whole when it seems to be antagonistic to the interests of the local districts. Questions of health, of education, of industry can no longer be considered in their local bearings alone, but must be dealt with in the light of national policy and to the end of national efficiency. As our population grows, means of communication perfected and the interests of the individual more closely interwoven with the interests of others, the opportunities for friction and conflict increases. So much the greater is the necessity for training the pupil to recognize the common general interest in the midst of conflicting group interests and for cultivating the will to subordinate the latter to the former.

On the other hand, there is another tendency which, though good in itself, sometimes has a tendency to undermine our sense of the importance of national solidarity. This is the conception of "internationalism," of "humanity as greater than its divisions," of a "world community." This conception indeed needs cultivation, as suggested in the following section; but it is necessary to keep our minds upon the elemental fact that before there can be effective "internationalism" there must be efficient and self-respecting nationalism; that the first step toward the realization of a "world community" must be the cultivation of sound ideals, and of efficiency in attaining these ideals, on the part of the several nations which must constitute the "world community."

The word "patriotism" has been much abused; but it is a good word. Instead of avoiding it because of its abuse, and instead of consciously or unconsciously giving young citizens the impression that the thing for which the word stands has somewhat lost its significance, every effort should be made to imbue it with real meaning and to make it a potent influence in the development of a sound national life. The committee submits that this should be a definite aim of secondary education, and that one of the means of attaining it is by applying to the study of our national interests, activities, and organization the point of view, the spirit, and the methods of community civics. This may be done in some measure in the eighth year and earlier, but it may be accomplished more fully and more effectively in the ninth year, and later, on the basis of the earlier work.

(b) *Amplification of world interests.*—As individuals within a community, or local communities within a State, or the States constituting the Nation, are dependent upon one another and are bound together into the larger community life by their common interests and cooperative action, so it can easily be shown that nations are becoming more and more closely dependent upon each other. Common world interests need emphasis, world sympathies need cultivation. Pupils will be quite prepared for instruction to this end on the basis of the principles developed in community civics. Such study should be concrete and based upon current events and problems. It offers a socially important line of development, and every available opportunity to this end should be seized upon.

(c) *Civic relations of vocational life.*—Still another opportunity presented in the ninth year is for the stressing of the civic relations of vocational life. There is evidence that, as a rule, ninth-year pupils have begun to think more or less earnestly about what they are "going to do," even though they may not have made any connection in their minds between their future vocations and the particular studies they are taking. Much of the mortality that occurs during the eighth and ninth years is due to the failure of pupils and parents to see the economic value of the high-school course. An opportunity exists to make high-school education seem "worthwhile" by taking the budding vocational or economic interest as one point of departure.

It is one of the essential qualities of the good citizen to be self-supporting, and through the activities necessary to his self-support to contribute efficiently to the world's progress. Not only is it important that this fact be emphasized in the civic education of the youth, but it is also appropriate that he be given as much enlightenment as possible to assist him in choosing his vocation wisely from the standpoint of social efficiency as well as from that of personal success.

The question of vocational guidance is very much in the foreground at present. While there is general agreement that the young need "guidance" for the vocational aspect of life, as for its other aspects, there is wide divergence of opinion as to the nature of this guidance and the means by which it may best be given. The committee on social studies believes that education as a whole should take account of vocational needs and should contribute to the preparation of the youth for an intelligent choice of vocation and for efficiency in it. As for the ninth-year study now under consideration, the committee is here interested in its vocational guidance aspect only as an incident to the broader social and civic training of the youth. If it can be made to contribute anything to his guidance toward a wise choice of vocation and intelligent preparation for it, it is that much gain.

The chief purpose of the phase of the ninth-year work now being emphasized should be the development of an appreciation of the social significance of all work; of the social value and interdependence of all occupations; of the social responsibility of the worker, not only for the character of his work but for the use of its fruits; of the opportunities and necessity for good citizenship in vocational life; of the duty of the community to the worker; of the necessity for social control, governmental and otherwise, of the economic activities of the community; and of the part that government actually plays in regulating the economic life of the community and of the individual. In other words, the work here proposed is an application of community civics to a phase of individual and community life that is now coming into the foreground of the pupil's interest. It has for its background the earlier work, and differs from it primarily in the larger emphasis given to the economic interest and its resulting activities. The other aspects of community life dealt with in the earlier course should receive renewed attention—the family, the protection of life, health, and property, education, recreation, etc.; but even they may be approached from the point of view of their relations to the activities and arrangements involved in "getting a living."

The term "vocational civics" has been suggested for this phase of the ninth-year work. The term is hardly adequate, however, since it is as important at this time to give instruction regarding the civic responsibility connected with the use of wealth as it is regarding responsibility in its production.

Community civics deals with real situations and relations in the pupil's own life. This vocational or economic phase of the subject should be no exception. It may well be approached through an examination of occupations or industries in which the pupils have some direct interest—those for which the several members of the class have a predilection, those in which their parents are engaged, or those of most importance in the immediate community.

4. *Relation of civics to history.*—The coordination of geography, history, and civics instruction in the years VII–IX and earlier has been referred to in preceding pages. The application to instruction in history of the principles which have already vitalized instruction in civics is discussed in detail in later pages. The principles there discussed, the committee believes, are equally pertinent to history in-

struction in both junior and senior cycles. The purpose of the present section is to emphasize the peculiar value of the civics proposed for the junior cycle from the standpoint of historical study.

History as it is usually taught in the first year of the high school is no better adapted to the educational requirements of that age than the old-time civil government. The committee further maintains that, even from the standpoint of the subsequent high-school courses in history, the latter should be preceded by a course in civics of the type described above. Children live in the present and not in the past. The past becomes educational to them only as it is related to the present. Hero stories and pioneer stories from history are of use in the early grades because children react naturally to them. Individuals are interested in the history of government, of education, of commerce, of industry, or of democracy, in proportion as they have a present interest in these things. Community civics endeavors to establish a consciousness of present community relations before discussing the more remote development of these relations.

On the other hand, the history of a thing may add to its present interest. Railroads assume a new significance when compared with the means of transportation in colonial times, or with the road system of the Roman Empire. Community civics affords opportunity for the actual use of much historical matter, for the development of the "historical sense," and for the creation of a desire to know more history. The best time to introduce history in the education of the child is when it is of immediate use. The traditional history course has given to the child a mass of facts, chronologically arranged, because, in the judgment of the adult, these facts may sometimes be useful, or for the purposes of that vague thing, "general culture." Community civics affords opportunity to use history to illuminate topics of immediate interest.

Local history finds its best opportunity in connection with community civics. There is hardly a topic in community civics that may not be made clearer by looking back to the simpler stages of its development. For developing an appreciation of what history means and for giving historical perspective to the present, local history is as useful as any other history. The most effective courses in community civics make large use of local history.

5. *Summary.*—Community civics is a course of training in citizenship, organized with reference to the pupil's immediate needs, rich in its historical, sociological, economic, and political relations, and affording a logical and pedagogically sound avenue of approach to the later social studies.

PART III.—SOCIAL STUDIES FOR YEARS
X–XIII.

(A) GENERAL ADMINISTRATIVE FEATURES.

1. *General outline.*—The committee recommends as appropriate to the last three years of the secondary school the following courses:

I. *European history to approximately the end of the seventeenth century*—1 year. This would include ancient and oriental civilization, English history to the end of the period mentioned, and the period of American exploration.

II. *European history (including English history) since approximately the end of the seventeenth century*—1 (or ½) year.

III. *American history since the seventeenth century*—1 (or ½) year.

IV. *Problems of American democracy*—1 (or ½) year.

These courses clearly repeat the cycle of social study provided for in years VII–IX. The principal of organization suggested in the pages following for all of these courses makes them extremely flexible and easily adaptable to the special needs of different groups of pupils, or of different high-school curriculums (commercial, scientific, technical, agricultural, etc.).

2. *Time allotment and minimum essentials.*—The course of social studies here outlined would constitute, if all were taken, from 2 ½ to 4 units, dependent upon whether one or one-half year is allotted to each of the last three courses. The committee believes that there should be a social study in each year of the pupil's course. It is,

however, conscious of the difficulty presented by the present requirements of the high-school program. The question then arises as to what would constitute a minimum course of social study under these existing conditions. To this question the committee would reply:

(a) The minimum essentials of the years X–XII should be determined by the needs of the particular pupil or group of pupils in question.

(b) Other things being equal, it would seem desirable for the pupil, whose time in the last three years is limited, to take those social studies which would most directly aid him to understand the relations of his own social life. If, for example, he had but one year out of the three for social study, and there were no special reason for deciding otherwise, it is probable that he might better take a half year of American history and a half year of European history (courses II and III); or, a half year of American history and a half year of the twelfth-year study of social problems (courses III and IV). The choice among these might be influenced by the trend taken by his social study in the ninth year (see the alternative possibilities of the ninth-year work).

(c) If the principles advocated in the following pages of this report for the organization of instruction in the social studies be adhered to, the apparent incompleteness of the cycle of social study, due to the impracticability of taking all the courses offered, will be in some degree obviated. Briefly stated, this means that any course of history instruction should be so organized that the pupil will inevitably acquire some familiarity with the economic, social, and civic factors in community life, just as in the study of civics or of social problems he should inevitably learn much history by using it.

(B) HISTORY.

I. GENERAL STATEMENT OF PRINCIPLES OF ORGANIZATION

1. *Reasons for the proposed organization of history courses.*— The committee recommends the organization of the history course in two or three units as indicated in the general outline in view of the following considerations.

(1) In small high schools more than two units of history are impracticable; and in large high schools, where more could be offered, few pupils would (or do) take more than two units, and these often unrelated.

(2) The long historical period included in course I offers a wide

range of materials from which to select, and makes possible the development of topics continuously and unhampered by chronological and geographical limitations.

(3) The assignment of an equal amount of time (or twice the time if a year is given to each of courses II and III) to the period since the seventeenth century as to the period prior to that time, expresses the committee's conviction that recent history is richer in suitable materials for secondary education than the more remote periods, and is worthy of more intensive study.

(4) The history of any two years that a pupil may elect under this plan will be related; that of courses II and III is contemporaneous and presents many points of contact, and that of either course II or III is continuous with that of course I.

(5) Under the present four-unit plan a premium is placed upon ancient and American history, all that goes between being left largely to chance. Under the plan proposed by the committee a much larger proportion of the pupils will secure the benefits of a study of the essentials of European history.

(6) It is important to remember that the cycle of history provided for in the years X–XII will have been once traversed, on narrower lines, in the years VII–IX. Consequently, the pupil who for any reason can not complete the cycle in the years X–XII will not be wholly deficient in the knowledge of any of its parts.

(7) Although many teachers are at present inadequately prepared to follow the method of instruction advocated by the committee, which requires the selection of materials on the basis of the pupils' own immediate interests and of current problems (see below), the compression of a longer historical period into a briefer course will bring pressure to bear to induce a more careful selection of facts and events for emphasis.

2. *Organization of subject matter within history courses.*— Within each course the committee recommends—

(1) The adoption to the fullest extent possible of a "topical" method, or a "problem" method, as opposed to a method based on chronological sequence alone.

(2) The selection of topics or problems for study with reference to (a) the pupil's own immediate interest; (b) general social significance.

The organization of history instruction on this basis unquestionably requires greater skill on the part of the teacher than the traditional method, less dependence upon a single textbook of the types now existent, and larger use of many books, or of encyclopedic books, for reference purposes. If the selection of materials is to be determined by immediate interests and current problems, it is manifestly impossible to furnish in advance a detailed and complete outline of topics for universal and invariable use. To attempt to do so would be contrary to the very spirit of the method. Whether Miss Harris, for example, should dwell at length upon the War of 1812 and the subjects of the rights of neutrals could not be determined for her in advance by a committee, nor even by an international lawyer to whom the question might seem of profound importance. The matter was determined for her by the exigencies of the hour and the interests of her pupils. So, also, was the method by which she approached and unfolded the subject.

In this there is suggested a possible organizing principle for history that is at once scientific and especially effective in teaching pupils who have had a course in community civics of the type described earlier in this report. This organizing principle is found in the "elements of welfare" or "fundamental interest," which afford an effective basis for the organization of the latter subject. It is a subjective rather than an objective basis. In the case just cited the pupils themselves have a more or less developed esthetic interest, which expresses itself in various elemental ways and reacts to conditions in the immediate community. This interest is common to all mankind and finds expression in a great variety of ways. It expressed itself in a remarkable manner among the Greeks, who developed certain standards of beauty that have profoundly influenced the world since their time.

Already the principle of organization here suggested is being adopted more or less completely in the treatment of one great phase of history—that which relates to the "economic interest" and is expressed in economic or industrial history. Not all industrial history has been written on this basis of organization. Reference is made to the type of industrial history to which Prof. Robinson evidently refers in the statement quoted in this report and which is clearly illustrated in the lesson described by Miss Hazard. The same principle is applied in the course suggested by Dr. Leavitt and Miss Brown in their chapter on history in "Prevocational Education in the Public Schools."[1]

But boys and girls, even in vocational and prevocational classes,

---

[1] Leavitt and Brown, Prevocational Education in the Public Schools, chap. viii. Houghton Mifflin Co.

have fundamental interests other than the economic. They are the interests or "elements of welfare" that serve as the organizing principle of community civics—physical, economic, intellectual, esthetic, religious, and social. Their relative prominence varies among nations as among individuals, partly because of temperament and partly because of physical and social influences; but the story of the life of any nation is the story of effort to provide for them. The life history of a nation, as of any community, consists of two great lines of endeavor which are, of course, closely interrelated: (1) The endeavor to establish permanent and definite relations with the land, which involves the geographical factor, and (2) the endeavor to establish effective means of cooperation to provide for the "elements of welfare," which involves the evolution of a form of government. The committee merely raises the question as a basis for discussion and experiment whether the principle of organization here suggested may not do as much to vitalize instruction in history as it has already done to vitalize instruction in government under the name of community civics.

3. *Important aims in teaching history.*—(1) A primary aim of instruction in American history should be to develop a vivid conception of American nationality, a strong and intelligent patriotism, and a keen sense of the responsibility of every citizen for national efficiency. It is only on the basis of national solidarity, national efficiency (economic, social, political), and national patriotism that this or any nation can expect to perform its proper function in the family of nations.

(2) One of the conscious purposes of instruction in the history of nations other than our own should be the cultivation of a sympathetic understanding of such nations and their peoples, of an intelligent appreciation of their contributions to civilization, and of a just attitude toward them. So important has this seemed that a proposal has recently been made that one year of the history course be supplanted by a course to be known as "A Study of Nations."[1]

In suggesting such a study, Clarence D. Kingsley says:

The danger to be avoided above all others is the tendency to claim that one nation has a sweeping superiority over others. The claim of such superiority, as among individuals, is a sure cause of irreconcilable hatred. The cure for this narrow and partisan attitude is to be found in the broad conception

---

[1] Kingsley, Clarence D., The Study of Nations: Its Possibilities as a Social Study in High Schools. School and Society, Vol. III, pp. 37–41, Jan. 8, 1916.

that humanity is greater than any one nation. The idea should be developed that every nation has, or may have, something of worth to contribute to other nations, and to humanity as a whole. This conception when thoroughly inculcated would lead to a national respect for other nations, and to the belief that the continued existence and development of all nations are essential to the development of civilization. We can not expect that a principle so fundamental and comprehensive can be inculcated in the abstract; but through a specific study of many nations, the achievements and possibilities of each of which have been studied in the concrete, this idea may become established.

This conception of the supplementary value of the dissimilarities of the different nations and peoples, together with the ideal of human brotherhood, which is generally thought of in terms of essential similarity, should do much to establish genuine internationalism, free from sentiment, founded on fact, and actually operative in the affairs of nations.

This "Study of nations," as Mr. Kingsley sees it, instead of focusing attention upon the past, would start frankly with the present of typical modern nations—European, South American, oriental—and would use history in explanation of these nations and of clearly defined problems of supreme social importance at the present time. Not only would the use of history organized in this way, according to Mr. Kingsley, "tend to reduce friction in international relations, as such friction often results from popular clamor, born of a lack of understanding of foreign nations," but "it would help to a truer understanding and appreciation of the foreigners who come to our shores," and "it would lead us to be more helpful in our relations with backward peoples, because it would help us to value them on the basis of their latent possibilities, rather than on the basis of their present small achievements."

(3) In connection with the several history courses, and especially in connection with courses II and III, due attention should be given to Latin America and the Orient, especially Japan and China, and to great international problems of social, economic, and political importance to America and the world at large.

II. DETAILED DISCUSSION OF PRINCIPLES UNDERLYING HISTORY INSTRUCTION.

1. *The position of history in the curriculum.*—History, which has long occupied the center of the stage among the social studies of the high school, is facing competition not only from other branches of study, such as science, but also from other social studies. The customary four units, which have been largely fixed in character by the

traditions of the historian and the requirements of the college, are more or less discredited as ill adapted to the requirements of secondary education.

In a recent address Miss Jessie C. Evans, of the William Penn High School for Girls, Philadelphia, said:

> There is a growing danger that the traditional history course will only be permitted to the college-preparatory student. I visited, the other day, one of the largest high schools in the country and found that the majority of the students took no history at all. The new definitions of culture and the new demands for efficiency are causing very severe tests to be applied to any subject that would hold its own in our schools.

This statement suggests certain questions:

2. *To what extent and in what ways are college requirements and life requirements mutually exclusive?*—In this connection the words of Prof. Dewey quoted are repeated with an interpolation:

> If we could really believe that attending to the needs of present growth would keep the child and teacher alike busy and would also provide the best possible guarantee of the learning needed in the future [in college or elsewhere], transformation of educational ideals might soon be accomplished, and other desirable changes would largely take care of themselves.

The problem of articulation between elementary and secondary schools, on the one hand, and between secondary schools and colleges, on the other, would take care of itself if elementary school, secondary school, and college would each give proper attention to the needs of present growth.

3. *To what extent does an increase in the amount of history offered insure more universal or better social education?*—The historical training acquired by the pupils is not proportional to the number of courses offered. Whether pupils elect history or not depends, first, upon whether they want it; and, second, upon the demands of other subjects upon their time. Those who are concerned for the prestige of history in the school program will find that their gains by adding courses are largely "on paper." In small high schools more than two or three units of history are impracticable; and in large schools few pupils take more than two units of the subject, these frequently disconnected; the majority take only what is required. Two or three units of history are ample in these years, provided they are adapted to the needs of the pupil and have been preceded by the cycle which this report recommends for the years VII–IX.

4. *What "tests" must the history course meet if it is "to hold its*

own in our schools"?—It is true that "the new definitions of culture and the new demands for efficiency are causing very severe tests to be applied" to all subjects, and the traditional type of history is in danger because it fails to meet the tests.

The ideal history for each of us would be those facts of past human experience to which we should have recourse oftenest in our endeavors to understand ourselves and our fellows. No one account would meet the needs of all, but all would agree that much of what now passes for the elements of history meets the needs of none. No one questions the inalienable right of the *historian* to interest himself in any phase of the past that he chooses. It is only to be wished that a greater number of historians had greater skill in hitting upon those phases of the past which serve *us* best in understanding the most vital problems of the present.—(Prof. James Harvey Robinson, in The New History.)

The italics in this quotation are our own. It is the chief business of the maker of the course of study, the textbook writer, and the teacher to do what the historian has failed to do, viz, to "hit upon those phases of the past which serve us" (the high-school pupil) "best in understanding the most vital problems of the present." Further, "the most vital problems of the present" for the high-school pupil are the problems which he himself is facing now or which are of direct value to him in his present processes of growth.

Prof. Mace had made the following statement:

To connect events and conditions with life as the pupil knows it will make history more or less of a practical subject. The pupil will see where his knowledge turns up in the affairs of everyday life. He will really discover how present-day institutions came to be what they are. Whenever or wherever he strikes a point in history, in Egypt, Greece, Rome, England, or even America, the point must be connected with modern life. Otherwise it may have only a curious or perhaps an academic interest for him, or it may have no interest whatever.

This connection may be worked out in several ways. The Egyptians had certain ideas about immortality, and therefore certain customs of burial. The Greeks probably took these up and modified them. The Romans changed them still further, especially after the coming of Christ. The Roman Catholic Church made still greater changes. The Reformation introduced new conceptions of the soul after death, and to-day the great variety of ideas on the subject show the tremendous differentiations that have come since the days of old Egypt. Likewise, it shows how tenacious the idea has been—its continuity. How much interest is aroused if the student is put to working out this problem of the life development of an idea! What sort of history is this? It is neither ancient, medieval, or modern, but all these in one. It is the new kind of general history—the kind that socializes the student. It makes him feel that history has some meaning when he sees ancient ideas functioning in the present.

Not every idea in history lends itself to such treatment. Many facts have not preserved their continuity in as perfect a way, but seem to have lost it before modern life is reached. But there is another relation—that of similarity. The reforms of Solon in Greece and of the Gracchi in Rome, the causes of Wat Tyler's rebellion, the measures of Lloyd George in England today, and the social-justice idea of the Progressive platform in the Presidential campaign of 1912 bear striking resemblance to each other. While they can not be connected by progressive evolution, they are richly suggestive in the lessons they teach.

Again, many events whose continuity we may not be able to trace have valuable lessons growing out of their dissimilarity. By making note of their contrasts we may see their bearing on modern life. The terrible Thirty Years' War, the Puritan Revolution, the Revolution of 1688, the American Revolution, and finally the French Revolution, present such striking contrasts as to give the student some notion of what might have been avoided for the betterment of the people. This means that when one of these upheavals is studied the rest should be made to yield their particular points of contrast, to the end that the student may see the lessons they present.

Another contribution to the discussion is the following, by Prof. Robinson. A portion of this is italicized for future reference.

One of our chief troubles in teaching history comes from the old idea that history is a record of past events; whereas our real purpose nowadays is to present past conditions, explain them so far as we can, and compare them with our own. . . .

While events can be dealt with chronologically, conditions have to be presented topically if they are to become clear. For example, we can select the salient events of the Crusades, and tell them in the form of a story; but the medieval church, castle, monastery, and farm have to be described in typical forms, as they lasted several centuries. The older textbooks told the events more or less dryly, gave the succession of kings, and the battles and treaties of their respective reigns. It was not deemed necessary to describe conditions and institutions with any care, and such terms as pope, king, bishop, church, baron, alchemy, astrology, witchcraft, were used as if every boy or girl of 14 knew exactly what they were.

A still unsolved problem is to determine what conditions and institutions shall be given the preference, considering the capacity of the student on the one hand and the limitations of time on the other. The committee should not undertake to pronounce on this matter, but should urge that teachers and textbook writers should be constantly asking themselves whether what they are teaching seems to them worth while. . . .

All instruction is, so to speak, the function of three variables—the pupils, the teacher, and the textbook. Every teacher is aware that pupils differ a good deal according to their environment, and, as we develop industrial and other forms of special education, it will be necessary to select our material to meet the special needs of the pupils. As for the teacher, no satisfactory results will be obtained until he learns to outrun the textbook and becomes really familiar, through judicious reading or university instruction, with the institutions which he proposes to deal with. Teachers should learn to deal with their subject topically, and should not be contented with reading historical manuals, which are usually poor places to go for information in regard to conditions and institutions. They should turn to the articles in the Encyclopedia Britannica and other similar works and to special treatments.

5. *Two questions at issue.*—There is general agreement that history, to be of value in the education of the boy or girl, must "function in the present." Disagreement arises over two questions: (1) What is meant by "functioning in the present"? (2) How shall the material of history be organized to this end?

(1) *What is meant by functioning in the present?*—There are two interpretations of this phrase: (a) The sociological interpretation, according to which it is enough if history be made to explain present conditions and institutions; (b) the pedagogical interpretation, according to which history, to be of value educationally, must be related to the present interests of the pupil. Many present-day problems are as far removed from the interests and experience of youth as if they belonged to the most remote historical epoch. It is not that a past event has its results, or its counterpart, or its analogy, or its contrast, in the present that gives it its chief educational value, but that it "meets the needs of present growth" in the pupil. We have learned to use hero stories and pioneer stories from any epoch of history in certain elementary grades because there is something in children that makes them want such stories as food for growth.

Recent periods are doubtless richer in materials of present application than the more remote periods. But children have very little chronological perspective. As one star seems as far away as another, although millions of miles may intervene between them, so American colonization may seem as remote to the child as the period of Athenian supremacy. The relative educational value of the wars of 1775, 1812, and 1861 does not depend upon their remoteness of proximity. It does not necessarily follow from the fact that trusts are a live, present issue, and negro slavery came to an end 50 years ago, that the slavery agitation preceding the Civil War is of less educational value than the agitation regarding the control of trusts at the present time.

Do not these considerations suggest a basis for a partial answer at least to Prof. Robinson's "still unsolved problem," stated above, viz, "to determine what conditions and institutions shall be given the preference," and to this question, "What is worth while?" The principle may be stated thus: *The selection of a topic in history and the amount of attention given to it should depend, not merely upon its relative proximity in time, nor yet upon its relative present importance from the adult or from a sociological point of view, but also and chiefly upon the degree to which such topic can be related to the present life interests of the pupil, or can be used by him in his present processes of growth.*

The committee does not imagine, however, that by stating this principle it has solved the problem of the organization of the history course. It has only recognized a new and most important factor in the problem. By so doing, it has even made the problem more difficult, for there are now raised the new questions, What history does meet the needs of the child's growth? and, How may a given topic be related to the child's interest? Acceptance of the principle throws the problem largely back upon the teacher, for the questions just stated are questions that she must answer for her particular group of pupils, and can not be disposed of once for all by a jury of historians or sociologists. The problem is only in part one of selection of topics; it is also one of method of approach. A topic that may be infused with vitality by a proper approach through the interests of the children may become perfectly barren of results through lack of such approach.

Illustrations of the principle.—The following type lessons illustrate, more or less perfectly, the application of this principle. The first is given by Miss Hannah M. Harris, of the State Normal School at Hyannis, Mass., and illustrates both the selection of topic and the method of approach with reference to the pupils' immediate interest.

Ordinarily we have regarded the War of 1812 as not closely related to those interests (of the children) nor essential to the development of the central theme of the term, "The building of the Nation"; hence we have passed over the subject rather lightly, and have saved time for the more intensive study of the Revolution and the making of the Constitution, topics which are necessary to the central theme, and which can be made real to the children by means of their activities in a school club. This club makes and amends its own constitution, earns money, votes its expenditures; in short, manages its own affairs on democratic principles, and so brings home to its members the meaning of certain political terms and situations involved in these topics, such as taxation without representation, majority rule, compromises, etc.

In 1915, however, the subject of the War of 1812 appeared to us in a different light. The children were reading headlines in the newspapers in which the word "neutrality" had a conspicuous place. They heard the word repeated at home and on every street corner, and were beginning to use it themselves, though with but vague notions of its meaning. Consequently the preceding topic in the history course was less fully treated than in ordinary years, and time was appropriated for a study of the War of 1812.

The study was approached in the following way: What is meant by the expression "a neutral nation," "belligerent nation"? What nations are now belligerent? Which ones neutral? What are some of the ways in which the citizens of a neutral nation come into contact with the citizens or with the government of a belligerent nation? (Some of the answers: "Buy things of them"; "sell them goods"; "have our goods carried in their ships": "travel in their countries.") So long as any nation remains neutral, what rights have its citizens in these matters and others? (So far answers all came from previous knowledge, casually acquired information.) Now, with some suggestions from the children and explanations from the teacher, the following outline was put upon the blackboard:

The main rights of neutrality:

1. To live peaceably at home; i.e., not to be forced to take sides in the war or to have life or property endangered by it.

2. To trade with any nation. Exceptions: Entrance to blockaded ports; dealing in contraband goods.

3. To travel peaceably on the high seas or anywhere permitted by existing treaties. Exceptions: Places in which belligerents are actually engaged in warfare.

The questioning was then resumed: Do neutral nations desire to keep up friendly relations with belligerents? What mistake on the part of a neutral nation may interfere with these friendly relations? (Showing more favor to one belligerent than to another.) Why does President Wilson ask us to be neutral (impartial, calm) in our talk and actions toward citizens of belligerent nations? What act on the part of a belligerent nation may interrupt these friendly relations? (The violation of any one of the rights of neutrality.)

The members of the class were referred to the textbook to find out how the United States tried in 1812 to maintain its neutrality and how it failed. The account in the textbook was found all too brief to satisfy the pupils' inquiries, and the study of the war was neither dry nor out of touch with reality.

(2) *How shall the course in history be organized for the purposes of secondary education?*

Each new writer of a textbook is guided, consciously or unconsciously, in his choice of topics by earlier manuals which have established what teachers and the public at large are wont to expect under the caption "history."

Until recently the main thread selected was political. Almost everything was classified under kings' reigns, and the policy of their government, and the wars in which they became involved were the favorite subjects of discussion. . . . Political history is the easiest kind of history to write; it lends itself to accurate chronological arrangement just because it deals mainly with events rather than with conditions. (Prof. Robinson, in The New History, chapter on "History for the Common Man," p. 136.)

The substitution of a sociological point of view for that of the mere annalist has led to the introduction of new threads of human progress and the subordination of wars and political policies. It has also led to a partial, but only partial, breaking down of the purely chronological basis of organization. But no substitute for the chronological organization of history has been found that adequately meets the conditions and needs of secondary education.

It is not meant to suggest that chronology can be disregarded. The gradual and orderly evolution, step by step, of institutions and conditions is of the very essence of history. It would be impossible, were it thought desirable, to eliminate this element from historical study. But the principle of organization is antiquated which results in what some one has called the "what-came-next" plan of English or Roman history on that of "reigns"; and in the organization of the entire history course in such a way that the pupil studies "ancient" history this year, "medieval" history next year, and "modern" history the year following—provided, indeed, that he happens to begin his history this year and continue it consecutively next year and the year following, which is by no means invariably true.

If, now, we accept the "pedagogical" interpretation of the principle that history must function in the present, namely, that history to be of educational value must relate to the present interests of the pupil, or meet the needs of present growth, in addition to explaining present-day conditions and institutions according to the sociological interpretation, what effect may this have upon the organization of the history course?

A statement by Miss Hannah M. Harris, of the State Normal School, at Hyannis, Mass., bears directly upon this question:

The moment we cut loose from the old method of trying to teach all the historical facts which may happen to be found between the covers of the textbook, the question of how to organize the material of history becomes an urgent one. The student of sociology desires to organize the subject matter primarily to exhibit some important phase or phases of the social evolution of the race or nation or of some smaller group. The student of children and their needs desires to start with their present interests and to select from the story of the past only such fragments as bear so close a relation to these interests that they are capable of being in some real sense understood by the children, and of proving incentives to further profitable interests and activities on their part. This second plan, if logically carried out, would leave the entire record of the past open as a field for selection at any stage of the child's education, and would thus impose upon the teacher a task immensely difficult if not impossible.

These two plans have a common purpose to make the study of history yield the help it should give in the social education of children and young people. Is it not possible to combine successfully certain features of both proposals?

Can we not heed the suggestions of modern pedagogy by starting with those contemporaneous matters in which the children have already some interest, and from this study of present-day community affairs be led naturally back into the past to find related material which is significant to the children because of this relationship, and valuable to them because it serves to make clearer or more interesting the present situation?

At the same time, can we not limit the field of history from which selection of material is to be made for any one year of school work to some one historical epoch, permitting the teacher free choice within these limits, the choice to be guided both by the present interests of the children and by the general rule that any historical facts considered must have some bearing upon the main lines of growth which are characteristics of the period being studied?

Plan of the University of Missouri elementary school.—One of the most radical experiments in the reorganization of history instruction to "meet the needs of present growth" is that of Prof. J. L. Meriam in the university elementary school of the University of Missouri. So far this experiment has been limited to the elementary school, but Dr. Meriam considers it a sufficient success to warrant its adaptation to the secondary school. He believes that "the present four units of history" in the secondary school are "quite out of date."

To quote from Dr. Meriam:

The university elementary school gives no instruction in history as such, although a great deal of historical material is very carefully studied. This policy is in accord with our policy in other subjects. We teach no arithmetic as such, but we do a great deal of arithmetical calculation in connection with special topics. We teach no geography as such, but we become acquainted with a great deal of geographical material in our study of various industrial and social activities. We teach no language as such, but language is in constant use in our efforts to express to the best of our ability the ideas we have in various other subjects.

History as usually taught is looked upon as a method of approach to the study of present-day problems. It is also used as a means of interpreting present-day problems. Thus history is usually studied before present-day problems. Further, history is usually studied by showing events in their chronological order. In the university elementary school no such purpose is present.

For us historical material is studied merely to satisfy interests and to further interests in present-day problems. Such study also provides at times inspiration and suggestion for the further study of problems that are of immediate interest. Such historical material frequently excites interest in reading and thus incidentally furnishes the pupil with certain information that may be of value later. This, however, must be looked upon as a mere by-product.

Thus, with us the study of historical material follows, rather than precedes, the study of similar events in the present, and there is no occasion for taking up these events in chronological order. The immature pupil is not yet prepared to understand and appreciate development of institutions merely because he has not yet had sufficient experience with details. He is, however, interested in isolated events, here and there, especially those which are similar in character to events taking place in the present time that are of interest to him. Thus we need no textbook as a guide, but we use many textbooks as mere reference books. Thus we have no course in history to follow and no given amount of historical study to complete. Within the elementary school field the pupil is not ready to summarize and organize this historical study.

One special illustration may be sufficient. In our sixth grade the subject of transportation is considered in so far as it is a present-day problem. Some eight weeks are spent on such topics as railways, steamship lines, public highways and animal power, use of electricity in travel, the automobile, the aeroplane. In the seventh or eighth grade the same topic is considered, but in certain historical aspects. For example, the growth of railways in the United States and elsewhere. Here would be considered change in the extent of mileage, change in location of roads as affected by needs in various parts of the country, change in the character of engines and cars as influenced by inventions, improvement made in roads, bridges, railway stations, and the like.

Such study calls for: (1) much reading; (2) geographical study concerning the trunk lines and lines of travel; (3) arithmetical calculations, especially in the change of mileage and the cost of construction of roads and trains; (4) some very elementary physics in the study of the steam engine, air brakes, and the like; (5) drawing as a means of illustration; (6) composition, spelling, and writing as a means of expression; (7) "history for the common boy and girl." (See Robinson's "The New History," chapter on "History for the Common Man.")

"History for the common man."—The chapter in Prof. Robinson's book to which Dr. Meriam alludes in the last clause constituted an

address before a meeting of school superintendents at which the subject of discussion was industrial education. Prof. Robinson introduced his address as follows:

Should the student of the past be asked what he regarded as the most original and far-reaching discovery of modern times he might reply with some assurance that it is our growing realization of the fundamental importance and absorbing interest of common men and common things. Our democracy, with all its hopes and aspirations, is based on an appreciation of common men; our science, with all its achievements and prospects, is based on the appreciation of common things. . . . We have come together with a view of adjusting our education to this great discovery.

It is our present business to see what can be done for that very large class of boys and girls who must take up the burden of life prematurely and who must look forward to earning their livelihood by the work of their hands. But education has not been wont, until recently, to reckon seriously with the common man, who must do common things. It has presupposed leisure and freedom from the pressing cares of life. . . .

It is high time that we set to work boldly and without any timid reservation to bring our education into the closest possible relation with the actual life and future duties of the great majority of those who fill our public schools. . . .

History is what we know of the past. We may question it as we question our memory of our own personal acts and experiences. But those things that we recall in our own past vary continually with our moods and preoccupations. We adjust our recollection to our needs and aspirations, and ask from it light on the particular problems that face us. History, too, is not fixed and immutable, but ever changing. Each age has a perfect right to select from the annals of mankind those facts that seem to have a particular bearing on the matters it has at heart. . . .

So, in considering the place to be assigned to history in industrial education, I have no intention . . . of advocating what has hitherto commonly passed for an outline of history. On the contrary, I suggest that we take up the whole problem afresh, freed for the moment from our impression of "history," vulgarly so called.

What Prof. Robinson suggests is that, given a group of boys and girls whose economic and social position is preordained to the ranks of the great majority of men and women "who do common things," the history instruction should be organized, not on the traditional basis of chronology and politics, but on that of their own immediate interests.

This is what Miss Hazard did in the case cited above. This is also what Dr. Meriam is doing—only he goes further. He maintains that, whether or not we know in advance that the pupils are to be "common men and women," they are at least "common boys and girls" with interests in the present. He would therefore organize all history instruction on the basis of these interests, selecting from any part of the past those facts that "meet the needs of present growth"; and he would utilize these facts at the time when the pupil has need for them in connection with any subject under discussion or any activity in progress.

Practical difficulties of radical reorganization.—It may be plausibly objected that, while such radical reorganization as that suggested by Dr. Meriam may succeed in a special experimental school under the direction of a Dr. Meriam and a well-trained, sympathetic staff, it could not succeed at present under the conditions of the ordinary school. Miss Harris refers to the difficulty and proposes to meet it by a compromise between the "chronological" and "pedagogical" methods, restricting the field from which the teacher shall draw her materials in any given year to a particular historical epoch.

The limitation of the ground to be covered makes it practicable for the average grammar-school teacher, who, of course, is not a specialist in history, to become very familiar with the possibilities of the history of the period in question, as a mine of valuable material. And it is only this familiarity on the teacher's part that will make this sort of teaching a success.

The difficulty to which Miss Harris here refers—unpreparedness in history on the part of the teacher—is perhaps not so much of a factor in the secondary school, especially in cities, as in the elementary school. Unpreparedness of the high-school teacher is likely to be of another kind, namely, unpreparedness in the art of teaching. The college-trained high-school teacher may be a specialist in his subject, but have no training whatever as a teacher.

This unpreparedness of teachers, the lack of suitable textbooks, natural conservatism, and the opposition of those whose chief apparent interest is to maintain the supremacy of a "subject," or who see in the traditional methods of history instruction a means of "culture" that the schools can not dispense with, cause school authorities and teachers to hesitate "to work boldly and without timid reservation," or to "take up the whole matter afresh, freed . . . from the impression of 'history' . . . so called," and to seek rather to modify the existing course of study, incorporating in it as much as possible of the new ideas in the hope that as they prove their worth they will gain favor and open the way for further improvement. The committee has taken account of this fact in arriving at its conclusions, and has made its recommendations in the hope that they will stimulate initiative and experiment rather than discourage effort at immediate improvement.

(C) PROBLEMS OF AMERICAN DEMOCRACY—ECONOMIC, SOCIAL, POLITICAL.

It is generally agreed that there should be a culminating course of social study in the last year of the high school, with the purpose of giving a more definite, comprehensive, and deeper knowledge of some of the vital problems of social life, and thus of securing a more intelligent and active citizenship. Like preceding courses, it should provide for the pupils' "needs of present growth," and should be founded upon what has preceded in the pupils' education, especially through the subjects of civics and history.

1. *Conflicting claims for the twelfth year.*—One fact stands out clearly in the present status of the twelfth-year problem, namely, the variety of opinion as to the nature of the work that should be offered in this year. Not to mention the claims of history, the principal claimants for position are political science (government, "advanced civics"), economics, and sociology in some more or less practical form.

A profitable course could be given in any one of these fields, provided only it be adapted to secondary-school purposes. Three alternatives seem to present themselves:

1. To agree upon some one of the three fields.
2. To suggest a type course in each of the three fields, leaving the choice optional with the local school.
3. To recommend a new course involving the principles and materials of all three fields, but adapted directly to the immediate needs of secondary education.

The traditional courses in civil government are almost as inadequate for the last as for the first year of the high school. Efforts to improve them have usually consisted of only slight modifications of the traditional course or of an attempted simplification of political science. The results have not met the needs of high-school pupils nor satisfied the demands of economists and sociologists.

A justifiable opinion prevails that the principles of economics are of such fundamental importance that they should find a more definite place in high-school instruction than is customary. Courses in economics are accordingly appearing in high-school curriculums with increasing frequency. To a somewhat less degree, and with even less unanimity as to nature of content, the claims of sociology are being pressed. A practical difficulty is presented by the resulting complexity of the course of study. The advocates of none of the social sciences are willing to yield wholly to the others, nor is it justifiable from the standpoint of the pupil's social education to limit his instruction to one field of social science to the exclusion of others. The most serious difficulty, however, is that none of the social sciences, as developed and organized by the specialists, is adapted to the requirements of secondary education, and all attempts to adapt them to such requirements have been obstructed by tradition, as in the case of history.

Is it not time, in this field as in history, "to take up the whole problem afresh, freed . . . from the impressions of" the traditional social sciences?

2. *Relation to preceding courses.*—The suggestion that follows with reference to the last-year course of social study must be considered in the light of the recommendations for the preceding years. The courses in community civics and in history, if developed along the lines suggested in this report, are rich in their economic, sociological, and political connotations. Even if no provision be made in the last year for the further development of the special social sciences, the committee believes that its recommendations for the preceding years still provide as never before for the education of the pupil regarding the economic and social relations of his life.

3. *Concrete problems in varied aspects.*—The only feasible way the committee can see by which to satisfy in reasonable measure the demands of the several social sciences, while maintaining due regard for the requirements of secondary education, is to organize instruction, not on the basis of the formal social sciences, but on the basis of concrete problems of vital importance to society and of immediate interest to the pupil.

In other words, the suggestion is not to discard one social science in favor of another, nor attempt to crowd the several social sciences into this year in abridged forms; but to study actual problems, or issues, or conditions, as they occur in life, and in their several aspects, political, economic, and sociological. These problems or issues will naturally vary from year to year, and from class to class, but they should be selected on the ground (1) of their immediate interest to the class and (2) of their vital importance to society. The principle suggested here is the same as that applied to the organization of civics and history.

4. *Illustrations.*—In actual life, whether as high-school pupils or as adults, we face problems or conditions and not sciences. We use sciences, however, to interpret our problems and conditions. Furthermore, every problem or condition has many sides and may involve the use of various sciences. To illustrate the point we may take the cost of living, which is a vital problem from the standpoint of

the individual and of society, and may readily have been forced upon the interest of the pupil through changes in mode of life, curtailment of allowance, sacrifice of customary pleasures, change in plans for education, etc. This problem involves, on the economic side, such fundamental matters as values, prices, wages, etc.; on the sociological side, such matters as standards of living, birth rate, etc.; on the political side, such matters as tariff legislation, control of trusts and the like, and the appropriate machinery of legislation, law enforcement, and judicial procedure.

The problem of immigration might impose itself upon attention for any one of a number of reasons. It will have been touched upon in an elementary way in community civics, and doubtless will have come up in a variety of ways in connection with history; but it may now be considered more comprehensively, more intensively, and more exhaustively. One of the chief aims should now be to organize knowledge with reference to the economic, sociological, and political principles involved.

Economic relations of immigration:

Labor supply and other industrial problems (on the side of "production").
Standards of living, not only of the immigrants, but also of native Americans as affected by immigration (on the side of "consumption").
Relation to the problem of land tenure in the United States.

Sociological relations of immigration:

Movements and distribution of population; congestion in cities; etc.
Assimilation of immigrant population; admixture of races.
Vital statistics, health problems, etc.
Educational and religious problems involved.
Social contributions of immigrants; art, science, ethics.

Political and governmental relations of immigration:

Political ideals of immigrants; comparison of their inherited political conceptions with those of the country of their adoption.
Naturalization; its methods, abuses, etc.
The courts in the light of the processes of naturalization.
Administration of immigration laws.
Defects and inconsistencies in the methods of our Government as shown in legislation regarding immigrants and in the administration of the laws.
Problems of municipal government arising from or complicated by immigration.

A study or series of studies of the type here suggested, developing from concrete issues, would afford opportunity to go as far as occasion demands and time allows into the fundamental economic and political questions of the time. In the field of political science, for example, problems can readily be formulated on the basis of particular cases involving a study of legislative methods of Congress and of State legislatures; the powers and limitations of Federal and State executives; judicial machinery and procedure; lack of uniformity in State legislation and its results; weakness of county government; comparison of administration of cities in Europe, South America, and the United States, etc.

There has not yet been the same insistent demand for sociology as a science in the high school that there has been for economics and the science of government. But there are many questions and principles of a more or less purely sociological character that are just as important for the consideration of a high-school boy or girl as many others of a more or less purely economic or political character. A course of the kind suggested by the committee should doubtless afford opportunity for some consideration of such vital social institutions as the family and the church. These institutions will, it is hoped, have been studied in some of their aspects and relations in connection with history courses and in community civics, but they may now be considered from different angles, the point of departure being some particular problem in the foreground of current attention, such as, for example, the strength and weakness of the church as a socializing factor in rural life, etc.

Again, there are certain facts relating to the "social mind" for which the high-school boy and girl are quite ready, provided the study has a sufficiently concrete foundation and a sufficiently direct application. Any daily paper, indeed the life of any large school, will afford numerous incidents upon which to base a serious consideration, for example, of the impulsive action of "crowds" in contrast with the deliberative action of individuals and of the consequences of such action in social conduct. The power and effects of tradition are another phenomenon of social psychology fully as worthy of study in the high-school as many of the other social facts and laws that seem indispensable; it is not necessary to go farther than the curriculum which the pupil is following and the methods by which he is instructed to find a starting point for a discussion of this question and abundant material for its exemplification.

These two particular illustrations of expressions of the "social mind" are taken from a description of the social studies in the curriculum of Hampton Institute.[1] It may be said in passing that

---

[1] Jones, Thomas Jesse. "Social Studies in the Hampton Curriculum." Hampton Institute Press, 1908.

this committee has found no better illustration of the organization of economic and sociological knowledge on a problem basis, and of the selection of problems for study with direct reference to the pupils' immediate interests and needs than that offered in the work of this institution.

5. *Summary of reasons for the proposed course.*—In making its suggestion for this study of concrete problems of democracy in the last year of the high school the committee has been particularly influenced by the following considerations:

(1) It is impracticable to include in the high-school program a comprehensive course in each of the social sciences. And yet it is unjust to the pupil that his knowledge of social facts and laws should be limited to the field of any one of them, however important that one may be.

(2) The purposes of secondary education and not the intrinsic value of any particular body of knowledge should be the determining consideration. From the standpoint of the purposes of secondary education, it is far less important that the adolescent youth should acquire a comprehensive knowledge of any or all of the social sciences than it is that he should be given experience and practice in the observation of social phenomena as he encounters them; that he should be brought to understand that every social problem is many-sided and complex; and that he should acquire the habit of forming social judgments only on the basis of dispassionate consideration of all the facts available. This, the committee believes, can best be accomplished by dealing with actual situations as they occur and by drafting into service the materials of all the social sciences as occasion demands for a thorough understanding of the situations in question.

(3) The principles upon which such a course is based are the same as those which have been successfully applied in community civics and, to some extent in isolated cases, to the teaching of economics, sociology, and even history.

6. *Experiment urged.*—The committee believes, however, that it should at this time go no further than to define principles, with such meager illustration as it has available, and to urge experiment. It would especially urge that the methods and results of experiment, either along the lines suggested in this report or in other directions, be recorded by those who make them and reported for the benefit of all who are interested.

PART IV.—STANDARDS—PREPARATION OF TEACHERS—AVAILABILITY OF MATERIAL.

I. STANDARDS BY WHICH TO TEST METHODS.

While the following statement[1] was made originally with specific reference to the teaching of civics, the committee sees in it a general application to all of the social studies.

While we are discussing ways and means of making the teaching of civics more effective, is it timely to consider by what standards we are to judge what is effective and what is not? If I examine your proposed course in civics, on what grounds shall I say that it is good or bad? If I visit your class and pronounce your teaching excellent or poor, by what standards do I estimate the value of your work? Why should you accept my judgment?. . . . Can standards be formulated so that we may have a common basis for comparison, and . . . so that any teacher may put her work to the test from day to day, or from week to week, and see, not whether it conforms to the opinions of some one, but whether it measures up to clearly recognized criteria?

There are those who say that we can not measure the results of teaching with a yardstick or a bushel measure. Neither can we so measure electricity or light. Nor, for that matter, do we measure potatoes with a yardstick nor cloth by the bushel. The standard must be appropriate to the commodity or force.

---

[1] Extract from an address by Arthur William Dunn on "Standard by which to Test the Value of Civics Instruction."

Those who say that the results of civics teaching can not be seen or measured until later years fall into one of the errors that have hindered the progress of civic education. This is the error of assuming that the child will be a citizen only at some future time; of forgetting that he is a citizen now, with real civic relations and interests. Civic education is a process of cultivating existing tendencies, traits, and interests. The gardener who cultivates a plant will, it is true, not know until the fullness of time how much fruit it will bear. Then he may measure his results by the bushel. But as he cultivates the plant day by day he appraises its growth by standards clearly recognized by all gardeners, and he varies his treatment according to the signs.

Civic education is . . . a cultivation of civic qualities which have already "sprouted", and which will continue to grow under the eyes of the teacher. . . . The first step is to define the civic qualities whose resultant we recognize as good citizenship, and whose cultivation should be the aim of civics teaching. . . .

First in importance is interest in one's civic relations. . . . Bad citizenship is more often due to lack of interest than to lack of knowledge. . . . It follows that it should be an important part of civic education to cultivate an abiding civic interest. . . . The only way to do this is to *demonstrate* that these relations *are* of vital moment to the individual. The present interest of the child must be kept in mind, and not his probable or possible interest of 10 years hence. . . .

1. *Civics teaching is good in proportion as it makes its appeal definitely and constantly to the pupil's own present interest as a citizen.*

Interest is closely allied to motive. But real or apparent interest may lead to the setting up of wrong motives. . . . Good citizenship can only grow out of right motives. It follows that it should be a part of civic education to cultivate right motives. Pupils should be led both to *want to know* about their civic relations and to *want to do* something as good citizens.

2. *Civics teaching is good in proportion as it provides the pupil with adequate motives for studying civics and for seeking opportunity to participate in the civic life of the community of which he is a member.*

Community of interests implies community of effort. . . . The proper conception of government is that of a means of cooperation for the common well-being. No man can . . . be effective in civic life unless his "teamwork" is good. The possession of a spirit and habit of *cooperation* is an essential qualification for good citizenship. . . .

3. *Civics teaching is good in proportion as it stimulates cooperation among the pupils, and on the part of the pupils with others, for the common interest of the community (school, home, neighborhood, city, State, or Nation).*

Given an interest in civic affairs, a right motive, and a willingness to work with others, a man's citizenship will not count for a great deal unless he is able to sift out the essentials from the nonessentials of a situation and to decide wisely as to the best method of dealing with it; and unless he has power to initiate action. . . . Civic education ought to include the cultiva-tion of civic judgment and civic initiative. . . .

4. *Civics teaching is good in proportion as it cultivates the judgment with reference to a civic situation and the methods of dealing with it; and in proportion as it cultivates initiative in the face of such situation.*

The only test that we have been in the habit of applying to our civics teaching is the informational test. We have contented ourselves with ask-ing, How much do the children know? A certain fund of information is essential to good citizenship. But mere knowledge . . . will not make a good citizen. Ignorance of government is more often a result than a cause of civic inefficiency. . . . The problem which confronts the teacher and the maker of the course of study is, How much and what kind of information should be acquired by the pupil? This question can not be answered by an enumera-tion of topics of universal application. But, in general,

5. *Civics teaching is good in proportion as its subject matter is selected and organized on the basis of the pupil's past experience, immediate inter-ests, and the needs of his present growth.*

It is not pretended that the standards here suggested are the only ones . . . to be adopted; it is hoped that better ones may be evolved. . . . It is not to be supposed that every half-hour class exercise will measure up to all of them. . . . What is suggested is that these or other standards be kept in view by every teacher as guides that will determine, with something like precision, the direction that he shall take.

NOTES

CHAPTER 1

1. The search for the beginnings of any curricular area is full of traps. The "trail" revealed from this search did not find any clear ladder proceeding from point A to B and outward. The "origins" traced here represent more an accounting of significant events and ideas that proved to shape the development of social studies in schools than a chronological log of linkages.

2. The 1913–1916 Social Studies Committee of the National Education Association was selected as the seminal organizing body of the social studies largely because it is popularly regarded as producing the initial prototype social studies program for secondary and middle schools. See Henry Johnson, *The Teaching of History in Elementary and Secondary Schools* (New York: Macmillan, 1940); Rolla M. Tryon, *The Social Sciences as School Subjects* (New York: Charles Scribner's Sons, 1935); Edgar Bruce Wesley, *Teaching the Social Studies* (New York: Heath, 1937), and more recently Hazel Hertzberg, *Social Studies Reform 1880–1980* (Boulder, Colo.: Social Science Education Consortium, 1981).

3. The traditional history curriculum/program identifies the course structure and intent that persisted through most of the twentieth century. This program was conceived at the Madison Conference of the Committee of Ten in 1892 and elaborated by the American Historical Association Committee of Seven in 1899.

4. One researcher claimed "it is probably a truism that secondary school social studies began with the study of history" (Oliver M. Keels, "Herbert Baxter Adams and the Influence of the American Historical Association on the Early Social Studies," *International Journal of Social Educa-*

tion, 3, no. 3 [winter 1988–1989], p. 37). Other writers have provided similar sentiments. See Alberta Dougan, "The Search for a Definition of the Social Studies: A Historical Overview," *International Journal of Social Education*, 3, no. 3 (winter 1988–1989): 13–15; Tryon, *Social Sciences*; Wesley, *Teaching*; N. Ray Hiner, "Professions in Process: Changing Relations among Social Scientists, Historians, and Educators, 1880–1920," *History Teacher*, 6, no. 2 (February 1973); Robert Barr, James L. Barth, and Samuel S. Shermis, *Defining the Social Studies* (Arlington, Va.: National Council for the Social Studies, 1977), p. 19.

5. For an overview of teaching in the public schools of the turn of the century, see Larry Cuban, *How Teachers Taught: Constancy and Change in American Classrooms 1890–1980* (New York: Longman, 1984); Theodore R. Sizer, *Secondary Schools at the Turn of the Century* (New Haven: Yale University Press, 1964); and for secondary schools, Bernard Mehl, "The High School at the Turn of the Century: A Study of the Changes in the Aims and Programs of Public Secondary Education in the United States 1890–1900," diss., University of Illinois, Urbana-Champaign (1954).

6. Thomas Jesse Jones, *Social Studies in the Hampton Curriculum* (Hampton, Va.: Hampton Institute Press, 1908).

7. National Education Association, *Report of the Committee of Ten on Secondary School Studies with the Reports of the Conferences Arranged by the Committee* (New York: American Book, 1894).

8. Andrew McLaughlin et al., *The Study of History in Schools: A Report to the American Historical Association by the Committee of Seven* (New York: Macmillan, 1899).

9. Henry Johnson, in an important little book, one of sixteen prepared from 1932 to 1937 for the Commission on Social Studies, claimed that not much was original. Johnson traced how people thought about teaching history from biblical times to the early twentieth century. Although Johnson's text was to be a "history" of social sciences in schools, he ignored these and concentrated exclusively on history. It was no surprise that Johnson's dislike of social studies, publicly voiced as early as 1915, was made clear too. To Johnson teaching about history was centered upon the principles of chronology and continuity, and should not be focused on using history merely to see what light it can shed on current problems. Johnson's distinction is made here also. See Johnson's *An Introduction to The History of Social Sciences in Schools* (New York: Charles Scribner's Sons, 1932).

10. Agnew O. Roorbach, "The Development of the Social Studies in American Secondary Education Before 1861," diss., University of Pennsylvania (1937). Roorbach attempts to trace the beginnings of the social studies (which includes Webster, Willard, and Parley) as defined by the 1913–1916 Social Studies Committee from the earliest dates in American history to

1861. This attempt, however, treats the "subjects" of social studies, not the developing conceptualization of social studies. See also Murry R. Nelson, "Emma Willard: Pioneer in Social Studies Education," *Theory and Research in Social Education*, 15, no. 4 (fall 1987).

11. These individuals as well as many unnamed others operated apart from association with "formalized" approaches to subject matter— that is, they did not follow the dictates of or were linked to either a history- or social studies-centered model. Rather, knowingly or not, they vacillated between methods and approaches or developed their own outside of any recognized or standardized model.

12. Barr, Barth, and Shermis, *Defining*. See also Shirley Engle and Anna Ochoa, *Education for Democratic Citizenship. Decision Making in the Social Studies* (New York: Teachers College Press, 1988), pp. 91–123, for similar discussion of definitions of social studies.

13. Harold Silver, *Education as History* (New York: Methuen, 1983). See also Harry Elmer Barnes, *An Introduction to the History of Sociology* (Chicago: University of Chicago Press, 1948); Bruce Watson and William Tarr, *The Social Sciences and American Civilization* (New York: John Wiley, 1964).

14. The issue of social control and the public schools ca. 1900–1920 as presented here is in contrast to the so-called revisionist interpretation of Michael Katz, Clarence Karrier, Paul Violas, and Joel Spring. These authors and others alleged that school leaders were not so much motivated by social service as by direct or extreme social control methods. As far as I can tell, the social studies of the 1916 Social Studies Committee *report* was egalitarian in form and spirit. The case made by the revisionists simply does not hold in the production or dissemination of the 1916 committee report. The problem, from the standpoint of this research, is perhaps not *with* the report but with the *use* of the report. In theory, a decided difference exists between supporting the status quo in social, political, and economic terms versus supporting and fostering a few, key underlying democratic ideals. The notion that the political-economic status quo as a group unduly influenced or directed educators to follow a uniform model has some merit. However, ultimately, it should be rejected in the case of social studies. The 1916 Social Studies sought to center their program on supporting/fostering democratic ideals. As part of their appeal, children were expressly encouraged to challenge and question the status quo, not blindly follow. For an early, although premature, appraisal of revisionist writings as applied to social studies beginnings, see David Paul Robinson, "Historical Models of the Emergence of Social Studies," diss., Stanford University (1977).

15. For a collection of original readings from authors of the "English Reform Tradition," see Sydney W. Jackman, ed., *The English Reform Tradition 1790–1910* (Englewood Cliffs, N.J.: Prentice-Hall, 1965).

16. *Constitution of the American Association for the Promotion of Social Science* (1865), p. 1. See also, Thomas Haskell, *The Emergence of Professional Social Science* (Urbana: University of Illinois Press, 1977).

17. Haskell, *Emergence*, p. vi.

18. See Carroll D. Wright, "Popular Instruction in Social Science," *Journal of Social Science*, 22 (June 1887): 28–35.

19. This is not to claim that formal investigations in science or social sciences did not precede the nineteenth century; however, the *organization* of social science subject/fields did occur in the nineteenth century.

20. In addition to Haskell, for a discussion on the beginnings of the social sciences in the United States, see Barnes, *Introduction;* Cynthia Eagle Russett, *Darwin in America: The Intellectual Response 1865–1912* (San Francisco: Freeman, 1976); Harold Y. Vanderpool, *Darwin and Darwinism* (Lexington: Heath, 1973); John Herman Randall, Jr., *The Making of the Modern Mind* (Boston: Houghton Mifflin, 1940).

21. The American Historical Association was formed at the 1884 annual meeting of the American Social Science Association.

22. For a sampling of interpretations, see Richard Hofstadter, *Social Darwinism in American Thought* (Boston: Beacon Press, 1955); Sidney Fine, *Laissez Faire and the General Welfare State* (Ann Arbor: University of Michigan Press, 1956); Henry Steele Commager, *The American Mind* (New Haven: Yale University Press, 1950); David W. Noble, *The Progressive Mind* (Chicago: Rand McNally, 1970); Robert H. Wiebe, *The Search for Order* (New York: Hill and Wang, 1967); and L.L. Bernard and Jessie Bernard, *Origins of American Sociology: The Social Science Movement in the United States* (New York: Russell and Russell, 1943).

23. For a general view of the development of the American Temperance Society, the Anti-Slavery Movement, Dorothy Dix and the treatment of the insane, Women's Rights (suffrage), and other social issues, see James MacGregor Burns, *The Workshop of Democracy* (New York: Vintage, 1986); Commager, *Mind;* Fine, *Laissez Faire;* Haskel, *Emergence;* Bernard and Bernard, *Origins.*

24. Edward Bellamy, *Looking Backward* (New York: New American Library, 1963), p. 222.

25. See Henry George, *Social Problems* (New York: Belford, Clarke, 1893), and Henry George, *Progress and Poverty* (New York: n.p., 1879).

26. Auguste Comte, *The Positive Philosophy of Auguste Comte* (London: John Edward Taylor, n.d.), II:472.

27. Dewey shifted from his positivistic beginnings and a Hegelian tradition by 1900. See Lawrence A. Cremin, *American Education: The Metropolitan Experience* (New York: Harper and Row, 1988), p. 166; and Clarence J. Karrier, *The Individual, Society, and Education* (Urbana: University of Illinois Press, 1986), p. 131.

28. See John Dewey, *How We Think* (Boston: D. C. Heath, 1909).

29. William Graham Sumner, *The Challenge of Facts and Other Essays* (New Haven: Yale University Press, 1914), p. 37.

30. George H. Hudson, "Herbert Spencer's Guiding Principles," *Education*, 16 (October 1895): 79.

31. This question was first introduced by Spencer in 1859.

32. Herbert Spencer, *Education: Intellectual, Moral, and Physical* (New York: Appleton, 1881), p. 31.

33. Ibid., p. 32. These five elements were first introduced in Spencer's 1859 essay, "What Knowledge is of Most Worth?" *Westminster Review*, (July 1859).

34. Earle Rugg, "How The Current Courses In History, Geography, and Civics Came To Be What They Are," in Harold Rugg, ed., *The Twenty-Second Yearbook of the National Society for the Study of Education*, Part II, "The Social Studies in the Elementary and Secondary School" (Bloomington, Ill.: Public School Publishing, 1923), pp. 67–70.

35. Lester Frank Ward, *Dynamic Sociology* (New York: Appleton, 1883), p. 589.

36. See Edward A. Ross, *Social Control* (New York: Macmillan, 1901). For a discussion of how this concept was used in education, see Edward Krug, *Shaping of the American High School* (New York: Harper and Row, 1964). For a more contemporary view, see Barry Franklin, *Building the American Community* (London: Falmer Press, 1986).

37. Shirley Engle and Anna Ochoa described this division as education for "socialization" and "counter-socialization," both necessary for citizenship education in a democracy. See Engle and Ochoa, *Education* (above, n. 12).

38. See Edward Ross, *Social Control* (New York: Macmillan, 1901).

39. In reading the work of the pioneer sociologists it is often difficult to isolate or even disentangle respective positions. A case in point is reflected in the writings of Franklin Giddings, who at one time has been labeled a Spencerian and at others a follower of Ward. Giddings, according to

Lybarger, contributed much to social studies and is due mention. See Michael Lybarger, "Origins of the Social Studies Curriculum: 1864–1916" diss., University of Wisconsin (1981).

40. See Tryon, *Social Sciences* (above, n. 2) and Lybarger, "Origins," for an extended discussion of the connection between sociology and the 1913–1916 Committee on Social Studies.

41. This thesis is explored in more detail in chapter 6. See works of Bessie Louise Pierce in the bibliography.

42. The contributions of these sociologists toward the social studies program of the 1910s can be found in the spirit and content of the 1913–1916 Social Studies prototype proposal. Furthermore, these contributions are evident in the work of their students, who became the principal authors of the social studies program. In the students of Small, Vincent, Ross, and Giddings, the most profound influence was felt. Arthur W. Dunn (secretary and compiler of each of the three Committee reports) was a student of Small and Vincent at the University of Chicago. Thomas Jesse Jones (chair of the committee), Clarence Kingsley (chair of the overall Reorganization Committee and Social Studies conferee), William Arey (first secretary of the committee), and Samuel Howe (conferee) were all students of Giddings at Columbia University. In addition, David Snedden (who contributed to the committee's second publication) was a student of Ross at Stanford. Columbia University also provided the services of James Harvey Robinson (also a member of 1916 Social Studies Committee) and John Dewey to committee members either directly or through their writings. The reader should note that these sociologists were critics of the Spencerian/Sumner camp.

43. Conway MacMillan, "The Sociological Basis of School Education," *Education*, 16, no. 6 (February 1896).

44. Ibid., pp. 333–34.

45. Ibid., p. 334.

46. Ibid., p. 335.

47. Charles DeGarmo, "Social Aspects of Moral Education," *The Third Yearbook of the National Herbart Society* (Chicago: University of Chicago Press, 1897), p. 41.

48. Ibid., p. 42.

49. Ibid., p. 47.

50. William Bishop Owen, "The Nineteenth Educational Conference of the Academies and High Schools in Relation with the University of Chicago," *The School Review*, 15, no. 1 (January 1907): 11.

51. Colin Scott, *Social Education* (Boston: Ginn, 1908). See also Scott, "Social Education," *Education*, 30, nos. 1, 2, 3 (October, November, December 1909).

52. See Otis H. Moore, "The Congress on Social Education," *Charities and the Commons*, 17 (1907): 439–45.

53. David Snedden, "History Study as an Instrument in the Social Education of Children," *Journal of Pedagogy*, 19 (June 1907): 260.

54. Ibid., p. 259.

55. Ibid., p. 266.

56. Interestingly, given his steady support of building a social studies base in education, curiously, Snedden was not called to be a member of the 1913–1916 Social Studies Committee. Although his name did appear in the credits of the second publication of the Committee, perhaps his more extreme position on social control (he favored tracking students) exempted him from direct service on the Committee.

57. Snedden, "History Study," p. 262.

58. Ibid., p. 266.

59. Charles Ellwood, "How History Can be Taught from a Sociological Point of View," *Education*, 30 (January 1910): 300.

60. At a special meeting of the Committee on History in the Schools (a joint effort of the American Historical Association and the Association of History Teachers' of the Middle States and Maryland) held in 1917, Johnson sharply criticized (without naming it) the insurgent social studies movement (see chapter 5). By 1932, although the social studies move to the curriculum was a fait accompli, Johnson still maintained the misguided nature of social studies; see Johnson, *Teaching* (n. 2, above).

61. The Committee on Social Science was one of the twelve subcommittees of the Committee of Nine on the Articulation of High School and Colleges of the NEA organized in 1912 to ascertain what work was being attempted in schools, to offer recommendations for modifications, and to suggest possible experimental programing. The Committee of Nine originated out of a request by NEA members in 1910 (headed by Clarence Kingsley, who later served as the chair of the Commission on the Reorganization of Secondary Education) to "discontinue entrance requirements of a second foreign language" as well as to accept all "well taught" elective subjects of the schools. Minutes from the 1911 and 1912 Committee of Nine reports mention social science as a field of studies that included "history, civics, economics, municipal affairs, and history of industry or commerce." It was after Thomas Jesse Jones was appointed chair of the social

science committee that the title of the committee was changed from social science to social studies. See NEA *Proceedings* (1911): 559–67; NEA *Proceedings* (1912): 667–69; and NEA *Proceedings* (1913): 489–91. In addition, the Committee of Nine was retitled (ostensibly to reflect the sweeping changes it was to proposed) to the Commission on the Reorganization of Secondary Education in 1913.

62. Thomas Jesse Jones, "Statement of the Chairman of the Committee on Social Studies," in Clarence Kingsley, chairman, *Preliminary Statements by Chairmen of the Committee of the Commission of National Education Association on Reorganization of Secondary Schools*, United States Bureau of Education, Bulletin, 1913, no. 41, whole 551 (Washington, D.C.: GPO, 1913). See also Thomas Jesse Jones, "NEA Committee on the Social Studies: Preliminary Recommendation," *History Teachers Magazine*, 4, no. 10 (December 1913): 291–96.

63. Jones's writings on social studies (by name) first appeared in issues of the *Southern Workman* beginning in 1905. Jones was, however, familiar to both social education and social studies terms (conceptualizations) prior to 1905. In the late 1890s Jones completed his master's degree at Columbia University with a thesis entitled "Social Education and the Elementary School" (master's thesis, 1899). Jones also contributed to a Columbia University bulletin that used "social studies" in its title (*Bulletin of Columbia University: Social Studies*). These articles largely concerned settlement issues from his dissertation , "Sociology of a New York City Block," diss., Columbia University (1903).

64. Murry R. Nelson, "Something Old, Something New, and All Borrowed," *Theory and Research in Social Education*, (Fall 1980).

65. Heber Newton, *Social Studies* (New York: Putnam, 1887).

66. Ibid., p. 43.

67. Sara Bolton, *Social Studies in England* (London: Lathrop, 1884).

68. Lady Jane Francesca Elgee Wilde, *Social Studies* (London: Ward and Downy, 1893).

69. Ibid., p. 155. Wilde's book is an eclectic mixture of essays ranging, for example, from the deplorable social status of women through the appropriate dress of literary people to discussions of life on other planets.

70. Ira Howerth, "A Programme for Social Study," *American Journal of Sociology*, 2, no. 6 (May 1897).

71. Albion W. Small and George E. Vincent, *An Introduction to the Study of Society* (New York: American Book, 1894).

72. Howerth, "Programme," p. 867.

73. Ibid., p. 852.

74. Edmund J. James, "Training for Citizenship," *The Third Year-book of the National Herbart Society* (Chicago: University of Chicago Press, 1897). See also Edmund J. James, in Samuel McCune Linsay, "The Study and Teaching of Sociology, Part III," *Annals of the American Academy of Political and Social Science*, 12 (July 1898): 39–41.

75. Edmund J. James, "The Place of Political and Social Sciences in Modern Education," *Annals of the American Academy of Political and Social Sciences*, 10 (November 1897): 53.

76. Ibid., pp. 104–5.

77. George Vincent, "Social Science and the Curriculum," *School Review*, 10 (1902): 186. Vincent's original presentation was published in the NEA *Proceedings* (1901)

78. Vincent, "Social Science," p. 125.

79. Arthur W. Dunn, "Is History in the High School a 'Snap'? If So, Why?," *Educational Review*, 24 (April 1905): 410.

80. Snedden, "History Study" (n. 52, above), p. 264.

81. Albion Small, "The Demands of Sociology Upon Pedagogy," *American Journal of Sociology*, 2, no. 6 (May 1897): 847. Small's original paper was published in the NEA *Proceedings* (1896).

82. Small, "Demands," p. 847.

83. See Johnson, *Teaching* (n. 2, above), chapter 2.

84. James, "Place," p. 75.

85. John Dewey, "Ethical Principles Underlaying Education," in *The Third Yearbook of the National Herbart Society* (Chicago: University of Chicago Press, 1897).

86. Earle Rugg, "Current Courses" (n. 33, above), pp. 69–70.

87. Johnson, *Teaching*, p. 114.

88. Ellen Condliffe Lagemann, "The Plural Worlds of Educational Research," *History of Education Quarterly*, 29, no. 2 (Summer 1989): 184–214.

89. See note 33, above.

90. C. C. Van Liew, "Training for Citizenship," *The Third Yearbook of the National Herbart Society* (Chicago: University of Chicago Press, 1897).

91. Henry Suzzalo, "Education as a Social Study," *School Review,* 16, no. 5 (May 1908): 330.

92. Ibid., p. 331.

93. Raymond Callahan, *Education and the Cult of Efficiency* (Chicago: University of Chicago, 1962). This is the most influential study of the efficiency movement in education.

94. Barbara Berman, "Business Efficiency, American Schooling, and the Public School Superintendency: A Reconsideration of the Callahan Thesis," *History of Education Quarterly,* 23, no. 3 (Fall 1983): 309.

95. See Merle Curti, *Social Ideas of American Educators* (New York: Charles Scribner's Sons, 1935), pp. 194, 256–57. This volume, created as part of the Commission on Social Studies in 1935, is a classic in the field. Chapter 6, "The School and Business Enterprise," is especially helpful in discussing the shift from Spencerian thought to social efficiency.

96. Suzzalo, "Education," pp. 332–33.

97. Ibid., p. 335.

98. Ibid.

99. Rolla M. Tryon, "Conference Upon Desirable Adjustments Between History and Other Social Studies in Elementary and Secondary Schools," *Historical Outlook,* 13, no. 3 (March 1921): 78.

100. The first social studies program that emerged following the initial social studies report in 1913 was the 1914 North Dakota project under the leadership of John Gillette. See John M. Gillette, "An Outline of Social Studies for Elementary Schools," *American Journal of Sociology,* 19 (1914): 491. See also Tryon, "Conference," p. 400, also chapter 4.

101. At the 1921 conference both Rolla Tryon and Bessie Louise Pierce noted the attention administrators gave to social studies. See Tryon, "Conference," p. 79. Pierce noted that the "NEA Committee" (Social Studies) had found "general acceptance among public school administrators," in Tryon, "Conference," p. 86. See also Charles H. Judd, "Report of the Committee on Social Science," *Third Yearbook* (National Association of Secondary School Principals, 1919). See also the *Fourth Yearbook* of the Association (1920).

102. The conditions for growth of secondary education from 1890 to 1912 appeared to strongly parallel the beginnings of social studies curricular programs. Among the factors that often are attributed to the growth of secondary education, which also appear to have contributed to the growth of social studies, are the urbanization of cities, growth of egalitarianism, the end of "free land," political stability, lack of war, growth of tax base, na-

tionalism, immigration, and the overall perception that education could elevate individuals.

103. See Bessie Louise Pierce, *Public Opinion and the Teaching of History* (New York: Knopf, 1926); and Pierce, *Civic Attitudes in American Schools* (Chicago: University of Chicago Press, 1930).

104. Mary D. Sheldon (Barnes), *Studies in General History* (Boston: Heath, 1885); Mary Sheldon Barnes and Earl Barnes, *Studies in American History* (Boston: Heath, 1891); and Mary Sheldon Barnes, *Studies in Historical Method* (Boston: Heath, 1896). See also R.U. Hilleman, "The Source Method of Teaching History," in National Council for the Social Studies, *The Historical Approach to Methods of Teaching Social Studies* (Philadelphia: McKinley Publishing, 1935); Robert Keohane, "The Great Debate Over the Source Method," *Social Education*, 13, no. 5 (May 1949); and David Warren Saxe, "Mary Sheldon Barnes and the Introduction of the Social Sciences in Public Schools: A Historical Perspective," *Social Studies*, 80, no. 5 (September/October 1989).

105. Paul Hanus, "Secondary Education," *Educational Review*, 17 (April 1899): 361.

106. Ibid.

107. Frank W. Blackmar, *The Study of History, Sociology, and Economics* (Topeka, Kansas: Crane and Company, 1901), p. 11.

108. Charles McMurry, *Special Method in History* (New York: Macmillan, 1903), p. 10.

109. Edward Krug, *Shaping of the American High School* (New York: Harper and Row, 1964), pp. 249–83. See also Herbert Kliebard, *The Struggle for the American Curriculum* (London: Routledge and Kegan Paul, 1986). Kliebard identifies the following three movements as affecting curricular matters during the early years of the century: child study, social efficiency, and social reconstruction. Another view of the historical context of the emerging school curriculum can be found in the work of Ivor F. Goodson: Ivor Goodson, ed., *Social Histories of the Secondary Curriculum: Subjects of Study* (London: Falmer Press, 1985); Ivor F. Goodson and Stephen J. Ball, eds., *Defining the Curriculum* (London: Falmer Press, 1984); and Clarence J. Karier, *The Individual, Society, and Education*, 2nd edition (Urbana: University of Illinois Press, 1986).

CHAPTER 2

1. Frederick Jackson Turner, "The Significance of the Frontier in American History," in *The Turner Thesis*, George Rogers Taylor, ed. (Boston: Heath, 1956), p. 4.

2. Ibid., p. 14.

3. David W. Noble, *The Progressive Mind, 1890–1917* (Chicago: Rand McNally, 1973), p. 24.

4. For a discussion of school history prior to the 1890s, see William F. Russell, "The Early Teaching of History in Secondary Schools," *The History Teachers Magazine*, 5, no. 7 (September 1914): 203–8; and Stuart Mc-Aninch, "Social Science, Social Cohesion, and Moral Uplift: The Historian and the Development of the Modern American Secondary School History Curriculum," diss., University of Illinois at Urbana-Champaign (1987).

5. See Stuart McAninch, and Howard Rai Boozer, "The American Historical Association and the Schools: 1884–1956," diss., Washington University (1960).

6. See Oliver M. Keels, "Herbert Baxter Adams and the Influence of the American Historical Association on the Early Social Studies," *International Journal of Social Education*, 3, no. 3 (Winter 1988–89).

7. N. Ray Hiner, "Professions in Process: Changing Relations Between Historians and Educators, 1896–1911," *History of Education Quarterly* (Spring 1972): 34.

8. By the early 1900s the leading history teaching textbooks were: Edward Channing and Albert Bushnell Hart, *Guide to the Study of American History* (Boston: Ginn, 1896); Mary Sheldon Barnes, *Studies in Historical Method* (Boston: Heath, 1896); Burton Hinsdale, *How to Study and Teach History* (New York: Appleton, 1893); William Mace, *Method in History* (Boston: Ginn, 1898); Frederick Fling and Howard Caldwell, *Studies in European and American History* (Lincoln, Nebr.: J.W. Miller, 1897); and Henry Bourne, *The Teaching of History and Civics in Elementary and Secondary Schools* (New York: Longman, Green, 1902).

9. G. Stanley Hall, ed., *Methods of Teaching History* (Boston: Heath, 1898), p. ix.

10. Ibid., p. xii.

11. Ibid.

12. Ibid., p. ix.

13. Ibid., pp. ix-x.

14. Ibid., p. x.

15. Ibid.

16. Ibid.

17. See Stanley Hall, child study movement, cultural epoch theory.

18. Cooperation between historians and schools waned considerably during the 1910s. After the social studies insurgents gained a foothold in the school curriculum, there was very little meaningful interaction between the two groups at a national committee level. Within the last forty years, only the 1988 Bradley Commission report could be counted as a joint effort.

19. That is, that university, scientifically-based history could be reduced for public school use.

20. William Torrey Harris, in Burton Aaron Hinsdale, *How to Study and Teach History* (New York: Appleton, 1893), p. vi.

21. Ibid., p. xii.

22. Ibid., p. xiv.

23. Ibid., p. 152.

24. Ibid., p. xiv.

25. Ibid.

26. Ibid., p. 72.

27. Ibid.

28. Ibid., p. 9.

29. Ibid., p. 10.

30. Ibid., p. 9.

31. Ibid., p. 11.

32. Ibid., p. 13.

33. Ibid., p. 14.

34. Ibid , p 16.

35. The other members of the Madison Conference were Edward G. Bourne, professor of history, Aldelbert College; Abram Brown, principal of Central High School, Columbus, Ohio; Ray Green Huling, principal of the High School of New Bedford, Mass.; Jesse Macy, professor of political science, Iowa College; William Scott, assistant professor of political economy, University of Wisconsin; and Henry P. Warren, Head Master of Albany Academy, New York.

36. National Education Association, *Report on Secondary School Studies* (Washington, D.C.: GPO, 1893), pp. 51–52. Hereafter cited as Committee of Ten.

37. Committee of Ten, p. 13.

38. Agnew O. Roorbach, *The Development of the Social Studies in American Education before 1861* (Philadelphia: University of Pennsylvania, 1937).

39. Committee of Ten, pp. 6–7.

40. Ibid., p. 28.

41. National Education Association, History Sub-Committee Report, "History, Civil Government, and Political Economy," as found in *Committee of Ten Report*, p. 200. Hereafter referred to as Madison Conference.

42. Henry Johnson, *Teaching of History in Elementary and Secondary Schools* (New York: Macmillan, 1940), p. 137.

43. Ibid., p. 138.

44. Earle Rugg, "How the Current Courses in History, Geography, and Civics Came To Be What They Are," in National Society for the Study of Education, *Twenty-Second Yearbook, Part II. The Social Studies in the Elementary and Secondary School* (Bloomington, Ill.: Public School Publishing, 1923), p. 48.

45. Ibid., pp. 60–61.

46. Charles W. Eliot, "The Unity of Educational Reform," in American Institute of Instruction, *Addresses and Proceedings* (1894), pp. 151–73.

47. Committee of Ten, pp. 15–16.

48. Madison Conference, p. 170.

49. Ibid., p. 169.

50. Ibid., p. 167.

51. Ibid.

52. Ibid.

53. Ibid.

54. Ibid.

55. Ibid., pp. 167–68.

56. Ibid., p. 163.

57. Ibid., p. 174.

58. Ibid.

59. Ibid., p. 187.

60. Ibid., p. 188.

61. Ibid., p. 189.

62. Ibid.

63. Ibid., pp. 189–90.

64. Ibid., p. 192.

65. Ibid., p. 195.

CHAPTER 3

1. See Walter S. Monroe, *Teaching-Learning Theory and Teacher Education* (New York: Greenwood Publishers, 1952).

2. Sidney S. Fine, *Laissez Faire and the General Welfare State* (Ann Harbor: University of Michigan Press, 1976), p. 253.

3. This mixing of traditions is one of the strange realities of American education—that is, over a period of time this emerging institution picked up a wide variety of influences, which were usually conflicting. Thus while it may appear to be a contradiction in terms to place liberal arts, Social Darwinism, and "scientific method" all in one sentence, in fact, this is exactly what happened.

4. Theodore R. Sizer, *Secondary Schools at the Turn of the Century* (New Haven: Yale University Press, 1964), pp. 199–200.

5. Ibid., p. 200.

6. Henry Johnson, *Teaching of History in Elementary and Secondary Schools* (New York: Macmillan, 1916), p. 138.

7. Joseph Rice, *The Public School System of the United States* (New York: Century, 1893). Rice's survey found that most schools offered the "old and antiquated education" where the function of the school consisted "primarily, if not entirely, in crowding into the memory of the child a certain number of cut-and-dried facts" (p. 20).

8. N. Ray Hiner, "Professions in Process: Changing Relations Between Historians and Educators, 1896–1911," *History of Education Quarterly* (Spring 1972): 36.

9. Andrew McLaughlin et al., *The Study of History in Schools, Report of the Committee of Seven to the American Historical Association* (New York: Macmillan, 1899).

10. Henry Johnson, *Teaching of History in Elementary and Secondary Schools With Applications to Allied Studies* (New York: Macmillan, 1940), p. 59.

11. Rolla M. Tryon, *The Social Sciences as School Subjects. A Report to the American Historical Association by the Commission on Social Studies* (New York: Charles Scribner's Sons, 1935), p. 22.

12. Edgar Bruce Wesley, *Teaching the Social Studies* (New York: Heath, 1937), p. 93.

13. Tryon, *Social Sciences*, pp. 22, 27.

14. Wesley, *Teaching*, p. 94.

15. *Study*, pp. 2–4.

16. Ibid., pp. 4–5.

17. Ibid., p. 17.

18. Ibid., pp. 16–17.

19. Ibid., pp. 16–26.

20. Tryon, *Social Sciences*, p. 24.

21. McLaughlin, *Study*, p. 34.

22. Ibid., pp. 34–35.

23. Ibid.

24. Ibid., p. 32.

25. Ibid., p. 42.

26. Ibid., p. 55.

27. Ibid.

28. Ibid., p. 56.

29. Ibid., p. 59.

30. Ibid., p. 64.

31. Ibid., pp. 65–66.

32. Ibid., pp. 60, 66.

33. Ibid., p. 67.

34. Ibid..

35. Ibid., p. 71.

36. Ibid., p. 74.

37. Ibid., pp. 77–78.

38. Ibid., pp. 79–80.

39. Ibid., p. 76.

40. Ibid., p. 87.

41. Ibid., p. 86.

42. Ibid., p. 91.

43. Ibid.

44. Ibid., p. 101.

45. Ibid., p. 91.

46. Ibid., p. 91.

47. Ibid., p. 92.

48. Ibid., p. 97.

49. Ibid., p. 113.

50. Ibid., pp. 113–14.

51. Ibid., p. 116.

52. Ibid., p. 117.

53. Ibid., p. 119.

54. Ibid., p. 120.

55. Ibid., pp. 119–20.

56. Ibid., p. 122.

57. Ibid., pp. 128–29.

58. Ibid., p. 131

CHAPTER 4

1. Woodrow Wilson, *The New Freedom* (New York: Doubleday, 1913), pp. 19, 21.

2. Arthur S. Link, *American Epoch: A History of the United States Since the 1890s* (New York: Knopf, 1958), p. 101.

3. Wilson, *Freedom*, p. 32.

4. Link, *Epoch*, p. 135.

5. Ibid., p. 115.

6. Michael B. Katz, as quoted in David Paul Robinson, "Historical Models of the Emergence of the Social Studies," diss., Stanford University (1977), p. 94; see also Michael B. Katz, *Class, Bureaucracy, and Schools: The Delusion of Educational Change in America* (New York: Praeger, 1971), pp. 122–23.

7. Michael Lybarger, "Origins of the Social Studies Curriculum: 1865–1916," diss., University of Wisconsin (1981), pp. 299–300.

8. Johnson's comments are discussed in chapter 5. See Henry Johnson, in "Proceedings of the Conference of Teachers of History," *American Historical Association Annual Report, 1917* (Washington, D.C.: GPO, 1920), pp. 220–26.

9. Correspondence between S. Samuel Shermis and David W. Saxe, December 16, 1989.

10. See James L. Barth and S. Samuel Shermis, "Nineteenth Century Origins of the Social Studies Movement: Understanding the Continuity Between Older and Contemporary Civic and U.S. History Textbooks," *Theory and Practice in Social Education*, 8, no. 3, Fall 1980.

11. Shermis letter.

12. Lester Frank Ward, *Dynamic Sociology*, vol. 2 (New York: Appleton, 1883), p. 589.

13. Raymond E. Callahan, *Education and the Cult of Efficiency* (Chicago: University of Chicago Press, 1962), pp. 18, 95.

14. See Callahan, especially chapters 4 through 7.

15. Edward A. Krug, *The Shaping of the America High School*, vol. 1 (New York: Harper and Row, 1964), pp. 282, 336.

16. See Dewey's *Interest and Effort in Education* (Boston: Houghton Mifflin, 1913), and his earlier "Ethical Principles Underlaying Education," *Third Yearbook of the National Herbart Society* (Chicago: University of Chicago Press, 1897).

17. See Bibliography for data on the Committee of Seven, especially Rolla M. Tryon, Edgar Dawson, Henry Johnson, and Edgar Bruce Wesley.

18. Howard Rai Boozer, "The American Historical Association and the Schools, 1884–1956," diss., Washington University (1960), p. 59.

19. "The Fifteenth Educational Conference of the Academies and High Schools Affiliated or in Cooperation with the University of Chicago," *School Review* (January 1902), p. 3.

20. Andrew C. McLaughlin et al., *The Study of History in Schools, Report to the American Historical Association by the Committee of Seven* (New York: Macmillan, 1906), p. 139.

21. Ibid., pp. 44–45, 46.

22. See John E. Stout, *The Development of High-School Curricula in the North Central States from 1860–1918*, Supplementary Education Monograph, no. 15 (Chicago: University of Chicago Press, 1921). In addition, Edgar Dawson found that schools drifted toward a "general history" offering between 1900 and 1924; see "History Inquiry," *Historical Outlook*, 15, no. 6 (June 1924).

23. Glenn Leroy Kinzie, "Historians and the Social Studies: A History and Interpretation of the Activities of the American Historical Association in the Secondary School Social Studies, 1884–1964," diss., University of Nebraska (1965), p. 43.

24. John Bach McMaster, as quoted in Kinzie, "Historians," p. 43; see also "Conference on Public School History Teachers," *American Historical Association Annual Report, 1904* (Washington, D.C.: GPO, 1905), p. 29.

25. Jane Addams, "The Influence of the Foreign Population on the Teaching of History and Civics," *Proceeding of the North Central History Teachers' Association, 1907* (Chicago: North Central History Teachers' Association, 1907), pp. 3–4.

26. Ibid., p. 4.

27. Ibid.

28. Ibid.

29. Boozer, "Association," pp. 60–61; see also "Meeting of the History Teachers' Association," *Educational Review* (April 1904): 429.

30. "Modifications in the Report of the Committee of Seven Recommended by the N. E. [New England Teachers'] Association," *History Teachers' Magazine*, 1, no. 4 (December 1909): 89–90.

31. Ibid., p. 90.

32. See Edward Eggleston, "The New History," presidential address, *American Historical Association Annual Report, 1900* (Washington, D.C.:

GPO, n.d.), pp. 37–47; also James Harvey Robinson, *The New History Essays Illustrating the Modern Historical Outlook* (New York: Macmillan, 1912); and Luther V. Hendricks, *James Harvey Robinson, Teacher of History* (Morningside Heights, N.Y.: King's Crown Press, 1946).

33. James Harvey Robinson, "Significance of History in Industrial Education," *Education Bi-Monthly*, 4 (June 1910): 370; see also Arthur William Dunn, *Social Studies in Secondary Education*, Report of the Committee of Social Studies of the Commission on the Reorganization of Secondary Education of the National Education Association, Bulletin, 1916, no. 28 (Washington, D.C.: GPO, 1916), p. 50.

34. Dunn, *Social Studies*, pp. 36–52.

35. Andrew McLaughlin, chairman, "Conference on History in Secondary Schools with Especial Reference to the Report of the Committee of Seven," *American Historical Association Annual Report, 1908* (Washington, D.C.: GPO, n.d.), pp. 65, 71.

36. Kinzie, "Historians," p. 48.

37. Ibid., p. 51; see also McLaughlin, "Conference on History," p. 71.

38. William MacDonald, "The Situation of History in Secondary Schools," *The Nation*, 85, no. 2202 (September 12, 1907): 226.

39. Ibid.

40. Macmillan published four texts edited and notated by MacDonald as "Source Books in American History." See advertisements in Andrew McLaughlin et al., *The Study of History in Schools, Report of the Committee of Five to the American Historical Association* (New York: Macmillan, 1912).

41. Frederick Jackson Turner, as noted in "American Historical Association Meetings," *History Teachers' Magazine*, 2, no. 5 (January 1911): 110.

42. Ibid.

43. James Harvey Robinson, as quoted in "American Historical Association Meetings," *History Teachers' Magazine*, 2, no. 5 (January 1911): 111; see also Robinson, "The Relation of History to the Newer Sciences of Mankind," *Journal of Philosophy, Psychology, and Scientific Methods*, 7, (March 1911): 141–57; and Robinson, *New History*, chapter 3, pp. 70–100.

44. Andrew McLaughlin, Charles H. Haskins, Charles W. Mann, James Sullivan, and James Harvey Robinson, *The Study of History in Schools, Report of the Committee of Five to the American Historical Association* (New York: Macmillan, 1912), p. 2.

45. Rolla Tryon, Henry Johnson, and Edgar Bruce Wesley are noted here as the "major writers on the early social studies." Although these three were certainly part of the shaping of the early social studies (especially Johnson), they are given the title "major writers" largely because they produced the only book-length works on the early years of social studies. In another sense, these authors may be considered the major historians of social studies for their contributions. Not to exclude Hazel Hertzberg's 1981 survey, it is an unhappy comment on the field that the last history of social studies was written in 1935 (Tryon).

46. Rolla M. Tryon, *The Social Sciences as School Subjects*, Part XI, Report of the Commission on Social Studies of the American Historical Association (New York: Charles Scribner's Sons, 1935), p. 31.

47. Ibid., p. 41.

48. Edgar Bruce Wesley, *Teaching the Social Studies Theory and Practice* (New York: Heath, 1937), p. 96.

49. Henry Johnson, *Teaching of History in Elementary and Secondary Schools* (New York: Macmillan, 1916), pp. 148, 149–50.

50. Henry Johnson, *Teaching of History in Elementary Schools with Application to Allied Studies* (New York: Macmillan, 1940), p. 63.

51. "History in the Secondary Schools, Is the Revision of the Course of Study in History Desirable? A Summary of the Report of the Committee of Five of the American Historical Association," *History Teachers' Magazine*, 2, no. 8 (April 1911): 181.

52. McLaughlin, Committee of Five, p. 6.

53. "History in the Secondary Schools," p. 183.

54. Ibid.

55. Ibid., pp. 182, 183.

56. Ibid., p. 182.

57. Ibid.

58. Boozer, "Association," p. 77.

59. Lucy M. Salmon, as quoted in Boozer, "Association," p. 74; see Salmon, "Some Principles in the Teaching of History," *The First Yearbook of the National Society for the Scientific Study of Education* (Chicago: University of Chicago Press, 1902).

60. Boozer, "Association," p. 79.

61. McLaughlin, Committee of Five, p. 39.

62. Ibid., p. 40.

63. Ibid., p. 41.

64. Ibid., p. 13.

65. "History in the Secondary Schools," p. 182.

66. Tryon, "Social Sciences" (n. 46, above), p. 33.

67. McLaughlin, Committee of Five, p. 64.

68. See "The Meeting of the American Historical Association in New York," *American Historical Review* (April 1910); see also *American Historical Association Annual Report, 1910* (Washington, D.C.: GPO, n. d.).

69. Henry E. Bourne, *The Teaching of History and Civics in the Elementary and Secondary School* (New York: Longman, Green, 1902), p. 104.

70. Tryon, "Social Sciences," pp. 154–55.

71. William MacDonald et al., "Text-Books in American History," Report of the Standing Committee on Text-books of the New England Teachers' Association, *Educational Review* (December 1898): 483.

72. Ibid., p. 485.

73. Tryon, "Social Sciences," p. 27.

74. Ibid., pp. 27, 190.

75. These texts were by no means the only history texts used during the period, or even the most popular. They were selected merely as representative of the work of several key historians of the era.

76. George Willis Botsford, *A History of the Orient, Greece, and Rome for High Schools and Academies* (New York: Macmillan, 1911).

77. Edward P. Cheyney, *A Short History of England* (Boston: Ginn, 1904).

78. James Harvey Robinson, *An Introduction to the History of Western Europe* (Boston: Ginn, 1903).

79. John Fiske, *A History of the United States* (Boston: Houghton, Mifflin, 1907).

80. John Bach McMaster, *A School History of the United States* (New York: American Book Company, 1897).

81. William C. Bagley and Harold O. Rugg, *Content of American History as Taught in the Seventh and Eighth Grades,* University of Illinois School of Education Bulletin 1916, no. 51 (August 21, 1916): 56–59.

82. Ibid., p. 56.

83. Ibid., p. 58.

84. Ibid., pp. 58–59.

85. Ibid., p. 58.

86. For additional data on school history, see Stout, *Development* (n. 22, above), and Edith W. Osgood, "The Development of Historical Study in the Secondary Schools of the United States," *School Review,* 22, no. 7 (September 1914), and 22, no. 8 (October 1914).

87. William MacDonald, "The Situation of History in Secondary Schools," *The Nation,* 85, no. 2202 (September 12, 1907): 225.

88. Ibid.

89. Ibid., pp. 225–26.

90. Ibid., p. 226.

91. Rolla M. Tryon, "A Brief Review of the Current Literature Relating to History and the Teaching of History in Junior and Senior High Schools," *School Review,* 25, no. 9 (November 1917): 668. Reviews of Bagley and Rugg, and Gold are found here.

92. Oriental history in this context includes those accounts that lead directly to later Western civilization, such as studies of Egypt, the Hebrews, and Persia. Connections to later Eastern civilizations were ignored.

93. Hugo H. Gold, "Methods and Content of Courses in History in the High Schools of the United States," *School Review,* 25, no. 2 (February 1917): 99–100; and no. 4 (April 1917): 281–82.

94. Leonard V. Koos, "History and other Social Studies," *The Administration of Secondary-School Units,* Supplementary Educational Monographs, 1, no. 3 (Chicago: University of Chicago Press, July 1917), 106–7.

95. Murry R. Nelson, "The Social Contexts of the Committee on Social Studies Report of 1916," paper presented at the National Council for the Social Studies Convention, St. Louis (November 10, 1989).

CHAPTER 5

1. William Chandler Bagley, *Craftsmanship in Teaching* (New York: Macmillan, 1911), p. 207.

2. Edward A. Krug, *The Shaping of the American High School*, vol. 1 (New York: Harper and Row, 1964), p. 296.

3. Elmer Ellsworth Brown, *The Making of Our Middle School. An Account of the Development of Secondary Education in the United States* (New York: Longman, Green, 1902), p. 436.

4. Ibid., p. 461.

5. Krug, *Shaping*, p. 274.

6. Ibid.

7. Edward Lee Thorndike, *Education. A First Book* (New York: Macmillan, 1912), p. 273.

8. Edward Lee Thorndike, *The Elimination of Pupils from Schools*, Bulletin no. 4, 1907, whole no. 379, Department of the Interior, Bureau of Education (Washington, D.C.: GPO, 1908), p. 10.

9. James Phinney Monroe, *New Demands in Education* (New York: Doubleday, Page, 1912), p. v.

10. Charles Hughes Johnston et al., *High School Education* (New York: Charles Scribner's Sons, 1912), pp. 3–4.

11. Monroe, *Demands*, pp. 207–8.

12. Thorndike, *Education*, pp. 145–46.

13. Johnston, *High School*, pp. 14, 22.

14. Wayland J. Chase, "History, Civil Government, and Political Economy," in Johnston, *High School*, p. 294.

15. Samuel Chester Parker, *Methods of Teaching in High Schools* (New York: Ginn, 1915), p. viii.

16. Henry Eastman Bennett, *School Efficiency. An Analysis of Modern School Management* (Boston: Ginn, 1917), p. 265.

17. Philander Priestly Claxton, *Report of the Commissioner of Education for the Year Ending June 30, 1912*, I (Washington, D.C.: GPO, 1913): 1.

18. Ibid., p. 2.

19. Ibid.

20. Ibid.

21. Ibid., p. 3.

22. Ibid., p. 129.

23. Ibid., p. 11.

24. Richard Hofstadter, *Anti-Intellectualism in American Life*, (New York: Knopf, 1963), p. 359.

25. John Dewey, "How Much Freedom in Schools?" *New Republic*, 63 (July 9, 1930): 204.

26. Christopher J. Lucas, *Our Educational Heritage* (New York: Macmillan, 1972), p. 527.

27. Ibid.

28. See Merle Curti, *The Social Ideas of American Educators*, A Report to the American Historical Association by the Commission on the Social Studies (New York: Charles Scribner's Sons, 1935).

29. For a discussion of the main features of Dewey's educational thought applied to social studies education, see Lawrence E. Metcalf, "An Overview of the Deweyan Influence on Social Studies Education," *International Journal of Social Education*, 3, no. 3 (Winter 1988–89).

30. Lucas, *Heritage*, p. 529.

31. Ibid.

32. John Dewey, *Democracy and Education* (New York: Macmillan, 1916), p. 212.

33. John Dewey, "The Psychological Aspect of the School Curricula," *Education Review*, 13 (April 1897): 362–63.

34. Leo J. Alilunas, "The Effects of the Changes in American Psychological Thought Upon the Study of History," *Educational Administration and Supervision*, 32 (1946): 488.

35. John Dewey, *Interest and Effort in Education* (Boston: Houghton Mifflin, 1913), pp. 14–15.

36. Henry Suzzallo, as quoted in Dewey, *Interest*, p. iv.

37. John Dewey, "Ethical Principles Underlying Education," *National Herbart Society Third Yearbook* (Chicago: University of Chicago Press, 1897), p. 21.

38. Ibid., p. 22.

39. Ibid.

40. Ibid.

41. Dewey, *Democracy*, pp. 250–51.

42. Ibid., p. 251.

43. John Dewey, *School and Society* (Chicago: University of Chicago Press, 1899), p. 151.

44. J. Madison Gathany, "The Reconstruction of History Teaching," *History Teacher's Magazine*, 5, no. 7 (September 1914): 223.

45. As noted in chapter 1, Snedden was quite active in his criticism of the traditional history curriculum since 1907.

46. David Snedden, "Teaching of History in Secondary Schools," *History Teacher's Magazine*, 5, no. 9 (November 1914): 279.

47. David Snedden, "History and Other Social Sciences in the Education of Youths Twelve to Eighteen Years of Age," *School and Society*, 5, no. 116 (March 17, 1917): 308.

48. David Snedden, *Problems of Educational Readjustment* (Boston: Houghton Mifflin, 1913), p. 2.

49. Ibid.

50. Snedden, "History," pp. 308–9.

51. Snedden, "Teaching of History," p. 277.

52. Snedden, *Problems*, p. iii.

53. David Snedden, as reported in Walter H. Drost, *David Snedden and Education for Social Efficiency* (Madison: University of Wisconsin Press, 1967), p. 141.

54. David Snedden, "The Certification of Teachers in the High School, with Special Reference to Certification in History," 3, 5 (May 1912), p. 104.

55. Snedden, *Problems*, p. 92.

56. Ibid., p. 94.

57. Snedden, *Problems*, pp. 94–95.

58. Ibid., p. 96.

59. Ibid., p. 97.

60. Ibid.

61. Snedden, "History," p. 311.

62. Snedden, "Teaching of History," p. 280.

63. Ibid., p. 281.

64. Ibid.

65. Snedden, *Problems*, pp. 103–7.

66. Snedden, "History," p. 311.

67. Snedden, *Problems*, pp. 109–10.

68. Ibid., p. 110.

69. Ibid., p. 111.

70. Snedden, "History," p. 311.

71. Herbert Spencer, *Education: Intellectual, Moral, and Physical* (New York: Appleton, 1881), p. 21.

72. Ibid., pp. 28, 29–30.

73. Ibid., pp. 69, 71.

74. Snedden, "Certification," p. 105.

75. Walter H. Drost, *David Snedden and Education for Social Efficiency* (Madison: University of Wisconsin Press, 1967), p. 128.

76. George L. Burr, "What History Shall We Teach?," *History Teacher's Magazine*, 5, no. 9 (November 1914): 286.

77. Drost, *Snedden*, p. 129.

78. Burr, "What History," p. 286.

79. Charles H. Fisher, as quoted in "Discussion," The Association of History Teachers of the Middle States and Maryland, *Proceedings, 1915*, no. 13 (n. p., n. d.), p. 112.

80. Snedden received credit for contributing to the community civics report; see J. Lynn Barnard, F.W. Carrier, Arthur William Dunn, and Clarence Kingsley, *The Teaching of Community Civics*, Prepared by a Special Committee of the Commission on the Reorganization of Secondary Education of the National Education Association, United States Bureau of Education, Bulletin, 1915, no. 23, whole number 650 (Washington, D.C.: GPO, 1915).

81. James Lynn Barnard, "The Teaching of Civics in the Elementary Schools," The Association of History Teachers of the Middle States and Maryland, *Proceedings, 1913*, no. 11 (n. p., n. d.): 46–47.

82. James Sullivan, "Civics in the High School and Training for Citizenship," The Association of History Teachers of the Middle States and Maryland, *Proceedings, 1913*, no. 11 (n. p., n. d.): 49.

83. Charles Beard, "Training for Citizenship," The Association of History Teachers of the Middle States and Maryland, *Proceedings, 1913*, no. 11 (n. p., n. d.): 53–54.

84. Beard, Ibid., p. 54.

85. Ibid.

86. Ibid.

87. Ibid.

88. The Association of History, *Proceedings, 1913*, p. 73.

89. Rolla M. Tryon, *The Social Sciences as School Subjects*, Part XI. Report of the Commission on Social Studies of the American Historical Association (New York: Charles Scribner's Sons, 1935), p. 208.

90. William E. Lingelbach, "The Content of the Course in European History in the Secondary Schools," The Association of History Teachers of the Middle States and Maryland, *Proceedings, 1915*, no. 13 (n. p., n. d.): 85.

91. bid.

92. See Koos, Gold, Stout, and MacDonald in chapter 4, above.

93. John R. Sutton, "The Report of the Committee of Seven in Relation to the Proposed Definition of the Course," *History Teacher's Magazine*, 7, no. 6 (June 1916): 207.

94. Henry Johnson, in "Proceedings of the Conference of Teachers of History," *American Historical Association Annual Report, 1917* (Washington, D.C.: GPO, 1920), p. 220.

95. Ibid., pp. 220–221.

96. Ibid., p. 221.

97. Ibid., p. 222

98. Ibid., p. 222.

99. Ibid.

100. Ibid., p. 224.

101. Ibid., p. 225.

102. Ibid., pp. 225, 226.

103. Marshall S. Brown, in Johnson, "Proceedings," p. 247.

CHAPTER 6

1. Edgar Bruce Wesley, *Teaching the Social Studies Theory and Practice* (New York: Heath, 1937), p. 278; see also Bradley Commission on History in the Schools, *Building a History Curriculum: Guidelines for Teaching History in Schools* (Washington, D.C.: Educational Excellence Network, 1988).

2. Clarence Kingsley, *The Reorganization of Secondary Education, Preliminary Report of Commission on the Reorganization of Secondary Education of the National Education Association*, United States Bureau of Education, Bulletin, 1913, no. 41 (Washington, D.C.: GPO, 1913), p. 7.

3. Walter H. Drost, *David Snedden and Education for Social Efficiency* (Madison: University of Wisconsin Press, 1967), pp. 156–57.

4. Besides Kingsley and Jones, the other members of the Social Studies Committee included: Arthur William Dunn, secretary, United States Bureau of Education; W. A. Arey, Hampton Institute, Hampton, Va.; James Lynn Barnard, School of Pedagogy, Philadelphia; George G. Bechtel, principal, Northwestern High School, Detroit; F. L. Boyden, principal, High School, Deerfield, Mass.; E. C. Branson, University of North Carolina, Chapel Hill; Henry R. Burch, West Philadelphia High School; F. W. Carrier, Sommerville High School, Sommerville, Pa.; Jesse C. Evans, William Penn High School for Girls, Philadelphia; Frank P. Goodwin, Woodward High School, Cincinnati, Ohio; W. J. Hamilton, superintendent of schools, Two Rivers, Wis.; Blanche C. Hazard, Cornell University; Samuel B. Howe, High School, Newark, N.J.; J. Herbert Low, Manual Training High School, Brooklyn, N.Y.; William H. Mace, Syracuse University; William T. Morrey, Bushwick High School, Brooklyn, N.Y.; John Pettibone, High School, New Milford, Conn.; James Harvey Robinson, Columbia University; and William A. Wheatley, superintendent of schools, Middletown, Conn.

5. Thomas Jesse Jones in Kingsley, *Reorganization*, pp. 16–17.

6. Arthur William Dunn, *The Social Studies in Secondary Education*, Report of the Committee on Social Studies of the Commission on the Reorganization of Secondary Education, National Education Association, United States Bureau of Education, Bulletin, 1916, no. 28 (Washington, D.C.: GPO, 1916): 51.

7. Ibid., p. 52.

8. The literal absence of elementary consideration hollows out the claim by present-day history advocates that the 1916 Social Studies is to

blame for displacing the traditional history curriculum in elementary schools. See Diane Ravitch, "Tot Sociology," *The American Scholar* (Summer 1987), pp. 343–54.

9. Dunn, *Social Studies*, p. 9.

10. Ibid.

11. Ibid.

12. Ibid., p. 10.

13. Ibid.

14. Ibid.

15. Ibid.

16. Ibid.

17. Ibid., p. 11.

18. Ibid., p. 12.

19. Ibid.

20. Ibid., p. 22.

21. Ibid.

22. Ibid.

23. Ibid., pp. 22–23.

24. J. Lynn Barnard, F. W. Carrier, Arthur William Dunn, and Clarence D. Kingsley, *The Teaching of Community Civics*, prepared by a Special Committee of the Commission on the Reorganization of Secondary Education of the National Education Association, United States Bureau of Education, Bulletin, 1915, no. 23, whole number 650 (Washington, D.C.: GPO, 1915): 12.

25. Ibid., pp. 12–13.

26. Clarence D. Kingsley, *Cardinal Principles of Secondary Education, Report of the Subject Committees of the Commission on the Reorganization of Secondary Education of the National Education Association*, United States Bureau of Education, Bulletin, 1918, no. 35 (Washington, D.C.: GPO, 1918).

27. Barnard et al., *Teaching*, p. 14.

28. Dunn, *Social Studies*, p. 14.

29. Ibid., p. 25.

30. Ibid., p. 26.

31. Ibid.

32. Ibid., p. 27.

33. Ibid.

34. Ibid.

35. Ibid., p. 32.

36. Ibid., p. 33.

37. Ibid., p. 28.

38. Ibid., p. 35.

39. Ibid.

40. Ibid., p. 37.

41. Ibid., p. 39.

42. Ibid.

43. Ibid. See also Clarence D. Kingsley, "The Study of Nations: Its Possibilities as a Social Study in High Schools," *School and Society*, 3, no. 54 (January 8, 1916): 37–41.

44. *Social Studies*, pp. 39–40.

45. Ibid., pp. 40–41.

46. Ibid., p. 43.

47. Ibid.

48. Ibid., p. 44.

49. Ibid.

50. Ibid., p. 51.

51. Ibid., p. 52.

52. Ibid.

53. Ibid., p. 53.

54. Ibid.

55. Ibid., p. 56.

56. A case could be made to support the notion that the sort of popular liberal attitude necessary for the successful implementation of this course had died out, or was dying, just as the Committee was formulating the report. Much to the dismay of other liberals, even John Dewey moved to support the war. See Allen F. Davis, *Spearheads for Reform* (New York: Oxford University Press, 1967); Henry Steele Commager, *The American Mind* (New Haven: Yale University Press, 1950); and David W. Noble, *The Progressive Mind, 1890–1917* (Chicago: Rand McNally, 1970).

57. Edgar Dawson, "The History Inquiry," *Historical Outlook*, 15, no. 6 (June 1924): 255.

58. Dunn, *Social Studies*, p. 24. See also Barnard, *Teaching*, pp. 13–14.

59. This issue will be treated in more detail in my projected continuing history of social studies from the Great War to sputnik (1916–1957).

60. For an early appraisal of the Problems course, see Rolla M. Tryon, "Thirteen Years of Problems of American Democracy in the Senior High School," *Historical Outlook*, 20, no. 8 (December 1929); and also Frances Purves Taylor, "Problems of American Democracy as a High School Subject," master's thesis, University of Chicago (1929).

61. Barry Franklin found that the efficiency movement, and, in particular, the 1916 social studies suggestion of a problems course did indeed exert an important influence upon schools. Franklin used a study of the Minneapolis public schools to support this conventional wisdom of curricular history. Although Franklin found that the course was initially popular among teachers and administrators, eventually it was abandoned. Franklin noted that the general failure of the course may have been that educators did not identify the exact function, content, and method of the course. In addition, other state requirements and demands of existing programs contributed to the course's falling from the curriculum. See Barry Franklin, "The Social Efficiency Movement and Curriculum Change 1939–1976," in Ivor Goodson, *Social Histories of the Secondary Curriculum: Subjects for Study* (London: Falmer Press, 1985), pp. 239–68.

62. Arthur William Dunn, *The Community and the Citizen* (Boston: Heath, 1907), pp. iii–v.

63. Kingsley, "Study" (n. 43, above), p. 17.

64. William Mace, *Method in History* (Boston: Ginn, 1898); see also David Warren Saxe, "Traditional History and the Social Studies in Secondary Education: A Historical Perspective, 1892–1916," diss., University of Illinois at Urbana-Champaign (1988), pp. 169–75.

65. See Office of Judge Advocate General of the Army, *Compilation of War Laws of the Various States and Insular Possessions* (Washington,

D.C.: GPO, 1919). For specific laws enacted for public schools, see Bessie Louise Pierce, *Public Opinion and the Teaching of History* (New York: Knopf, 1926).

66. Repression is certainly a harsh word, with negative connotations. The term is used here to place American government policy on the freedom-conformity continuum. A repressive policy, that is, one that aims to confine, obstruct, or prohibit open dialogue on issues is, of course, an extreme course of action. Although such policies are on the continuum between freedom and conformity, they should not be interpreted that they were used to reconcile the freedom-conformity paradox. Indeed, such actions are the antithesis of reconciliation.

67. Henry J. Perkinson, *The Imperfect Panacea: American Faith in Education, 1865–1965* (New York: Random House, 1968), p. 197.

68. Richard Hofstadter, *The Age of Reform* (New York: Vintage, 1955), p. 278.

69. Richard Hofstadter, as quoted in Perkinson, *Panacea*, pp. 197–98.

70. Arthur Link claimed that "probably a majority of Americans were mildly pro-Allied . . . by 1914," and despite German and British propaganda they most likely decided upon the rightness of the Allied cause long before America's entry into the war. Therefore, the notion of debating war issues was not viewed as thoughtful thinking; it was viewed as treason. See Arthur Link, *Woodrow Wilson and the Progressive Era* (New York: Harper Torchbooks, 1963), pp. 145–73. By contrast, Christopher C. Gibbs argued that many Americans, particularly those living in Missouri, were actually against the war and maintained a certain silence about the war and war issues; see Gibbs, *The Great Silent Majority* (Columbia: University of Missouri Press, 1988). For a related position, see Henry May, *The Discontent of the Intellectuals: A Problem of the Twenties* (Chicago: Rand McNally, 1963).

71. See Pierce, *Public Opinion*. For a general view of repression areas other than education, see Merle E. Curti, *Peace or War: The American Struggle, 1636–1936* (New York: Norton, 1936); H.C. Peterson and Gilbert C. Fite, *Opponents of War, 1917–1918* (Madison: University of Wisconsin Press, 1957); and Frederick C. Giffin, *Six Who Protested* (Port Washington, N.Y.: Kennikat Press, 1977).

72. The irony between historians and social studies insurgents on war issues was that the historians supported the Allied cause, although they owed much of their tradition to Germany; the social studies insurgents remained silent on the war in the 1916 report, although they owed much of their tradition to the earlier English reform movement.

73. Trustees of the Carnegie Endowment for International Peace, as quoted in *History Teachers' Magazine*, 8, no. 7 (September 1917): 231.

74. Nicholas M. Butler, president of Columbia University, was the chairman of the Carnegie Foundation Education Division and later president of the organization.

75. The Board was designed to serve the country during the war years and was dissolved in 1919. The organization of the Board was continued as part of the American Historical Association. In fact, Board members Schafer (who was named chair) and Johnson (who wrote major sections of the report) served on the Committee on History and Education for Citizenship that sought to extend the Board's agenda into the "return to normalcy."

76. See C.H. Hamlin, *Educators Present Arms* (Zebulon, N.C.: Record Publishers, 1939), and, in particular, Albert E. McKinley, *Collected Materials for the Study of War* (Philadelphia: McKinley Publishing, 1918).

77. Henry Johnson, "The School in History: Some Precedents and a Possible Next Step," *History Teacher's Magazine*, 9, no. 2 (February 1918): 75. Johnson's presentation was part of a joint session of the Association of History Teachers of the Middle States and Maryland and the American Historical Association, December 29, 1917.

78. Karl von Clausewitz, *On War*, translated by Col. J. J. Graham (London: Trubner, 1873), I: 4.

79. General William T. Sherman, as quoted in Gwyenne Dyer, *War* (New York: Crown, 1985), p. 99d.

80. See Robert H. Weibe, *The Search For Order* (New York: Hill and Wang, 1967), pp. 256–85; Link, *Wilson*, pp. 145–282; and Hofstadter, *Reform*, pp. 272–82. In addition, for a general treatment of the war's effects on the people of the United States from the beginning of the war up to the Great Depression, see Ellis W. Hawley, *The Great War and the Search for a Modern Order* (New York: St. Martin's Press, 1979).

81. The *History Teacher's Magazine*, retitled *The Historical Outlook* in 1918, filled every issue between late 1916 and 1919 with war-related articles. Amid an almost rabid devotion to the Allied cause and, consequently, a savage anti-German attitude, the magazine printed teaching ideas, readings, course outlines, and more, all slanted toward Allied powers and policy. Several key articles were reprinted and distributed to schools by McKinley's press. Factual materials that would have cast doubts upon the "rightness" of the Allied cause (and America's entry into the war) were not treated seriously or were omitted entirely. For example, Senator William Stone, chair of the Senate Foreign Relations Committee, who represented

Missouri, a state whose people silently opposed the war and had a large German-American population (see Christopher C. Gibbs) raised many important issues in a lost cause for peace that McKinley saw fit to leave out of his magazine. See Stone's plea for peace, *Congressional Record*, 64th Congress, 2nd Session (March 3, 1917), pp. 4886–93. Many factual materials that may have revealed the inaccuracy and incompleteness of the magazine's articles were published after the war. For examples, see Albert Jay Nock, *The Myth of a Guilty Nation* (New York: B.W. Huebsch, 1922); Stewart E. Bruce, *The War Guilt and Peace Crime of the Entente Allies* (New York: McArdle Press, 1920); and Arthur Ponsonby, *Falsehood in War-Time* (New York: Dutton, 1928).

82. See James Lynn Barnard, "A Program of Civics Teaching for War Times and After," *Historical Outlook*, 9, no. 9 (December 1918): 492–500.

83. Dunn, *Social Studies*, pp. 44–45. The reference to the War of 1812 may provide an example of the Committee's political context—that is, a balanced, if not, "openly" neutral, position. The question of maintaining neutrality was hotly contested on the approach of "Mr. Madison's War" in America ca. 1812. Therefore, the analogy, by supposition, is that given the facts, the prudent course for America ca. 1916 would be to remain neutral and let the Europeans fight it out. The popularity of the War of 1812 and the shift toward an intense nationalistic fervor came after the war, not before. In using this example, the Committee may have been hopeful that teachers would lead students to consider a peace-neutrality (thus keeping an open mind) as an alternative to war.

84. Lawrence E. Metcalf, "Final Impressions," a statement following the Lawrence E. Metcalf Colloquium, University of Illinois, Urbana (September 26, 1986).

85. These were issues that Professor Metcalf prized dearly and sought to "instil" in his students. See Maurice P. Hunt and Lawrence E. Metcalf, *Teaching High School Social Studis* (New York: Harper and Row, 1955).

86. Besides articles in *The History Teacher's Magazine*, later *The Historical Outlook*, a large number of books and pamphlets related to war issues slanted toward the Allied cause were made available to teachers through newspapers, major printing houses, military, other governmental agencies, and private organizations. A sampling of wartime books would include: Gerald Stanley Lee, *WE* (New York: Doubleday, 1916); H.G. Wells, *The War That Will End War* (New York: Duffield, 1914); Oliver Perry Chitwood, *The Immediate Causes of the Great War* (New York: Thomas Crowell, 1917); Douglas Sladen, *The Real "Truth about Germany." Facts about the War* (New York: Putnam's Sons, 1914); James M. Beck, *The Evidence in the Case* (New York: Putnam's Sons, 1914, 1915); A German, *I*

Accuse (New York: George H. Doran, 1915); and Hermann Fernau, *Because I am a German* (New York: Dutton, 1916).

87. Harold Rugg, "Needed Changes in the Committee Procedure on Reconstructing the Social Studies," *Elementary School Journal*, 21 (May 1921): 689.

88. Hamlin, *Educators*, p. 34.

89. Nicholas Butler, as quoted in Hamlin, *Educators*.

90. For a brief discussion of the effect of World War I on the social studies, see George L. Mehaffy, "Social Studies in World War One: A Period of Transition," *Theory and Research in Social Education*, 15, no.1 (Winter 1987).

91. Rugg, *Needed Changes*, p. 690.

92. The Council emerged from faculty members and others associated with Columbia University. The NCSS was organized during the NEA Atlantic City conference on March 3, 1921. Albert McKinley was named president, with Edgar Dawson as secretary, and Earle Rugg as assistant secretary.

93. Raymond E. Callahan, *Education and the Cult of Efficiency* (Chicago: University of Chicago Press, 1962).

94. John Dewey, "Ethical Principles Underlying Education," *National Herbart Society Third Yearbook* (Chicago: University of Chicago Press, 1897), pp. 7–34.

95. "Notes from the Historical Field," *The Historical Outlook*, 11, no. 5 (May 1920): 203. The Committee did endeavor, however, to further their work through a "propaganda" committee, but this attempt did not yield any significant results. See "Committee on Teaching Citizenship," *Historical Outlook*, 10, no. 6 (June 1919): 340–41.

96. "Notes from the Historical Field," p. 203.

97. J. Montgomery Gambrill, "Some Tendencies and Issues in the Making of Social-Studies Curricula," *Historical Outlook*, 15, no. 2 (February 1924): 84–89.

98. Edgar Dawson, "The History Inquiry," *The Historical Outlook*, (formally *The History Teacher's Magazine*), 15, no. 6 (June 1924): 246–49.

99. "The History of the Social Studies," *Theory and Practice in Social Education*, 8 (Fall 1980); Virginia A. Atwood, ed., "Historical Foundations of Social Studies," special topic of *Journal of Thought* (Fall 1982); John Weakland, ed., "Founders of the Social Studies," *Indiana Social Studies*

Quarterly, 38, no. 3 (Winter 1985–86); "Old Masters and Founders," *International Journal of Social Education*, 3 (Winter 1988–89); and James L. Barth, ed., *Foundations of the Social Studies Special Interest Group*, Bulletin 1, January 1989.

100. This book is the first of my projected three-volume history of the social studies.

BIBLIOGRAPHY

SOURCES TO 1921

Addams, Jane. "The Influence of the Foreign Population on the Teaching of History and Civics." *Proceedings of the North Central History Teachers' Association, 1907.* Chicago: North Central History Teachers' Association, 1907.

"American Historical Association Meetings." *The History Teacher's Magazine,* 2, no. 5, January 1911.

Bagley, William C., and Harold Rugg. *Content of American History as Taught in the Seventh and Eighth Grades.* University of Illinois School of Education Bulletin 1916, no. 51, August 21, 1916.

————. *Craftsmanship in Teaching.* New York: MacMillan, 1911.

Barnard, James Lynn. "A Program of Civics Teaching for War Times and After." *The Historical Outlook,* 9, no. 9, December 1918.

————. "The Teaching of Civics in the Elementary Schools." The Association of History Teachers of the Middle States and Maryland. *Proceeding, 1913,* no. 11, n.p., n.d.

————, F. W. Carrier, Arthur William Dunn, and Clarence D. Kingsley. *The Teaching of Community Civics.* Prepared by a Special Committee of the Commission on the Reorganization of Secondary Education of the National Educational Association, United States Bureau of Education, Bulletin, 1915, no. 23, whole no. 650. Washington, D.C.: GPO, 1915.

Barnes, Mary Sheldon. "History: A Definition and Forecast." *Annals of the American Academy of Political and Social Science,* 6, July 1895. Philadelphia: American Academy of Political and Social Science, 1895.

———. *Studies in General History.* Boston: Heath, 1885.

———. *Studies in Historical Method.* Boston: Heath, 1896.

Beard, Charles. "Training for Citizenship." The Association of History Teachers of the Middle States and Maryland. *Proceedings, 1913,* no. 11, n.p., n.d.

Bellamy, Edward. *Looking Backward.* New York: New American Library, 1963.

Bennett, Henry Eastman. *School Efficiency. An Analysis of Modern School Management.* Boston: Ginn, 1917.

Blackmar, Frank. *The Study of History, Sociology, and Economics.* Topeka: Crane and Company, 1901.

Bolton, Sara. *Social Studies in England.* London: Lathrop, 1884.

Botsford, George Willis. *A History of the Orient, Greece, and Rome for High Schools and Academies.* New York: Macmillan, 1911.

Bourne, Henry E. *The Teaching of History and Civics in the Elementary and Secondary Schools.* New York: Longman, Green, 1902.

Brown, Elmer Ellsworth. *The Making of Our Middle Schools. An Account of the Development of Secondary Education in the United States.* New York: Longman, Green, 1902.

Burr, George L. "What History Shall We Teach?" *The History Teachers Magazine,* 5, no. 9, November 1914.

Channing, Edward, and Albert Bushnell Hart. *Guide to the Study of American History.* Boston: Ginn, 1896.

Cheyney, Edward P. *A Short History of England.* Boston: Ginn, 1903.

Claxton, Philander Prestley. *Report of the Commissioner of Education, 1912.* Washington, D.C.: GPO, 1913.

Comte, August. *The Positive Philosophy of August Comte.* London: John Edward Taylor, n.d.

"Conference on Public School History Teachers." *American Historical Association Annual Report, 1904.* Washington, D.C.: GPO, 1905.

Degarmo, Charles. "Social Aspects of Moral Education." *The Third Yearbook of the National Herbart Society.* Chicago: University of Chicago Press, 1897.

Dewey, John. *Democracy and Education.* New York: Macmillan, 1916.

——. "Ethical Principles Underlying Education." *The Third Yearbook of the National Herbart Society for the Scientific Study of Teaching.* Chicago: University of Chicago Press, 1897.

——. *How We Think.* Boston: Heath, 1910.

——. *Interest and Effort in Education.* Boston: Houghton Mifflin, 1913.

——. "The Psychological Aspect of the School Curricula." *Education Review,* 12, April 1897.

——. *School and Society.* Chicago: University of Chicago Press, 1899.

"Discussions." The Association of History Teachers of the Middle States and Maryland. *Proceedings, 1915,* no. 13. n. p., n.d.

Dunn, Arthur William. *The Community and the Citizen.* Indianapolis: Echo Press, 1906. Boston: Heath, 1907.

——. "Is History in the Schools a 'Snap'? If So, Why?" *Educational Review,* 24, April 1905.

——. *The Social Studies in Secondary Education.* Report of the Committee on Social Studies of the Commission on the Reorganization of Secondary Education, National Education Association. United States Bureau of Education, Bulletin, 1916, no. 28. Washington, D.C.: GPO, 1916.

Eggleston, Edward. "The New History." *American Historical Association Annual Report, 1900.* Washington, D.C.: GPO, n.d.

Eliot, Charles W. "The Unity of Educational Reform." American Institute of Instruction. *Addresses and Proceedings,* 1894.

Ellwood, Charles. "How History Can Be Taught from a Sociological Point of View." *Education,* 30, January 1910.

"The Fifteenth Educational Conference of the Academies and High Schools Affiliated or in Cooperation with the University of Chicago." *The School Review,* January 1902.

Fiske, John. *A History of the United States.* Boston: Houghton, Mifflin, 1897.

Fling, Fred Morrow, and Howard W. Caldwell. *Studies in European and American History.* Lincoln, Nebr.: J. W. Miller, 1897.

Gathany, J. Madison. "The Reconstruction of History Teaching." *The History Teachers Magazine,* 5, no. 7, September 1914.

George, Henry. *Progress and Poverty.* New York: n.p., 1879.

———. *Social Problems*. New York: Belford, Clarke, 1893.

Gillette, John M. "An Outline of Social Studies for Elementary Schools." *American Journal of Sociology*, 19, 1914.

Gold, Hugo H. "Methods and Content of Courses in History in the High Schools of the United States." *School Review*, 25, no. 2, February 1917; 25, no. 3, March 1917; and 25, no. 4, April 1917.

Hall, G. Stanley. *Educational Problems*, vol. 2. New York: Appleton, 1911.

———, ed. *Methods of Teaching History*. 2nd ed. Boston: Heath, 1898.

Hanus, Paul. "Secondary Education." *Educational Review*, 17, April 1899.

Hart, Albert Bushnell. *Studies in American Education*. New York: Longman, Green, 1895.

Hinsdale, Burton Aaron. *How to Study and Teach History*. New York: Appleton, 1893.

"History in the Secondary Schools, Is the Revision of the Course of Study in History Desirable?" *The History Teacher's Magazine*, 2, no. 8, April 1911.

Howerth, Ira. "A Programme for Social Study." *The American Journal of Sociology*, 2, no. 6, May 1897.

Hudson, George H. "Herbert Spencer's Guiding Principles." *Education*, 16, October 1895.

James, Edmund J. "The Place of Political and Social Sciences in Modern Education." *Annals of the American Academy of Political and Social Sciences*, 10, November 1897.

———. In Samuel McCune Linsay, "The Study and Teaching of Sociology, Part III." *Annals of the American Academy of Political and Social Sciences*, 12, July 1898.

———. "Training for Citizenship." *The Third Yearbook of the National Herbart Society*. Chicago: University of Chicago Press, 1897.

Jones, Thomas Jesse. *Essentials of Civilization*. New York: Henry Holt, 1929.

———. *Four Essentials of Education*. New York: Charles Scribner's Sons, 1926.

———. *Social Studies in the Hampton Curriculum*. Hampton, Va.: Hampton Institute Press, 1908.

————. *Sociology of a New York City Block*. New York: Columbia University Press, 1904.

————. "Statement of the Chairman of the Committee on Social Studies." In Clarence Kingsley, ed., *Preliminary Statements by Chairman of the Committee of the Commission of National Education Association on Reorganization of Secondary Schools*. United States Bureau of Education, Bulletin, 1913, no. 41. Washington, D.C.: GPO, 1913.

Johnson, Henry. "Proceedings of the Conference of Teachers of History." *American Historical Association Annual Report, 1917*. Washington, D.C.: GPO, 1920.

————. "The School in History: Some Precedents and a Possible Next Step." *The History Teacher's Magazine*, 9, no. 2, February 1918.

————. *The Teaching of History in Elementary and Secondary Schools*. New York: Macmillan, 1916.

Johnston, Charles, et al. *High School Education*. New York: Charles Scribner's Sons, 1912.

Judd, Charles H. "Report of the Committee on Social Science." *Third Yearbook*. National Association of Secondary School Principals. n. p.

Kingsley, Clarence D. *Cardinal Principles of Secondary Education*. Report of the Subject Committees of the Commission on the Reorganization of Secondary Education of the National Education Association. United States Bureau of Education, Bulletin, 1918, no. 35. Washington, D.C.: GPO, 1918.

————. *The Reorganization of Secondary Education*. Preliminary Report of the Commission on the Reorganization of Secondary Schools of the National Education Association. United States Bureau of Education, Bulletin, 1913, no. 41. Washington, D.C.: GPO, 1913.

————. "The Study of Nations: Its Possibilities as a Social Study in High Schools." *School and Society*, 3, no. 54, Saturday, January 8, 1916.

Koos, Leonard V. *The Administration of Secondary-School Units*. Supplementary Educational Monographs, I, no. 8, July 1917. Chicago: University of Chicago Press, 1917.

Lingelbach, William E. "The Content of the Course in European History in the Secondary Schools." The Association of History Teachers of the Middle States and Maryland, *Proceedings, 1915*, n.p., n.d.

MacDonald, William. "The Situation of History in Secondary Schools." *The Nation*, 85, no. 2202, September 12, 1907.

MacDonald, William, Charles F. A. Currier, Edward G. Bourne, Caroline Close, Elizabeth Holbrook, and J. Eston Phyfe. "Text-books in American History." Report of the Standing Committee on Text-Books to the New England History Teachers' Association. *Educational Review*, December 1898.

Mace, William. *Method in History*. Boston: Ginn, 1898.

MacMillan, Conway. "The Sociological Basis of School Education," *Education*, 16, no. 6, February 1896.

McKinley, Albert E. *Collected Materials for the Study of War*. Philadelphia: McKinley Publishing, 1918.

McLaughlin, Andrew. "Conference on History in Secondary Schools with Especial Reference to the Report of the Committee of Seven." *American Historical Association Annual Report, 1908*. Washington, D.C.: GPO, n.d.

———, Charles Haskins, Charles W. Mann, James Sullivan, and James Harvey Robinson. *The Study of History in Schools*. Report to the American Historical Association by the Committee on Five. New York: Macmillan, 1912.

———, et al. *The Study of History in Schools*. Report to the American Historical Association by the Committee of Seven. New York: Macmillan, 1899.

McMaster, John Bach. *A School History of the United States*. New York: American Book Company, 1897.

McMurry, Charles. *Special Method in History*. New York: Macmillan, 1903.

"Modifications in the Report of the Committee of Seven Recommended by the N. E. Association." *The History Teacher's Magazine*, 1, no. 4, December 1909.

Monroe, James Phinney. *New Demands in Education*. New York: Doubleday, Page, 1912.

Moore, Otis. "The Congress of Social Education." *Charities and the Commons*, 17, 1907.

National Education Association. *Proceedings*, 1911, 1912, 1913.

———. *Report of the Committee of Ten on Secondary School Studies with Reports of the Conferences Arranged by Committee*. New York: American Book Company, 1894.

———. *Report on Secondary School Studies*. Washington, D.C.: GPO, 1893.

Newton, Reverend Heber. *Social Studies*. New York: Putnam, 1886.

Office of the Judge Advocate General of the Army. *Compilation of War Laws of the Various States and Insular Possessions*. Washington, D.C.: GPO, 1919.

Osgood, Edith. "The Development of Historical Study in the High Schools of the United States." *School Review*, 22, no. 7, September 1914; 22, no. 8, October 1914.

Owen, William Bishop. "The Nineteenth Educational Conference of the Academies and High Schools in Relation with the University of Chicago." *The School Review*, 15, no. 1, January 1907.

Parker, Samuel Chester. *Methods of Teaching in High Schools*. New York: Ginn, 1915.

Rice, Joseph. *The Public School System of the United States*. New York: Century, 1893.

Robinson, James Harvey. *An Introduction to the History of Western Europe*. Boston: Ginn, 1907.

———. "Mediaeval and Modern History in the High Schools." *The Fifth Yearbook of the National Herbart Society for the Scientific Study of Teaching*. Chicago: University of Chicago Press, 1899.

———. *The New History: Essays Illustrating the Modern Outlook*. New York: Macmillan, 1912.

———. "The New History." *Proceedings of the American Philosophical Society*, 50, no. 199, May-August 1911. Philadelphia: American Philosophical Society, 1911.

———. "The Relationship of History to the Newer Sciences of Mankind." *Journal of Philosophy, Psychology, and Scientific Methods*, 7, March 1911.

———. "The Significance of History in Industrial Education." *The Education Bi-Monthly*, 4, June 1910.

Ross, Edward A. *Social Control*. New York: Macmillan, 1901.

Rugg, Harold. "Needed Changes in the Committee Procedure on Reconstructing the Social Studies." *The Elementary School Journal*, 21, May 1921.

Russell, William F. "The Early Teaching of History in Secondary Schools." *The History Teacher's Magazine*, 5, no. 7, September 1914.

Salmon. Lucy. "Some Principles in the Teaching of History." *The First Year-book of the National Society of the Scientific Study of Education.* Chicago: University of Chicago Press, 1902.

Scott, Colin. *Social Education.* Boston: Ginn, 1908.

———. "Social Education." *Education,* 30, Nos. 1, 2, 3, October, November, December 1909.

Small, Albion W. "The Demands of Sociology upon Pedagogy." *The American Journal of Sociology,* 2, no. 6, May 1897.

———, and George E. Vincent. *An Introduction to the Study of Society.* New York: American Book Company, 1894.

Snedden, David. "The Certification of Teachers in the High School, with Special Reference to Certification in History." *The History Teachers Magazine,* 3, no. 5, May 1912.

———. "History and Other Social Sciences in the Education of Youths Twelve to Eighteen Years of Age." *School and Society,* 5, no. 115, March 10, 1917; 5, no. 116, March 17, 1917.

———. "History Study as Instrument in the Social Education of Children." *Journal of Pedagogy,* 19, June 1907.

———. *Problems of Educational Readjustment.* Boston: Houghton, Mifflin, 1913.

———. "Teaching of History in Secondary Schools." *The History Teachers Magazine,* 5, no. 9, November 1914.

Spencer, Herbert. *Education: Intellectual, Moral, and Physical.* New York: Appleton, 1881.

Stone, Senator William. *Congressional Record,* 64th Congress, 2nd Session, March 3, 1917. Washington, D.C.: GPO, 1918.

Stout, John Elbert. *The Development of High-School Curricula in the North Central States from 1860–1918.* Chicago: University of Chicago Press, 1921.

Sullivan, James. "Civics in the High School and Training for Citizenship." The Association of History Teachers of the Middle States and Maryland. *Proceedings, 1913,* n.p., n.d.

Sumner, William Graham. *The Challenge of Facts and Other Essays.* New Haven: Yale University Press, 1914.

Sutton, John R. "The Report of the Committee of Seven in Relation to the Proposed Definition of the Course." *The History Teachers Magazine,* 7, no. 6, June 1916.

Suzzalo, Henry. "Education as a Social Study." *The School Review*, 16, no. 5. May 1908.

Thorndike, Edward. *Education. A First Book*. New York: Macmillan, 1912.

———. *The Elimination of Pupils from Schools*. Department of the Interior, Bureau of Education Bulletin, no. 4, 1907. Washington, D.C.: GPO, 1907.

Tryon, Rolla M. "A Brief Review of the Current Literature Relating to History and the Teaching of History in Junior and Senior High Schools." *The School Review*, 25, no. 9, November 1917.

———. "Conference Upon Desirable Adjustments Between History and Other Social Studies in Elementary and Secondary Schools." *The Historical Outlook*, 13, no. 3, March 1921.

Turner, Frederick Jackson. "The Significance of the Frontier in American History." *The Fifth Yearbook of the National Herbart Society*. Chicago: University of Chicago Press, 1899.

Van Liew, C. C. "Training for Citizenship." *The Third Yearbook of the National Herbart Society*. Chicago: University of Chicago Press, 1897.

Vincent, George. "Social Science and the Curriculum." *School Review*, 10, 1902.

Ward, Mark Lester. *Dynamic Sociology, II*. New York: Appleton, 1883.

Wilde, Lady Jane Francesca Elgee. *Social Studies*. London: Ward and Downy, 1893.

Wilson, Woodrow. *The New Freedom*. New York: Doubleday, 1913.

Wright, Carroll D. "Popular Instruction in Social Science." *Journal of Social Science*, 22, June 1887.

SOURCES 1922 AND LATER

Alilunas, Leo J. "The Effects of Changes in American Psychological Thought Upon the Study of History." *Educational Administration and Supervision*, 32, 1946.

Atwood, Virginia A., ed. "Historical Foundations of Social Studies." *Journal of Thought*, Fall 1982.

Barnard, L. L., and Jessie Barnard. *Origins of American Sociology: The Social Science Movement in the United States*. New York: Russell and Russell, 1943.

Barnes, Henry Elmer. *An Introduction to the History of Sociology*. Chicago: University of Chicago Press, 1948.

Barr, Robert, James L. Barth, and Samuel S. Shermis. *Defining the Social Studies*. Arlington, Va.: National Council for the Social Studies, 1977.

Barth, James L., ed. *Foundations of the Social Studies Special Interest Group*. Bulletin 1, January 1989.

Berman, Barbara. "Business Efficiency, American Schooling, and the Public School Superintendency: A Reconsideration of the Callahan Thesis." *History of Education Quarterly*, 23, no. 3, Fall 1983.

Bradley Commission on History in the Schools. *Building a Histor Curriculum: Guidelines for Teaching History in Schools*. Washington, D.C.: Educational Excellence Network, 1988.

Burns, James MacGregor. *The Workshop of Democracy*. New York: Vintage, 1986.

Butts, R. Freeman, and Lawrence A. Cremin. *A History of Education in American Culture*. New York: Henry Holt, 1953.

Callahan, Raymond E. *Education and the Cult of Efficiency*. Chicago: University of Chicago Press, 1962.

Commager, Henry Steele. *The American Mind. An Interpretation of American Thought and Character Since the 1880s*. New Haven: Yale University Press, 1950.

Cremin, Lawrence A. *The Transformation of the School*. New York: Knopf, 1961.

Cuban, Larry. *How Teachers Taught: Constancy and Change in American Classrooms 1890–1980*. New York: Longman, 1984.

Cubberley, Ellwood P. *Public Education in the United States*. Boston: Houghton, Mifflin, 1946.

Curti, Merle. *Peace or War: The American Struggle, 1636–1936*. New York: Norton, 1936.

———. *The Social Ideas of American Educators*. A Report to the American Historical Association by the Commission of Social Studies. New York: Charles Scribner's Sons, 1935.

Davis, Allen F. *Spearheads for Reform*. New York: Oxford University Press, 1967.

Dawson, Edgar. "The History Inquiry." *Historical Outlook*, 15, no. 6, June 1924.

Dewey, John. "How Much Freedom in Schools?" *New Republic*, 63, July 9, 1930.

Dougan, Alberta. "The Search for a Definition of Social Studies: A Historical Overview." *The International Journal of Social Education*, 3, no. 3, Winter 1988–89.

Drost, Walter H. *David Snedden and Education for Social Efficiency.* Madison: University of Wisconsin Press, 1967.

Engle, Shirley, and Anna Ochoa. *Education for Democratic Citizenship Decision Making in the Social Studies.* New York: Teachers College Press, 1988.

Fine, Sidney. *Laissez Faire and the General Welfare State.* Ann Arbor: University of Michigan Press, 1956.

Franklin, Barry F. *Building the American Community.* London: Falmer Press, 1986.

———. "The Social Efficiency Movement and Curriculum Change 1939–1976." In Ivor Goodson, ed., *Social Histories of the Secondary Curriculum: Subjects for Study.* London: Falmer Press, 1985.

Gambrill, J. Montgomery. "Experimental Curriculum-Making in the Social Studies." *Historical Outlook*, 14, no. 9, December 1923; 15, no. 1, January 1924.

———. "Some Tendencies and Issues in the Making of Social Studies Curricula." *The Historical Outlook*, 15, no. 6, June 1924.

Gibbs, Christopher C. *The Great Silent Majority.* Columbia: University of Missouri Press, 1988.

Ginger, Ray. *Age of Excess.* New York: Macmillan, 1965.

Goodson, Ivor, ed. *Social Histories of the Secondary Curriculum: Subjects of Study.* London: Falmer Press, 1985.

Griffin, Frederick C. *Six Who Protested.* Port Washington, N.Y.: Kennikat Press, 1977.

Hamlin, C. H. *Educators Present Arms.* Zebulon, N.C.: Record Publishers, 1939.

Haskell, Thomas. *The Emergence of Professional Social Science.* Urbana: University of Illinois Press, 1977.

Hawley, Ellis W. *The Great War and the Search for a Modern Order.* New York: St. Martin's Press, 1979.

Hendricks, Luther V. *James Harvey Robinson, Teacher of History.* Morningside Heights, N.Y.: King's Crown Press, 1946.

Hertzberg, Hazel Whitman. *Social Studies Reform 1880–1980.* Boulder, Colo.: Social Science Consortium, 1981.

"The History of the Social Studies." *Theory and Practice in Social Education,* 8, no. 3, Fall 1980.

Hilleman, R.U. "The Source Method of Teaching History." In National Council for the Social Studies, *The Historical Approach to Methods of Teaching Social Studies.* Philadelphia: McKinley Publishing, 1935.

Hiner, N. Ray. "Professions in Process: Changing Relations Between Historians and Educators, 1896–1911." *History of Education Quarterly,* Spring 1972.

———. "Professions in Process: Changing Relations Among Social Scientists, Historians, and Educators, 1880–1920." *The History Teacher,* 6, no. 2, February 1973.

Hofstadter, Richard. *Age of Reform.* New York: Vintage Press, 1965.

———. *Anti-Intellectualism in American Life.* New York: Knopf, 1963.

———. *Social Darwinism in American Thought.* Philadelphia: University of Pennsylvania Press, 1944.

Hunt, Maurice P. and Lawrence E. Metcalf. *Teaching High School Social Studies.* New York: Harper and Row, 1955.

Jackman, Sydney W., ed. *The English Reform Tradition 1790- 1910.* Englewood Cliffs, NJ: Prentice-Hall, 1965.

Johnson, Henry. *An Introduction to the History of Social Sciences in Schools.* New York: Charles Scribner's Sons, 1932.

———. *Teaching of History in Elementary and Secondary Schools With Applications to Allied Studies.* New York: Macmillan, 1940.

Karrier, Clarence. *The Individual, Society, and Education.* Urbana: University of Illinois Press, 1986.

Katz, Michael B. *Class, Bureaucracy, and School: The Delusion of Educational Change in America.* New York: Praeger, 1971.

Keels, Oliver M. "Herbert Baxter Adams and the Influence of the American Historical Association on the Early Social Studies." *The International Journal of Social Education,* 3, no. 3, Winter 1988–89.

Keohane, Robert. "The Great Debate Over the Source Method." *Social Education,* 13, no. 5, May 1949.

Kliebard, Herbert. *The Struggle for the American Curriculum.* London: Routledge and Kegan Paul, 1986.

Krug, Edward A. *The Shaping of the American High School,* vol. 1. New York: Harper and Row, 1964.

Lagemann, Ellen Condliffe. "The Plural Worlds of Educational Research." *History of Education Quarterly,* 29, no. 2, Summer 1989.

Link, Arthur S. *American Epoch: A History of the United States Since the 1890s.* New York: Knopf, 1958.

————. *Woodrow Wilson and the Progressive Era.* New York: Harper Torchbooks, 1963.

Lucas, Christopher J. *Our Educational Heritage.* New York: Macmillan, 1972.

May, Henry. *The Discontent of Intellectuals: A Problem of the Twenties.* Chicago: Rand McNally, 1963.

Mehaffy, George L. "Social Studies in World War One: A Period of Transition." *Theory and Research in Social Education,* 15, no. 1, Winter 1987.

Metcalf, Lawrence E. "Final Impressions." A Statement following the Lawrence E. Metcalf Colloquium. University of Illinois, Urbana, September 26, 1986.

————. "An Overview of the Deweyan Influence on Social Studies Education." *The International Journal of Social Education,* 3, no. 3, Winter 1988–89.

Monroe, Walter S. *Teaching-Learning Theory and Teacher Education.* New York: Greenwood, 1952.

Nelson, Murry R. "Emma Willard: Pioneer in Social Studies Education." *Theory and Practice in Social Education,* 15, no. 4, Fall 1987.

————. "The Social Contexts of the Committee on Social Studies Report of 1916." Paper presented at the National Council for the Social Studies Convention, St. Louis, November 10, 1989.

Noble, David W. *The Progressive Mind.* Chicago: Rand McNally, 1970.

Perkinson, Henry J. *The Imperfect Panacea: American Faith in Education, 1865–1965.* New York: Random House, 1968.

Peterson, H. C., and Gilbert C. Fite. *Opponents of War, 1917–1918.* Madison: University of Wisconsin Press, 1957.

Pierce, Bessie Louise. *Civic Attitudes in American Schools.* Chicago: University of Chicago Press, 1930.

———. "Propaganda in Teaching Social Studies." *Historical Outlook,* 20, no. 8, December 1929.

———. *Public Opinion and the Teaching of History.* New York: Knopf, 1926.

Randall, John Herman, Jr. *The Making of the Modern Mind.* Boston: Houghton Mifflin, 1940.

Ravitch, Diane. "Tot Sociology." *The American Scholar,* Summer 1987.

Rugg, Earle. "How the Current Courses in History, Geography, and Civics Came To Be What They Are." National Society for the Study of Education, *Twenty-Second Yearbook, Part II. The Social Studies in the Elementary and Secondary Schools.* Bloomington, Ill.: Public School Publishing, 1923.

Rugg, Harold O. "The Social Studies in the Elementary and Secondary Schools." National Society for the Study of Education, *Twenty-Second Yearbook, Part II. The Social Studies in Elementary and Secondary Schools.* Bloomington, Ill.: Public School Publishing, 1923.

Russett, Cynthia Eagle. *Darwin in America: The Intellectual Response 1865–1912.* San Francisco: W. H. Freeman, 1976.

Saxe, David Warren. "Mary Sheldon Barnes and the Introduction of the Social Sciences in Public Schools: A Historical Perspective." *The Social Studies,* 80, no. 5, September/October 1989.

Silver, Harold. *Education as History.* New York: Methuen, 1983.

Sizer, Theodore R. *Secondary Schools at the Turn of the Century.* New Haven: Yale University Press, 1964.

Tryon, Rolla M. "Thirteen Years of Problems of American Democracy." *The Historical Outlook,* 20, no. 8, December 1929.

———. *The Social Sciences as School Subjects.* A Report to the American Historical Association by the Commission on Social Studies. New York: Charles Scribner's Sons, 1935.

Vanderpool, Harold Y. *Darwin and Darwinism.* Lexington: Heath, 1973.

Watson, Bruce, and William Tarr. *The Social Sciences and American Civilization.* New York: John Wiley, 1964.

Weakland, John, ed. "Founders of the Social Studies." *Indiana Social Studies Quarterly,* 38, no. 3, Winter 1985–86.

————, ed. "Social Studies: Old Masters and Founders." *The International Journal of Social Education*, 3, no. 3. Winter 1988–89.

Wesley, Edgar Bruce. *Teaching the Social Studies*. New York: Heath, 1937.

Wiebe, Robert H. *The Search For Order*. New York: Hill and Wang, 1967.

DISSERTATIONS

Alilunas, Leo J. "Genesis of the Social Studies Movement in American Secondary Education." Diss., University of Michigan, 1946.

Boozer, Howard Rai. "The American Historical Association and the Schools, 1884–1956." Diss., Washington University, 1960.

Cruikshanks, Andrew Norman. "The Social Studies Curriculum in the Secondary School 1893–1955." Diss., Stanford University, 1957.

Glasheen, Patricia. "The Advent of Social Studies, 1916: An Historical Study." Diss., Boston University, 1973.

Hiner, Norville Ray, Jr. "The Changing Role of History and Social Sciences in the Schools, 1892–1918." Diss., George Peabody College, 1967.

Jones, Thomas Jesse. "Social Education and the Elementary School." Master's thesis, Columbia University, 1899.

Kinzie, Glenn Leroy. "Historians and the Social Studies: A History and Interpretation of the Activities of the American Historical Association in the Secondary Social Studies." Diss., University of Kansas, 1965.

Lybarger, Michael Bruce. "Origins of the Social Studies Curriculum: 1865–1916." Diss., University of Wisconsin, 1981.

McAninch, Stuart A. "Social Science, Social Cohesion, and Moral Uplift: The Historian and the Development of Modern American Secondary School History Curricula." Diss., University of Illinois, 1987.

Mehl, Bernard. "The High School at the Turn of the Century: A Study of the Changes in the Aims and Programs of Public Secondary Education in the United States 1890–1900." Diss., University of Illinois, 1954.

Robinson, David Paul. "Historical Models of the Emergence of the Social Studies." Diss., Stanford University, 1977.

Roorbach, Agnew O. "The Development of the Social Studies in American Education before 1861." Diss., University of Pennsylvania, 1937.

Saxe, David Warren. "Traditional History and the Social Studies in Secondary Education: A Historical Perspective, 1892–1916." Diss., University of Illinois, 1988.

Taylor, Frances Purves. "Problems of American Democracy as a High School Subject." Master's thesis, University of Chicago, 1929.

INDEX

A

Acculturation, 3
Adams, Charles Kendall, 30–31, 39, 42
Adams, Herbert B., 30–31, 55
Addams, Jane, 86–87, 119
Alilunas, Leo J., 121
American Historical Association, beginning of, 31; control of history curriculum, 85–87; passage of influence from, 148; sponsor of Committee of Five, 83; sponsor of Committee of Seven, 54; sponsor of National Board for Historical Service, 148; sponsor of the History Inquiry, 178; under criticism, 85–87
American Social Science Association (ASSA), 3–4
Association of History Teachers of the Middle States and Maryland, 83, 87, 135, 138
Arey, William, 147

B

Bagley, William C. 102, 109, 111, 138

Ballinger, Richard, 78
Barnard, James Lynn, 135, 138, 146; with Committee on Social Studies, 166–67, 172, 178
Barnes, Mary Sheldon, 26, 31, 75, 99
Barr, Robert, 2
Barth, James, 2
Beard, Charles, 135–36, 143
Becker, Carl, 143
Bellamy, Edward, 5
Bennett, Henry Eastman, 114–115
Berman, Barbara, 24
Blackmar, Frank W., 26–27
Bolton, Sarah, 18
Botsford, George Willis, 100–02
Bourne, Henry, 31, 99, 100, 138
Bradley Commission on History in Schools, 144
Brown, Elmer Ellsworth, 111
Brown, Marshall S., 140
Burch, Henry R., 167
Burr, George L., 133–34
Butler, Nicholas, 173

C

Caldwell, Howard, 31
Callahan, Raymond, 24, 81